Women in Executive Power

Women in Executive Power studies the participation of women in the political executive around the world – notably in cabinet positions as ministers and sub-ministers and as heads of government and state.

Providing multiple case studies in each chapter, the book provides regional overviews of nine different world regions covering those with the fewest to the most women in executive power. Evaluating the role of socio-cultural, economic and political variables on women's access to cabinet positions and positions of head of state and government, the book shows that women are increasingly moving into positions previously considered "male." Tracing the historical trends of women's participation in governments that has markedly increased in the last two decades, the book assesses the factors that have contributed to women's increasing presence in executives and the extent to which women executives, once in office, represent women's interests.

With case studies from Europe, the Americas, Asia, Africa, the Arab World and Oceania, *Women in Executive Power* will be of interest to scholars of comparative politics, gender and women's studies.

Gretchen Bauer is professor and chair in the Department of Political Science and International Relations, University of Delaware, USA.

Manon Tremblay is professor at the School of Political Studies at the University of Ottawa, Canada.

Routledge research in comparative politics

Women in Executive Power

A global overview

Edited by
Gretchen Bauer and Manon Tremblay

Routledge
Taylor & Francis Group

LONDON AND NEW YORK

First published 2011
by Routledge
2 Park Square Milton Park Abingdon Oxon OX14 4RN

Simultaneously published in the USA and Canada
by Routledge
711 Third Avenue, New York, NY 10017

Routledge is an imprint of the Taylor & Francis Group, an informa business

British Library Cataloguing in Publication Data
A catalogue record for this book is available from the British Library

Library of Congress Cataloging in Publication Data
A catalog record for this book has been requested

ISBN: 978-0-415-60380-5 (hbk)
ISBN: 978-0-203-82998-0 (ebk)

Typeset in Times New Roman
by Wearset Ltd, Boldon, Tyne and Wear

Contents

Figures and tables

Figures

Tables

Contributors

Tiffany D. Barnes is a doctoral candidate in the Department of Political Science at Rice University. Her dissertation explores the relationship between gender and representation via a study of Argentine provincial legislatures. Her research has been supported by a United States National Science Foundation Doctoral Dissertation Research Improvement Grant and an Ora N. Arnold Fellowship.

Gretchen Bauer is professor and chair of the Department of Political Science and International Relations at the University of Delaware. Her current research focuses on women's under-representation in politics in Botswana and on women chiefs in Botswana.

Christina Bergqvist is associate professor of political science and lecturer at the Department of Government, Uppsala University. Her research fields include gender and political representation, gender and public policy and feminist comparative policy.

Fiona Buckley is a lecturer in the Department of Government, University College Cork, Ireland. Her teaching and research interests cover the areas of gender politics, Irish politics and electoral behavior. She is currently a doctoral candidate in the School of Politics, International Studies and Philosophy at Queen's University Belfast. Her thesis examines the concept of gender power and relations in cabinet government in Europe.

Vânia Carvalho Pinto is a National Council of Technological and Scientific Development Post-Doctoral Fellow at the University of Brasilia in Brazil, conducting research on Arab-Latin American relations. She is the author of *Women, State, and the Genderframing of Women's Rights in the United Arab Emirates (1971–2009)* (2010).

Jennifer Curtin teaches comparative politics and policy at The University of Auckland. She has published widely on women and politics and is the author of *Women and Trade Unions: a Comparative Perspective* (1999) and co-editor of *Globalising the Antipodes?* (*Australian Journal of Political Science* 2006).

Andrea Fleschenberg works as research fellow and lecturer for comparative politics and international development studies at the Philipps-University Marburg, Germany. Her research interests include gender and politics, democratization and participation studies, and transitional justice and state-building with an area focus on South and Southeast Asia.

Maxime Forest is QUING (6th EU framework) post-doctoral fellow at the Complutense University in Madrid. His research investigates the gendered dimension of post-communist politics and the Europeanization of gender equality policies. He is the co-editor with Emanuela Lombardo of *The Europeanization of Gender Equality Policies: a Sociological-Discursive Approach* (forthcoming).

Yvonne Galligan is professor of comparative politics at Queen's University Belfast, Northern Ireland. She has been researching various aspects of women and politics since the mid 1980s, and since 2007 leads a five-year project on gender justice and democracy.

Farida Jalalzai is assistant professor in the Department of Political Science at the University of Missouri-St. Louis. Her research analyzes the role of gender in the political arena. Her work has been published in *Politics and Gender*, *International Political Science Review*, *Women, Politics and Policy* and *Politics and Religion*.

Mark P. Jones is the Joseph D. Jamail Chair in Latin American Studies, as well as chair of the Department of Political Science, at Rice University. His research focuses on the effect of political institutions on governance, representation and voting.

Marian Sawer is an emeritus professor in the School of Politics and International Relations, Australian National University. She has published 16 books, most recently *Federalism, Feminism and Multilevel Governance* (co-edited, 2010), and is currently working for the Australian government on gender assessment of policy.

Manon Tremblay is a professor of political science at the University of Ottawa. Her research interests lie in the study of gender and politics. Her current research includes a study of women cabinet ministers in Canada from 1921 to 2007.

Acknowledgments

Gretchen Bauer began work for this book during her 2009 sabbatical leave in Gaborone, Botswana during which she was a visiting researcher in the Department of Sociology. She would like to thanks her colleagues there for their warm reception and support. Manon Tremblay worked extensively on this book during her sabbatical leave, in the 2010 winter semester; she was then a visiting fellow at the Political Science Program, Research School of Social Science, Australian National University (from December 2009 to March 2010) in Canberra, and at the Centre de recherches politiques de Sciences Po, Centre national de la recherche scientifique (from March to June 2010) in Paris. She would like to thank both the Political Science Program (ANU) and the Cevipof (CNRS) for welcoming and supporting her.

Assembling such a book, with many contributors from around the world, is an arduous process made somewhat easier by electronic communications. We would like to thank our contributors for participating in this project, for adhering closely to our guidelines and for responding cheerfully to our many queries. We would also like to thank Sarah Andrews, a master's student in political science at the University of Ottawa, for completing the tedious task of formatting the lengthy bibliography.

Additionally, the editors would like to thank anonymous reviewers at Routledge for their helpful comments. Finally, we are grateful to Hannah Shakespeare and Harriet Frammingham for their patience and for guiding us through the publication process.

1 Introduction

Gretchen Bauer and Manon Tremblay

In early 2010 just over a dozen women served as heads of state or government around the world – as presidents or prime ministers; additionally, a mere 16.9 percent of cabinet ministers and secretaries across the globe were women.[1] While these numbers are very low, they represent a significant increase over women's presence in executive positions just 50 years ago. Whereas only three women served as heads of state in the 1960s, six in the 1970s and seven in the 1980s, in the 1990s 26 women served as president or prime minister and in the first decade of the 2000s 29 have done so. Women's presence in cabinets world-wide has nearly doubled in the last decade, from just under 9 percent in 1999 to just under 17 percent in 2010. As is more widely known, in the last few decades women have also made great strides in national legislatures with women out-numbering men for the first time ever in a legislative body – in the Chamber of Deputies in Rwanda. Indeed, in mid 2010 more than 26 countries had 30 percent women or more in their single or lower house of parliament, for a worldwide average of 19 percent.

Historically, access to the executive branch – "the highest glass ceiling" – has been considerably more difficult for women than has access to the legislative branch (Reynolds 1999: 572). Watson *et al.* (2005: 55–6) suggest that executive positions are "the most gendered of all political offices," with public perceptions of "the maleness of high office" raising concerns about women's ability to make critical decisions particularly in areas of defense, economics, and foreign policy. Indeed, while women's access to both branches has improved markedly in recent years, the pace has been somewhat slower for women entering the executive branch. So, for example, women were reportedly 8.7 percent of cabinet ministers worldwide in 1999 rising to 15.2 percent by 2007 and 16.9 percent in early 2010 (WEDO 2007; IPU 2010d). According to the Inter-Parliamentary Union (n.d.), women occupied 13.1 percent of seats in lower or single houses of parliament in 1999, up to 17.5 percent of seats in 2007 and 19 percent in mid 2010.

This book provides a comprehensive overview of women's increasing partici-pation in political executives around the world today. Whereas several recent books examine women's increased legislative representation around the world and in specific regions (Dahlerup 2006a; Bauer and Britton 2006; Tremblay 2008a; Rueschemeyer and Wolchik 2009), few recent books have investigated women's executive representation in the same manner. Those books that have focused on women executives have privileged women presidents and prime ministers and largely ignored women cabinet ministers and secretaries; moreover, they have tended to narrate individual women leaders' stories rather than to analyze more broadly women's participation in political executives (see Genovese 1993; Opfell 1993; Jackson-Laufer 1998; Hoogensen and Solheim 2006; Liswood 2007; Jensen 2008). As such, this book fills a void in the literature on women's participation and representation in political executives.

While we do not argue that the focus on women's recent dramatic increased access to national legislatures is misplaced, we suggest that a failure to recognize the importance of women's increasing access to executives, especially cabinets, is regrettable. Indeed, in most parliamentary systems at least, cabinet ministers play a large role in setting the legislative agenda and they are often the ones to introduce new legislation. Cabinet ministers control substantial portions of the national budget and are responsible for not only initiating but also implementing policy. Cabinet level appointments are key indicators of executive priorities and emphasis, with stronger ministers better able to articulate, defend or promote their policy arenas. Just as importantly, cabinet ministers may engage in "negative agenda control," that is, in blocking policies that they do not support (Atchison and Down 2009: 6). In terms of the pinnacle of power, it may also be argued that cabinet ministers represent important potential recruits for the position of chief executive. Presidents and prime ministers, meanwhile, set the national policy agenda as well as represent their nations internationally.

Women in Executive Power: A global overview takes a comparative approach to women in political executives – as heads of state and government and in cabinets – with material gathered from nearly every region of the world. Nine regional chapters provide a general overview of women in executives in that region and an in-depth examination of two or three cases in the region. With regional overviews and case studies from across the globe, the book offers the most comprehensive analysis of women in executives around the world to date; drawing together observations from all of the regional chapters, the concluding chapter provides a compelling set of lessons learned.

Overview of the literature

The existing literature on women in executive power has tended to focus on women presidents and prime ministers or women in cabinets but rarely both. In bringing the two elements of the executive together, this book represents an important departure from past volumes. In general, the little work on women executives has privileged those women at the apex of power rather than those women in cabinets – a situation our book seeks to redress. As mentioned above, probably because there have been so few women leaders in the last 50 years, much of the literature on women heads of state and government has provided interviews with and profiles of individual women rather than attempting to aggregate their experiences. At the same time, some of the early studies seem to have provided enduring insights that continue as the state of the art today. So, for example, in the conclusion to his edited book that portrays several women leaders from around the world, Genovese (1993: 211) relates several patterns gleaned from the individual portraits: most women executives (up until the time of writing in the early 1990s) held office in less developed countries and most came to power during times of "social or political distress," often inheriting their positions in one way or another from male relatives. At the same time, he also notes that most of the women leaders were highly educated and many had prior political experiences. Genovese also suggests that women leaders were more likely to be found in secular political regimes and those with "some form of democracy." Genovese was unable to evaluate women executives' substantive representation of women.

Published around the same time, Richter's (1991) study of South and Southeast Asian women executives reveals findings that are still widely reported today. Richter homes in on the apparent contradiction between the overall low status of women in much of Asia and a fairly hefty presence of Asian women leaders, beginning with the first woman prime minister in the world in Sri Lanka in 1960. According to Richter, the explanation lies in Asian women leaders' elite status and their familial ties to prominent male politicians who have died, been assassinated or somehow martyred (1991: 528). A similar phenomenon has been asserted for Latin America as well (Jalalzai 2004; Watson *et al.* 2005). Richter is also unable to evaluate the policy impact of Asian women leaders, but does suggest a role model effect for other women in Asian societies (1991: 539). Unfortunately, she concludes, the exceptional and tragic means by which most Asian women attain executive power suggests that women executives are unlikely to grow in number in the years ahead (1991: 539).

More recently, Watson *et al.* (2005: 71–3) again seek to extract some commonalities from among women executive leaders based on their respective profiles. Like others, they find that many, though not all, women leaders hail from wealthy, prominent families, indeed, often families with ties to high office. Similarly, they find that several women leaders in the late twentieth century attained executive office during times of "social and political strife" which, in some cases, contributed to shorter terms in office. They also note that "women's leadership is an international phenomenon" with women executives to be found in nearly all world regions.

Jalalzai (2004, 2008) and Jalalzai and Krook (2010) summarize some of the existing literature on women executives and seek to make their own contributions based on their analysis of women leaders since 1960. In her early article, Jalalzai (2004) confirms the observation that Latin American and Asian women leaders have tended to attain power through family ties but notes that this has not been the case in Africa (2004: 103). Jalalzai's survey also reveals that most women leaders have very high levels of political experience and are relatively well educated (2004: 99). In her more recent article, Jalalzai (2008) reiterates earlier findings that women's overall status in a society seems to have little bearing on women's access to executive positions given that more often than not women attain executive office as members of privileged groups. She also notes, as have others, that "political transitions and instability have coincided with women's ascension to executive office all over the world" (2008: 223; see also Hoogensen and Solheim 2006). Finally, she claims that women are more likely to hold executive power when their powers are "relatively few and generally constrained" (2008: 208); thus they are more likely to be prime ministers than presidents and more likely to be presidents in systems in which they share power. More recently, Jalalzai and Krook (2010: 17) conclude that there appear to be important role model effects from women presidents and prime ministers, given that 15 countries have had not just one but two women executives. They further suggest that while some women executives have actively promoted women into cabinet and have advocated women-friendly policies, others quite clearly have not (2010: 17). These questions – concerning the extent to which women heads of state and government substantively represent women and the extent to which they bring more women into cabinets – are addressed in the regional chapters that follow. In addition, the regional chapters address questions of the individual characteristics of women leaders and how they have reached the pinnacle of executive power.

The scant literature on women in cabinets has tended to treat the subject from a regional perspective with the exception of some studies of women in cabinets in the United States in particular (see Carroll 1987; Martin 1989; Borrelli and Martin 1997; Borrelli 2002). Moreover, the bulk of studies concern women in cabinets in the developed rather than developing world. Most of the literature seems to rely upon mid 1990s data, thus missing out on the most recent developments in women's access to executive office. In one of the few global studies, Whitford *et al.* (2007) seek to uncover differences in women's representation and policymaking authority at the ministerial and sub-ministerial levels. Data from the mid 1990s are drawn from 72 countries. The study finds that women's presence at the ministerial level is positively associated with the proportion of women in the national legislature (assuming a parliamentary system) and the use of an open-list proportional representation electoral system. Women's presence at the sub-ministerial level, by contrast, is influenced by national supply factors such as women's educational attainment and women's economic roles as administrators and managers (2007: 560–1). Further, the study finds that the two levels of representation are conjoined: an increase in women at the ministerial level is associated with an increase in women's presence at the sub-ministerial level – and vice versa (2007: 573). Whitford *et al.* (2007: 575) suggest that the major significance of their study lies in the conclusion that women's ability to attain ministerial positions is attributable to political forces and initiatives rather than demographic and socioeconomic changes over time. Using data from a similar time period Reynolds (1999: 572) reports similar findings, namely, that the presence of women in cabinets is closely correlated with a government's political orientation and women's presence in the national legislature. He finds that in the mid 1990s women cabinet ministers were still far more likely to be occupying the "softer" socio-cultural portfolios than the four "harder" and more prestigious ministerial positions, namely, defense, finance, home affairs, and foreign affairs (1999: 564).

Mathiason and Dookhony (2006), with more recent data, make the same finding: that women's presence in ministerial positions is most strongly correlated with women's presence in parliament, with the closest correlations with the most recent parliaments. Siaroff (2000) probes Davis' (1997) work on cabinets in western Europe that identified "generalist" versus "specialist" recruitment norms for cabinet – with the former pulling ministers able to move from portfolio to portfolio from parliament and the latter selecting ministers based on their policy expertise and generally from outside the ranks of parliament. Davis found that women were much less likely to be selected for cabinet in generalist systems – among other reasons, because of the smaller pool of women in parliament, at least in the past. Siaroff's expanded study (in terms of number of countries) of industrial democracies confirmed that specialist recruitment patterns lead to more women in cabinets, as do more egalitarian political cultures and left and centrist governments (2000: 209). (Davis' other major finding was that women are more likely to be appointed to cabinet after an election than during midterm reshuffles, 1997: 85.)

While these studies have investigated women's descriptive representation in cabinets around the world, Atchison and Down (2009) examine women cabinet ministers' substantive representation in 18 advanced industrial democracies between 1980 and 2003. Noting that women's greater presence in national legislatures has had a beneficial impact on the adoption of social policy favorable to women, they seek to determine if a similar relationship exists between women in cabinets and female-friendly social policy (2009: 1). Investigating family leave policy in 18 parliamentary democracies, they find that the proportion of women in cabinet is positively associated with total weeks of maternity and parental leave guaranteed by the state. Moreover, given the role of executives in proposing and passing legislation, the authors assert that having women in cabinet is of even greater importance than having women in parliament (2009: 17). On a related note, in their study of the recent rapid proliferation of state bureaucracies for gender mainstreaming across the world, True and Mintrom (2001: 49) find that the proportion of women cabinet members has a statistically significant impact on the adoption of those bureaucracies whereas the proportion of women members of parliament does not.

Considerably less optimistic about the potential impact of women heads of government or cabinet ministers, Sykes (2009) argues that in the Anglo-American nations (Australia, Canada, Ireland, New Zealand, the United Kingdom, and the United States) several factors converge to thwart women executives' substantive representation of women. Sykes (2009: 37–8) suggests that Anglo-American institutions, ideology, and political development are highly masculinist, privileging traditional masculine traits in leaders and placing "women executives at a distinct disadvantage." Anglo-American political systems, Sykes continues (2009: 38–9), are adversarial systems with power heavily concentrated in the executive; indeed, only three women have ever been elected head of state in one of these countries. Worse yet, Sykes asserts (2009: 39), because of the "presidentialization" of the executive, "just as women reached cabinet level in greater numbers, the leadership opportunities associated with that office were eroding." Anglo-American women cabinet ministers, meanwhile (some notable exceptions aside), have largely held portfolios dealing with domestic policies and programs, such as education, health, and welfare – with the worry being that these positions "threaten to become regendered as 'women's posts'" (2009: 40).

Russell and DeLancey (2002), again relying upon data up to 1996, investigate women's presence in ministerial and sub-ministerial positions in Africa. In 1996, 26 African countries were below the world average percentage of women in ministerial positions (6.8 percent), while 25 were above. They seek to identify the determinants of women's representation in cabinets. In testing the relationship between gross national product per capita, literacy, life expectancy, and women's presence in cabinets, only higher life expectancy was found to be positively associated with more women in cabinet (2002: 160), thus confirming the findings of other studies that women's overall socioeconomic status in a polity may have no direct bearing on women's access to executive offices. In general, they conclude that during the period under study, 1970 to 1996, women were under-represented in cabinets in Africa, though there were signs of improvement, and that women were generally to be found in the less significant and less powerful ministries, a finding that had not changed during the period under study. Russell and DeLancey do not consider the education or health portfolios to be among the more important ministerial posts, despite their vital roles in African societies.

In two articles, Escobar-Lemmon and Taylor-Robinson (2005, 2009) investigate women in cabinets in 18 Latin American democracies from 1980 to 2003. In the first article (2005), they investigate some of the same issues treated in studies above – what factors seem to affect women's access to executive posts, the frequency with which women are appointed, and to which portfolios they are most likely to be assigned. They note that by the early 2000s women were represented in significant proportions in an increasing number of Latin American countries; indeed, they were 50 and 29 percent of ministers in Colombia and Honduras in 2003 and 2002, respectively. They conclude that by the mid 2000s it was unusual to find a Latin American cabinet without at least one woman minister. Further, in these 18 Latin American countries having more women in the national legislature was associated with more women in cabinet. In addition, Escobar-Lemmon and Taylor-Robinson found that presidents from leftist parties and presidents who found themselves in more partisan political environments were likely to appoint more women to their cabinets. Finally, they cite international pressure, in other words, a diffusion effect, as having a powerful impact on women's presence in Latin American executives as well. In their subsequent study, Escobar-Lemmon and Taylor-Robinson (2009) seek to determine whether Latin American cabinets are "gendered institutions," meaning, among other things, that "they may operate in a way that systematically denies women an equal opportunity to participate" – and that with a few exceptions women in cabinets will largely be tokens (2009: 685). They conclude that, overall, there are gendered patterns to cabinet appointments in the 18 Latin American democracies, but (and in contrast to the Anglo-American countries) that as the number of women in cabinets increases it is likely that women will also increasingly be appointed to the more prestigious ministries to which they are not typically appointed (2009: 696–7). All of the regional chapters in this volume address the issue of the portfolios to which women cabinet members tend to be assigned, in many cases questioning the accuracy of a hierarchical dichotomy of "hard" and "soft" portfolios.

Overview of the book

These findings and remaining questions from the literature on women executives to date form the backdrop for the rest of our book. Our cursory review of the literature reveals that there appear to be geographic patterns in women's participation and representation in executives and so we have organized the book into regional chapters, albeit with each regional chapter also providing an in-depth analysis of two or three cases within the region. The chapters are presented in an ascending order in terms of average regional (or sub-regional) presence of women in cabinets in early 2010 – with our regions representing the full range for women in cabinets around the world – from 7.6 percent in the Arab states to 49.7 percent in the Nordic countries.[2] So, Chapters 2 and 3 cover the Arab states and South and Southeast Asia, with case studies of Morocco and the United Arab Emirates, and Burma and Pakistan, respectively. Chapters 4, 5, and 6 treat Oceania, with focus on Australia and New Zealand, Central and Eastern Europe with focus on Croatia, the Czech Republic, and Lithuania, and sub-Saharan Africa, with focus on Liberia and Rwanda. Chapters 7 and 8 cover Latin America and North America, with case studies of Argentina and Chile, and Canada and the United States, respectively. Finally, Chapters 9 and 10 present Western Europe and the Nordic states, with cases studies of Germany, Spain and the United Kingdom and Norway and Sweden, respectively. A concluding chapter summarizes the main observations drawn from the regional chapters and provides a set of lessons learned from a comparative politics perspective.

Each of the regional chapters follows a framework established by the editors and drawn from the literature. Each regional chapter begins with an introduction and regional overview which provides an overview of the region, including historical trends in women's participation in executives since World War II. Some of the regional trends captured in these chapters include women's historic participation in politics in the region, women's access to executives as compared to legislatures in the region and the pace at which women are entering executives as heads of state and government and cabinet members. As noted previously, women's access to executives still lags slightly behind their access to legislatures and we seek to uncover whether this is consistent across regions. The regional overviews may also shed light on the importance that women attach to appointed executive positions as compared to elected legislative positions.

Next, each of the regional chapters focuses on two or three country cases in order to provide a more in-depth study of women's participation in executives in the region. Each of the contributors selected their country cases – based on interest, expertise, and available data and research, among other things. In general, the case studies tend to feature countries with more women in cabinets and/or with women as president or prime minister – with the idea being that those cases will have more insights to impart about women's access to executives. (Given this selection method for our case studies, however, it is largely impossible for us to draw broad generalizations from our findings.) Taking our cues from discussions of the importance to women's executive access of type of political regime, type of electoral system, and "generalist" versus "specialist" recruitment norms, we begin the country cases with a description of the political regime and the formal and informal rules of access to the executive. This section also provides an analysis of the evolution of the proportion of women in executives in the countries since World War II.

Debates around women's descriptive representation led us to query a series of socio-cultural, economic, and political factors to try to determine their influence over women's access to executive office. So, for example, the chapters seek to determine what, if any, influence the following factors have on women's access to executives: religion, education, views of gender-based social roles, the Human Development Index, the birth rate, the proportion of women in the labor market, the female/male revenue ratio, the per capita gross national product, public expenses in education and healthcare, the urbanization rate, the year women attained the right to vote and run in national legislative elections, the nature (parliamentary versus presidential) of the political regime, the nature (majoritarian, proportional or mixed) of the electoral system, and the political party system. As suggested by the literature that shows, for many societies, little relationship between women's overall socioeconomic status and some women's access to executives, these somewhat circumscribed socio-cultural, economic, and political factors may not be nearly as salient as larger and more complex phenomena. These more complex phenomena include the political opportunities offered by democratic transitions and post-conflict situations, the influence of national and international women's movements, the rise or demise of military regimes, and diffusion effects, among others. Ultimately the case studies provide us with a nuanced array of factors influencing women's access to executives around the world.

Before concluding, each regional chapter turns to women executives' substantive representation, a topic not well addressed in the literature. Indeed, as we also find, this is likely because the numbers are so small and modest increases in women's access to executives is very recent and therefore tracing women executives' substantive representation may be premature if not impossible.[3] This section of the regional chapters seeks to elaborate, in particular, the (potential) impact of executive women on women's legislative representation and on women's interests. Some of the answers to these questions lie in the portfolios for which cabinet women are responsible; thus we seek to ascertain whether women remain ghettoized at the bottom of an executive hierarchy or whether women are moving into the most significant ministerial posts – or even redefining what the most important posts are. We are also keen to ascertain to what extent women presidents and prime ministers bring in more women cabinet members and are able to or interested in advancing women-friendly policy agendas. Finally, we revisit the issue of the relationship between numbers of women executives and numbers of women legislators.

Our contributors are a balanced mix of junior and senior academics from universities around the world, all of whom have been engaged in significant women and politics scholarship in their own right, many for numerous years. This book has brought them together to interrogate the fairly discreet phenomenon of women in executive power in a given world region. As such, we are making a small but significant contribution to the overall scholarship on gender and politics. Many questions remain for future research, for example on the symbolic representation impacts of more women political executives or women's role in the third branch of government, the judiciary. Similarly, moving beyond the state, future research should interrogate women's descriptive and substantive representation in international financial institutions and international organizations. The relationships between women and political power around the world are complex and their explication requires a multilayered approach. We hope that *Women in Executive Power: A global overview* has contributed to a better understanding of women in politics and to these future research endeavors.

Notes

1 Numbers in this paragraph come from the following sources: Inter-Parliamentary Union (2010b, 2010c, 2010d), Hoogensen and Solheim (2006: 146–50), Jalalzai and Krook (2010: 6), WEDO (2007).
2 The nine regions utilized in this book present a mix of "regions" and "sub-regions" as identified by the Inter-Parliamentary Union (2010d), from which these figures are drawn. Table 11.1 in the Conclusion provides a complete rendering of women's average regional sub-regional participation in cabinets around the world.
3 Limited access to generally confidential executive documentation also makes this research undertaking more difficult.

2 Arab states

Vânia Carvalho Pinto

Introduction[1]

The term "neopatriarchal state" has been proposed by Sharabi (1988) to describe the general gender regimes of the Arab states.[2] This term refers to the impact of modernization on traditional patriarchal structures. According to Sharabi (1988: 4), material modernization only served to remodel and reorganize patriarchal structures and relations and to reinforce them by giving them "modern" forms and appearances. Furthermore, religion is bound to power and state authority, and the family, not the individual, constitutes the basis of society (Moghadam 2008: 427). Despite the commonality of socioeconomic and political factors, the actual ways in which women's political status is defined depends on the internal dynamics within each country (Sabbagh 2005: 52).

The expansion of women's rights in the Arab world has been intimately connected to both political movements for independence and decolonization processes, which unfolded throughout the late nineteenth and twentieth centuries. During both colonization and independence, gender issues occupied a paramount place within general discourses and programmatic reforms. The so-called backward status of Arab women was then politicized, and the modernization of women's roles, as mothers and as wives, was indicated as a necessary means for the development of society, the education of future generations, and the overall assertion of a national identity (see Abu-Lughod 1998). Thus, since the rights of women were defined along nationalistic lines, such delimitation determined the degree of political participation available to them within their respective societies (see Kandiyoti 1991; Moghadam 2008; Carvalho Pinto 2010).

This chapter discusses women in executives in the Arab states. The following section provides an overview of the participation of women in governments across the region since the second half of the twentieth century. Next, two country cases are investigated, beginning with a description of the political regimes in Morocco and the United Arab Emirates (UAE), continuing with an overview of the participation of women in executives in both countries and outlining the variables that influence women's access to executive positions. Finally, the chapter evaluates the potential impact that the presence of women in executives may have on women's legislative representation and women's interests.

Regional overview

Around the world, access to executive office is influenced by gender. Since men are usually depicted as the norm or as "natural leaders" (Jalalzai 2008: 206), this often leads to situations of discrimination and to the undervaluing of women's personal and political capabilities. The fact that so far there has been no female prime minister or head of state in the Arab region speaks to the prevalence and deep-rootedness of traditional views and religious interpretations that are unfriendly to the participation of women in politics (Schmidt 2008: 121). Nevertheless, despite these constraints, women have been making inroads in the political field throughout the last 60 years, and they have been part of all Arab executives at one time or another (UNDP 2005: 9).[3]

The first Arab country to appoint a woman minister was Iraq, with the nomination of Dr. Naziha al-Dulaimi. She took office in 1959 and was given the portfolio of municipalities (Worldwide Guide to Women Leadership 2009a). In the same year, Dr. Nafissa Sid Cara became secretary of state in charge of social affairs in Algeria, in the French colonial government (Suffrage Universel: Citoyenneté, démocratie, ethnicité et nationalité en France 2009). Her appointment was followed by the nomination of Dr. Hikmat Abu-Zeid as minister of social affairs in Egypt in 1962 (Egypt State Information Service 2009). Mauritania nominated its first female minister in 1971, Toure Aissata Kone, to the portfolio of family and social welfare. Since then, women have been present in the Mauritanian executive, either as ministers or secretaries of state, usually, but not exclusively, with the portfolios of women's issues or social affairs (Worldwide Guide to Women in Leadership 2009b). Sudan also nominated its first woman minister in 1971, Deputy Minister of Youth and Sport Nafisah Ahmad al-Amin. In 1975 Fatima Abd el-Mahoud became the minister of state of social welfare, the first woman to have a full portfolio. Throughout the years, women have also been present as ministers in the Sudanese government, usually as ministers of state, and assigned to different portfolios such as the environment, international cooperation, and the economy (Worldwide Guide to Women in Leadership 2008a).

Syria's first woman in the executive was Dr. Naja al-Attar appointed minister of culture in 1976; in Jordan In'am al-Mufti was appointed minister of social development in 1979. Still in Jordan, Laila Sharaf was appointed minister of information in 1984 (Worldwide Guide to Women in Leadership 2009a). In 1982, this time in independent Algeria, another woman, Z'hour Ounissi, assumed the position of secretary of social affairs; in 1984 she became the first female minister of the country, with the portfolio of social affairs. In 1997, Dr. Aziza Bennani was assigned to the portfolio of culture as a secretary of state in Morocco (Worldwide Guide to Women in Leadership 2009a). The first female minister delegate was appointed in 2002, and only in 2007 did a woman obtain a full portfolio as minister (Worldwide Guide to Women in Leadership 2007). In this year, the number of women ministers in Morocco reached an all time high with the appointment of five females, thus allowing the country to become the Arab state with the highest proportion of female ministers, 19.2 percent, according to January 2008 data. This number fell following a June 2009 cabinet reshuffle, after which the number of female ministers was only three. Lebanon's first female ministers were appointed in 2004, Leila Solh as minister of industry, and Wafaa Hamza as minister of health. Both stayed in office for only one year. Nayla Moawad was minister of social affairs from 2005 to 2008; and Bahia Hariri ascended to the education ministry in 2008 (Worldwide Guide to Women in Leadership 2009c).

The outline above shows that women's participation in the executive has been sparse in the Arab world, usually limited to one to three portfolios that are more often than not related to "soft" issues, such as social affairs and women's issues. That tendency is beginning to subside, albeit very slowly, as in 2005 when Egypt gave a woman, for the first time, the portfolio of manpower and immigration (UNDP 2005: 30). Until now, Jordan is the only Arab country to appoint a woman deputy prime minister (UNDP 2005: 203, fn. 3).

Other countries that nominated women to the executive only in the last decade are the Gulf states, thus confirming that political participation for women in that region only began from 2000 onwards (in both the legislature and the executive). The first woman with the rank of minister was Sheikha Hessa al-Thani, who was nominated by her brother, the Emir of Qatar, to the vice-presidency of the Supreme Council for Family Affairs. She did not sit in cabinet, however. Qatar was the first country to nominate a female full-fledged minister, Sheikha al-Mahmood, to the education ministry in 2003. In the same year, Aisha al-Siabia was appointed minister without portfolio in charge of the handicraft industry in Oman (al-Kitbi 2004: 9–10). Qatar was followed by the UAE, with the appointment of Sheikha Lubna al-Qasimi to the economy portfolio and by Kuwait with the assigning of the planning ministry to Dr. Massouma al-Mubarak in 2005. Dr. Mubarak later resigned and was elected into the Kuwaiti parliament in 2009. Other female ministers in the region include Dr. Fatima al-Balushi, nominated as the Bahraini minister of social development in 2005; and Dr. Nuria al-Subeih (education) and Dr. Modhi al-Homoud (housing), nominated in 2007 in Kuwait.

Currently, Oman and the UAE have the highest number of women ministers in the Gulf region, both with a total of four. Even Saudi Arabia, a country whose conservative religious interpretations strongly prevent women from conducting activities in the public domain, has a female deputy minister. She is Noura al-Faiz and was assigned to women's education. Her appointment was widely considered as a milestone for Saudi women's rights (Shaheen 2009).

Table 2.1 offers an overview of the participation of women in Arab executives in January 2008. As Table 2.1 indicates, until January 2008 the percentages of female ministers in the region ranged from zero (Saudi Arabia and Libya) to 19.2 percent (Morocco), percentages that are still below world regional averages of between 7.7 and 28.1 percent (UNIFEM 2009b). Further, according to Table 2.1, the Arab states with more women ministers up until January 2008 were Morocco and Jordan, the latter with 14.8 percent. However, since these data were compiled, some noteworthy changes have altered the picture. Due to a June

Table 2.1 Women in executive positions in the Arab world, January 2008

	Total ministers	*Number of women*	*% of women*
Algeria	37	4	10.8
Bahrain	23	1	4.3
Egypt	31	2	6.5
Iraq	39	4	10.3
Jordan	27	4	14.8
Kuwait	15	1	6.7
Lebanon	22	1	4.5
Libya	18	0	0.0
Mauritania	25	3	12.0
Morocco	26	5	19.2
Oman	33	3	9.1
Qatar	13	1	7.7
Saudi Arabia	28	0	0.0
Sudan	32	2	6.3
Syria	32	2	6.3
Tunisia	28	2	7.1
United Arab Emirates	25	2	8.0

Source: Inter-Parliamentary Union (2008).

2009 cabinet reshuffle in Morocco, the number of women ministers decreased to three, thus lowering the percentage of women from 19.2 percent to 11 percent (also the number of cabinet members increased from 26 to 27); in the UAE, two more women were appointed ministers, thus raising the total to four (while the number of cabinet members was reduced from 25 to 22). In percentage terms, this represents an increase from 8 to 18 percent women. Therefore, numbers from 2009 indicate that the Arab state with the greatest percentage of women ministers is the United Arab Emirates, located in the Gulf region, followed by Jordan, located in the Fertile Crescent, and finally Morocco, located in the north-western part of Africa. There was also a reshuffle in the Jordanian cabinet, but the number of female ministers remained the same (UAE 2008a; Gouvernement du Royaume du Maroc 2006; *Jordan Times* 2009).

These three countries, located in quite different areas of the Arab region, do share one attribute in terms of their political systems – they are all monarchies. For reasons of space and complexity, only Morocco and the UAE will be comparatively examined in this chapter. The UAE, on the one hand, despite having been the last of the Arab states to award women the right to vote and stand for election, has impressively topped the charts in terms of female presence in the government (and in the parliament). Morocco, on the other hand, despite a gender quota in parliament, has an unremarkable record in terms of percentage of female legislators, though it briefly occupied the top position for number of female ministers. Furthermore, a North African and a Gulf country are seldom grouped together for the purposes of comparison – except when they are both monarchies as in the case at hand – particularly as concerns gender matters.

Issues of geographical distance, divergent modern histories and, as Mernissi (2006: 123) notes, "very little cultural exchange" between the two regions, have generally not encouraged comparative examination. But the numbers presented here do encourage a closer comparison with regard to women in executives.

Country cases: Morocco and United Arab Emirates

Description of the political regimes

Both Morocco and the UAE are monarchies; the former is a constitutional monarchy, whereas the latter is a federation of seven tribal hereditary monarchies. The head of state in Morocco is the king, whereas in the UAE the head of state is the president of the federation, chosen by the seven rulers of the seven emirates that compose the country. They are all members of the Federal Supreme Council, the highest institution in the land. The presidency has so far belonged to the ruler of Abu Dhabi, which is the largest and wealthiest emirate. The states that make up the Emirati federation are the following: Abu Dhabi, Ajman, Fujairah, Sharjah, Dubai, Ras al-Khaimah, and Umm al-Qaywayn. Each of these regions has its own local government and ruling family.

In early 2010 Morocco was led by King Mohammed VI, enthroned in July 1999, and the UAE by Sheikh Khalifa al-Nahyan, head of the federation since November 2004. The Moroccan kingship has a religious component, as the king is also the "Commander of the Faithful" by virtue of his direct descent from Prophet Mohammed, the founder of the Islamic religion. There is no such component to the UAE leadership, although it is generally expected that rulers uphold and defend religious values.

Both states were subject to colonial domination, Morocco until 1956 by France, and the UAE until 1971 by the United Kingdom. Unlike the UAE, Morocco awarded suffrage a few years after independence, though it only became universal in January 2003 (CIA 2009c). The UAE, by contrast, is yet to render suffrage universal. In the country's first ever election, held in 2006 for the election of half the members of parliament – the Federal National Council – the system chosen was indirect elections by an appointed electoral college, made up of members selected by the seven rulers. Only these appointed members could vote and stand as candidates, which meant that only 6,689 citizens, or about 0.08 percent of the population, could participate in the elections. Of these, only 1,189 were women (Ameinfo 2006). There are no political parties in the UAE, and until 2006 formal political participation was only possible through royal appointment, a situation that has now changed.

In Morocco, the legislative branch is made of a bicameral parliament – a Chamber of Counsellors and a Chamber of Representatives. The first has 270 seats, whose members are elected indirectly by local councils, professional organizations, and labor syndicates. The second chamber has 325 seats, elected by popular vote from a proportional list system. For the 2002 elections, the political parties signed a national charter whereby 30 seats from the 325 would be reserved for women to be elected nationwide. The agreement was not made binding on the political parties, however (Naciri 2005).

As for the formation of cabinet in both countries, in the UAE the government is appointed by the president of the federation and the premiership is usually allocated to the ruler of Dubai. Ministers, according to article 56 of the constitution (UAE 2008b), are to be drawn from across the country, but in practice, the vast majority of the positions, particularly the most sensitive ones, are in the hands of male members of the ruling al-Nahyan family from Abu Dhabi. In Morocco, following legislative elections, the king selects the prime minister in consultation with the political parties. The governments are usually based on a coalition of parties that have the largest share of seats in the House of Representatives. Following consultations with the parties, the king nominates the prime minister and the members of cabinet. Since the formation of the cabinet is a royal prerogative, the cabinet may or may not be drawn from the legislature. Previous to the 1996 constitution, the cabinet was fully formed by the king, but since then, the king may take into account the prime minister's recommendations regarding the formation of cabinet, advice which is not binding (Storm 2007: 82, 125, 147).

Evolution of women's presence in the executive

Even though the constitutions of both countries do not discriminate against women in terms of enjoyment of political rights (Tahri 2003: 1–2; al-Kitbi 2004: 2), these rights in both countries have only started being truly implemented quite recently. In Morocco, this coincided with the reform of the political system in the 1990s (Naciri 2005), and in the UAE, despite a discussion period of about ten years (from roughly 1997 to 2006), a woman was only appointed minister in 2004. She is Sheikha Lubna al-Qasimi, a known professional and member of the Emirate of Sharjah ruling family. She kept her original portfolio until 2008 when she assumed foreign trade. She was joined in the government by Maryam al-Roumi as minister of social affairs in 2006, who had been an undersecretary in the same ministry since 1999. In 2008, two more women were nominated, Dr. Maitha al-Shamsi and Reem al Hashimi, both ministers of state without portfolio.

Before women joined the cabinet, undersecretary or assistant vice minister[4] was most senior position a woman could occupy in the UAE government. Dr. Aisha al-Sayar was the first female assistant vice minister, having occupied that position from 1981 to 1998, first in the social services department and later in the educational and central activities department at the minister of education. Thus, in the Emirati case, women became ministers (2004) before they became members of parliament (MPs) (2006).

In Morocco, the order was reversed. Women were first elected into parliament in 1993, and only joined the executive in 1997. Four women were at the time nominated as secretaries of state, and assigned the portfolios of youth and sports, education, mining, and social affairs. The situation was reversed in the following year, with merely two women remaining in the executive (Pennell 2000: 387). The 2002 cabinet had the first woman minister with a full-fledged portfolio. Her name is Yasmina Baddou, an attorney, who was appointed minister of family affairs. Two deputy ministers were then also nominated: Dr. Nezha Chekrouni, in charge of the Moroccan diaspora; and Dr. Nejma Thay Rhozali, in charge of battling illiteracy (Laskier 2003: 18). The Moroccan government that resulted from the 2007 elections had the highest proportion of women to date. Seven women were nominated to the executive, five of whom held the rank of ministers and two the rank of secretaries of state. These ministers were Dr. Amina Benkhadra, who was assigned the portfolio of energy, mines, water, and the environment. She had already been part of the 1997–8 government as a secretary of state of energy and mines. The same was true for Nawal El Moutawakil who was secretary of state of youth and sports in the 1997–8 government. She was the first Moroccan to win an Olympic medal in the 1984 Olympics in Los Angeles and the first Arab woman to win gold. According to Pennell (2000: 387), her accomplishments became the symbol of the regime's gender liberalism.

Other female ministers included once again Yasmina Baddou with the health portfolio; Nouzha Skalli as the minister of social development, family, and solidarity; and Touria Jabrane as the minister of culture. The two secretaries of state were Latifa Labida, in the ministry of education; and Dr. Latifa Akherbach in foreign affairs and cooperation (Bismi Infos 2007; Worldwide Guide to Women in Leadership 2007). This government meant Morocco was the most gender-friendly in the Arab region, with 19.2 percent women in the executive. A cabinet reshuffle in July 2009 resulted in the exit of two female ministers: Nawal al Moutawakil and Touria Jabrane, the minister of sports and the minister of culture, respectively. All other women ministers and secretaries of state remained in their positions (Gouvernement du Royaume du Maroc 2006). The loss of two women ministers meant a fall to 11 percent women in the executive, thus stripping Morocco of the prime position it had hitherto occupied.

The obvious questions that these percentages raise are the following: what reasons can be put forward to explain this downturn? And why has the UAE, the last Arab country to enable female participation, been rising in the statistics thus setting an example in terms of female participation?

Factors explaining women's access to the executive

In seeking to answer these questions, it is worth examining some socioeconomic indicators. As Table 2.2 illustrates, the starkest differences between the two countries are in terms of gross domestic product (GDP), female literacy, rate of urbanization, and the Human Development Index (HDI). In all three indicators, the UAE is clearly ahead with an almost 100 percent female literacy rate, a more urban population, and an overall better quality of life as expressed in the HDI. However, despite these differences, the two countries have similar birth rates, percentages of women in the labor force, and ratio of female to male earned income. Both countries are also predominantly Muslim.

Table 2.2 Socioeconomic statistics: Morocco and United Arab Emirates in comparison

Variables	United Arab Emirates	Morocco
Birth rate (2009 est.)	2.4	2.5
Female literacy (%) (1997–2007)[a]	91.5	43.2
Public expenses on education (%, 2000–7)	28.3	26.1
Urbanization (%) (2010)	78.0	56.7
Religion (% of Muslim)[b]	96.0	98.7
Human Development Index (HDI) (2007, per rank)	35 (very high)-value 0.903	130 (medium)-value 0.654
Women in labor force (%, 2005)	38.2	26.8
Estimated ratio of female to male earned income (2007)	0.27	0.24
Gross domestic product (GDP) per capita (US$) (2009 est.)	42,000	4,600
Public expenses on healthcare (%, 2009)	8.7	5.5

Sources: CIA (2009c, 2009d); UNDP (2009f).

Notes

a Data refer to national literacy estimates from censuses or surveys conducted between 1999 and 2007, unless otherwise specified. Due to differences in methodology and timeliness of underlying data, comparisons across countries and over time should be made with caution. For more details, see UNESCO (2010).

b CIA, *The World Factbook*, page last updated on May 27, 2010.

Indeed, prevailing religious interpretations are seen to legitimate conservative gender norms, but the former should not be held as possessing full explanatory potential with regard to the enjoyment of female political rights. This is primarily because religion is not monolithic; it is lived differently over time and space and deeply enmeshed in local traditions and cultural practices (al-Ali 2003: 218; Moghadam 2008: 425–6). Thus, due attention must also be paid to traditional gender views. Women are primarily seen as wives and mothers, and the wording of the personal status laws in both countries reflects that view. For example, women still encounter difficulties in engaging in public domain activities, especially because they require consent from their male guardians.[5] In Morocco, even though a new family code was approved in 2004 that includes a disposition that effectively removes the male right of guardianship, in practice, the new code has been facing difficulties in implementation due to the judges' lack of preparation to apply the new dispositions, and a generalized rejection and lack of knowledge of its provisions (Naciri 2005; Stauffer 2006).

Other traditional gender views are related to stereotypes regarding women's capabilities to enter the political arena. More specifically, men (and some women) tend to think little of females' capabilities and knowledge. Even if women may be well prepared by education and/or professional experience to become political officials, there is still a tendency to minimize their potential contributions. Part of this mindset is a belief in women's weakness, inability to take tough decisions, and lack of knowledge (Abou-Zeid 2006; Carvalho Pinto 2010; Naciri 1998: 19). Perhaps the pervasiveness of this mindset and the need to confront it whenever a woman joins politics helps explain the tendency for the nomination of highly educated women for ministerial positions, and for the election to parliament of similarly highly qualified females. As I have argued elsewhere (Carvalho Pinto 2010), this trend is particularly evident in the Gulf states, but also in Morocco (e.g. the first woman to be part of the executive, Dr. Aziza Bennani, has a PhD, as do several other female members of cabinets). In other Arab states, this trend is also apparent as many of the female ministers throughout the past 60 years are in possession of a PhD or are otherwise highly educated. They also tend to hail from an upper middle class background.

Although more research is necessary to further establish the link between Arab women's political participation and their educational levels, it can be suggested that in countries where the opposition to women's political participation is strong and largely rooted in traditional gender beliefs, women with high educational qualifications are the ones more likely, not only to enter the political arena but also, to be nominated to the executive. This may be because accusations of lack of knowledge are difficult to level in these cases, and because women with high academic qualifications may feel more secure in entering a predominantly male and hostile environment (Carvalho Pinto 2010).

Women's presence in Arab executives has been characterized as symbolic, limited to specific ministries, and conditional (fluctuating with changes in governments) (UNDP 2005: 202–3). While this may be so in Morocco where since 1997 women's presence in the executive has fluctuated a great deal, usually as a result of government reshuffles that lowered the number of women, in the UAE, the number of female ministers has been steadily rising. This may be seen as indicative of a political will to promote women into cabinet positions. Female access to sensitive portfolios (such as defense or the interior) seems very difficult to come by, as these ministries tend to stay in the hands of male members of the al-Nahyan family of Abu Dhabi. Similar difficulties in accessing these posts are experienced by women all over the world.

Given the constraints that surround female access to the executive, it is, in my view, unproductive and unfair to designate the few women who succeed in joining the executive as mere tokens. Not only does that charge minimize their efforts and achievements in reaching (and keeping) these positions, but it also ignores that men can also be tokens and, similarly to women, they are also part of their country's elite (Dahlerup 2006b: 297; Naciri 1998: 20).

Since in both countries the access of women (and men) to executive positions is largely dependent on the head of state, the Moroccan king or the Emirati sheikhs, to what extent do gender state policies offer clues to the reasons for the appointment of women to the executive? In the UAE, it should be noted that the past 30 to 40 years were devoted to ensuring female education and women's entrance into the labor force. For several decades after independence in 1971, there were portions of the population who did not believe in the usefulness of female education and who married off their daughters upon puberty. These cases still exist but are far less common than in the past. Such perceptions were largely rooted in a population that for decades lived a difficult existence, marked by poverty, illiteracy, and high mortality rates. Female political participation was even more controversial because it requires a high degree of exposure of women politicians to their constituents, which is culturally frowned upon. This issue was under public discussion since the late 1990s and it took almost ten years for the first woman to join cabinet. This can be ascribed to a number of reasons, chief among them that the state preferred not to touch such a sensitive matter given the strong opposition to it. However, the fact that the country is a federation and that policy is dependent upon the agreement of the seven rulers may also account for these difficulties. Each emirate has a different record in terms of gender issues, and securing universal agreement on this matter may explain why it took a decade-long discussion in order to nominate a woman to cabinet.

In Morocco, Sultan Mohammed V, the monarch that led the country to independence from France, was a supporter of woman's rights. He educated his daughters and encouraged his subjects to do the same. During the struggle for independence, women participated actively and they began expanding their scope for action within the public domain. For some time, the two struggles were synonymous. Similarly to the UAE, upon self-determination, the doors of administration were open to women although not at the top levels. Advances for women were made, but the Istiqlal party, which was for some time the only party, soon lost interest in women's concerns, such as illiteracy and political participation (Howe 2005: 147, 149–50). The accession of the current monarch, King Mohammed VI, marked a turning point in terms of Moroccan women's rights. He undertook a number of measures of high symbolic importance such as the closing down of the palace harem, and marrying an educated professional woman. For the first time, news of the engagement was made public, and information and photographs of the bride were sent to the press. She was also given an official title, which was a novelty for royal brides (Howe 2005: 10, 21).

Further innovations under King Mohammed's reign have been the women's quota in parliament and the increase in number of women ministers. In addition, an important change during this period was the alteration to the Personal Status Law, a long-standing fight from women's groups (Maddy-Weitzman 2005), notwithstanding the difficulties in implementing the law. In general, state policy in both countries on gender issues, despite shortcomings connected to personal law, tends to be characterized by an emphasis on the contributions that females can make to national development (Naciri 1998: 15; Carvalho Pinto 2010). In the last few years, particularly after 9/11 and subsequent calls for democracy, human rights, and the empowerment of women, measures to increase females' political participation have been stepped up (Fauss 2003: 88). The determination of these countries to display a progressive image internationally and be recognized as a modern country has certainly also played a role.[6]

Do women executives represent women?

Since both countries only recently experienced their first women ministers, it is still early to examine the impact that they or their appointments might have in terms of women's legislative representation and the furthering of women's inter-ests. Still, some departure points for future research can be identified. In the UAE it may be argued that the fact that a woman was first a minister and then an MP might have somehow prepared the population to see women as politicians. Research conducted in the post-election context, however, suggests otherwise (al-Dabbagh and Nusseibeh 2009; Carvalho Pinto 2010). People seemed unpre-pared to see women MPs in the legislature even though there was already a woman in the executive. Since this minister belongs to the ruling family of the emirate of Sharjah, her nomination may have been perceived more as a royal occupying a cabinet position, rather than a woman occupying that position. While her position in cabinet was a statement for women's political rights, it may not have been popularly perceived in that way.

In both countries, women's chances of becoming a minister depend almost exclusively on royal recognition of their work. In Morocco, with the introduc-tion of the constitutional disposition allowing the prime minister to recommend the cabinet, women have a further possibility to reach the executive, depending on their positioning within the political parties. The Moroccan king's appoint-ment of seven women to the executive upon the 2007 legislative elections was perceived by some as compensation for women's poor legislative results in pre-vious elections, and as a desire among state leaders to recognize female capabil-ities and strengthen their position within society (Touahri 2007). The latter perception exists in the UAE as well.

Given the context in both countries whereby female (and male) access to the executive is dependent on the head of state, what are the changes that women ministers can pursue to effectively further women's interests? Molyneux (1985: 232) long ago argued that it is "difficult, if not impossible, to generalize about the interests of women." This is so, she argued, because women are differently positioned within their societies and separated by differences of class, ethnicity, religion, and the like. Despite differences in the conceptualization of women's interests, however, female legislators are more likely than male legislators to advocate policies that promote the rights of women (Trimble 1998: 257–8).

Differences among women and the ways this may impact their mobilization is particularly evident in the two cases at hand. In the UAE, affiliation is expressed in terms of tribal belonging. Hence, from this perspective, it would be very difficult, at least in the foreseeable future, to see women organizing along other lines. In Morocco, even though the country has a vibrant women's move-ment, deep cleavages remain, particularly in terms of class. As Naciri (1998: 19–20) so forcefully argues, in Morocco, feminist demands are often presented as opposed to the "real" needs of women. Indeed, she claims that rural women, who make up half of the total female population, are presented as having con-cerns "very far from the extravagant demands of the feminists." She further argues that, from this vantage point, demands for formal political rights are seen as ridiculous given the physical and moral destitution of the great majority of women. These demands are seen as originating from a minority who represent only themselves and who constitute a marginalized westernized elite.

Still, in both countries, much of the impact that the appointment of women might produce is similar to impacts found elsewhere. They can:

1   provide role models for other women by symbolically displaying the message that, similar to men, women are entitled to participate in politics;
2   contribute to the legitimacy of political regimes (Tremblay 1998: 435); and
3   eventually draft or support legislation that would improve the status of women in family and labor law (Moghadam 2008: 429).

Fostering points 1 and 2 have undoubtedly been at the center of the appointment of women ministers in both Morocco and in the UAE. As regards 3, the extent to which women in the executive could influence gender politics would depend first, on whether they are interested in pursuing these matters; and second, on whether they have a feminist consciousness (see Tremblay and Pelletier 2000).

It would, however, be incorrect to place the onus of female participation in executives on royal will exclusively, and deny the role that several groups within both societies play in lobbying for female political inclusion. In Morocco, there is a vibrant women's movement that has been lobbying the government for several decades to expand women's rights. In the UAE, even though a comparable women's network does not exist, there are formal and informal channels by which the population can access the rulers and their wives, and put forward their claims. Due to the gender-segregated nature of society, women can have access to female members of the ruling families through kin connections, or through women's associations and Ladies' Clubs. These settings are often home to events focusing on the status of UAE women, and have constituted a privileged way of mainstreaming ideas that, through female members of the ruling families, may eventually reach the country's male leaders (Carvalho Pinto 2010).

Conclusion

Women have been participating in Arab executives since the late 1950s, although in limited numbers. Their portfolios are usually restricted to soft issues and they are rarely, if ever, assigned to more sensitive ministries. The variables which were found to more closely affect the access of women to the executive in the two countries under consideration were of a socio-cultural and political nature. The socio-cultural variables include religion, education, and the gender culture, and the political variables include the specifics of the monarchical regimes that characterize both countries.

A link between women's executive and legislative representation does not seem to exist at the moment (apart from the fact that, in Morocco, women were seemingly appointed to cabinet in order to compensate for their poor legislative representation), although this potential relationship warrants further investigation particularly as female presence in the executive becomes more common. Women's interests seem to be articulated more in terms of class in both countries, although in the UAE there is a further cleavage, that of tribal belonging.

Due to the recentness of women's accession to the executive, the dearth of research on the topic, and the fact that the monarchs from both Morocco and the UAE determine who will become minister, there is not, at the moment, an obvious connection between the presence of women in the executive and the furthering of women's interests in general, however they may be defined.

Notes

1 The transliteration of Arabic terms into English has generally followed the recommendations of the *International Journal of Middle Eastern Studies*. Adjustments were made in some cases so as to facilitate reading. They include the elimination of diacritical marks, and the favoring of certain spellings of words whose usage became more common among specialized English language literatures. For example, using the spelling "Sheikh" instead of "Shaykh." The spelling of names as they appeared in printed and online materials was maintained so as to keep accuracy in the referencing of the sources.

2 This contribution will adopt the Inter-Parliamentary Union (IPU) definition of Arab states, encompassing 19 countries. Those are the North African countries of Algeria, Egypt, Libya, Morocco, Sudan, Tunisia, and Mauritania; the Fertile Crescent countries of Iraq, Syria, Lebanon, Jordan, and the Palestinian territories; as well as the Arab Gulf states of United Arab Emirates, Kuwait, Qatar, Saudi Arabia, Oman, Bahrain, and Yemen (Inter-Parliamentary Union 2009a).

3 Information about women ministers in the Arab states is sparse and sometimes contradictory, particularly as regards the year in which women were first nominated. I drew extensively on the website Worldwide Guide to Women in Leadership (2010) for information, but whenever possible I tried to use official government sources.

4 In the website Worldwide Guide to Women in Leadership (2008b), Dr. Aisha al-Sayar is listed as an undersecretary. According to information she provided to me, she describes herself as having occupied the position of assistant vice minister. Since this may be an issue of translation, it will be assumed that both women occupied a similar position in the Emirati government.

5 In Muslim societies, men are considered the legal guardians of women. This means that women are in a situation of perpetual minority whereby their fathers and then their husbands are their legal guardians.

6 Dahlerup (2006b: 295) makes a similar case for the introduction of gender quotas across the world.

3   South and Southeast Asia

Andrea Fleschenberg

Introduction

There has been an overall increase in women's representation in executives worldwide in the past few decades, although the majority of countries is still far away from parity arrangements such as in Sweden and Norway (since 1988) or in Spain and Chile more recently. During the past six decades, women in worldwide executives remained largely compartmentalized:

> women ministers have been concentrated in departments that deal with traditional concerns of women. Fifty-six percent of the women cabinet ministers headed departments focusing on health, education, welfare, and consumer affairs, while only 15 percent held posts dealing with the economy.
>
> (Jensen 2008: 7; see also Stokes 2005: 143; United Nations 1991)

Reviewing women's representation and participation in Asian executives appears, at first glance, an impossible task given the diversity and heterogeneity of the region, its political systems and cultures, gender ideologies and political developments. At second glance, however, when analyzing the statistical data on women's inroads into the political mainstream and the top echelons of political power, certain patterns and trends emerge for the "region" as well as for the specific sub-regions.[1]

This chapter begins its journey through Asian countries with an investigation of the evolution of the proportion, patterns, trends and types of women in Asian executive positions since the end of World War II, a period when a significant number of Asian countries gained independence from colonial rule. The next section presents the reader with case studies from Pakistan (South Asia) and Burma[2] (Southeast Asia) – two countries heavily influenced by male-exclusive military regimes but with different policies and outcomes for women's political representation and participation. The case studies section provides a description of the political regimes of Burma and Pakistan, an overview of women's progress in their political executive positions, an analysis of how far socio-cultural, economic or political factors mediate women's access to cabinet and

positions as head of state and government and an evaluation – or rather estima-
tion – of the (potential) impact of women ministers and heads of executives on
the representation of women's interests.

Regional overview

From a worldwide perspective, Asian women were at the cutting edge of female
political participation and have set significant historical precedents: as the
world's first female prime minister (Sri Lanka), first prime minister and president of a Muslim country (Pakistan, Indonesia) or first female double-executive
(Sri Lanka). Female prime ministers and presidents repeatedly governed several
Asian nations: Bangladesh, the Philippines, Sri Lanka, India and Pakistan (see
Table 3.1). Women politicians have also been at the forefront of reform and
opposition as well as autonomy movements across Asia, for example Wan
Azizah Wan Ismail in Malaysia, Aung San Suu Kyi in Burma or Rebiya Kadeer
in China.

This outstanding participation of women, most of them coming from political
dynasties, is not met by an equal number of women at other levels of political
decision- and policy-making across Asia. As Table 3.2 shows, the level of executive and parliamentary representation of women varies to a significant degree
within Asia, but it is fair to say that most nations are far away from giving women
a just share of representation and participation. Access to the top political office
has not led to an increase in female political participation at the sub-national or
the national level, neither in parliament, bureaucracy nor government.

At the same time, women have made inroads into Asian politics in diverse and
intricate ways – via dynastic descent, quota regulations and civil society activism,

Table 3.1 Asian women as presidents and prime ministers, 1953–2009

	Country	*Year elected*
Presidents		
Suhbaataryn Yanjmaa	Mongolia	1953
Corazon Aquino	Philippines	1986
Chandrika Kumaratunga	Sri Lanka	1994
Gloria Macapagal-Arroyo	Philippines	2001, 2004
Megawati Sukarnoputri	Indonesia	2001
Pratibha Patil	India	2007
Prime ministers		
Sirimavo Bandaranaike	Sri Lanka	1960, 1970, 1994
Indira Gandhi	India	1966, 1980
Benazir Bhutto	Pakistan	1988, 1993
Khaleda Zia	Bangladesh	1991, 2001
Chandrika Kumaratunga	Sri Lanka	1994
Sheikh Hasina Wajed	Bangladesh	1996, 2009
Han Myeong-sook	Korea (Republic)	2006

Sources: Center for Asia-Pacific Women in Politics (2009).

Table 3.2 Proportion of women in parliament and ministerial positions in Asia, 1987–2008[a]

| | Percentage of women in... | | | | | | | | | |
| | ...parliament | | | | | ...ministerial positions | | | | |
	1987	1995	2000	2005	2008	1987	1995	2000	2005	2008
Afghanistan	n.a.	n.a.	n.a.	n.a.	25.8	n.a.	n.a.	n.a.	10.0	3.7
Bangladesh[b]	9.0	10.6	9.1	2.0	6.0	2.8	5.0	9.5	8.3	8.3
Bhutan	1.0	0.0	2.0	9.2	4.2	28.6	13.0	n.a.	0.0	0.0
Brunei Darussalam	No parliament					0.0	0.0	0.0	9.1	7.1
Cambodia	n.a.	5.8	9.3	10.8	17.9	n.a.	0.0	7.1	7.1	6.9
China	21.0	21.0	21.8	20.2	20.6	0.0	6.0	5.1	6.3	8.6
India[b]	8.0	8.0	8.9	9.2	9.1	0.0	4.0	10.1	3.4	10.3
Indonesia[b]	12.0	12.2	8.0	11.3	11.6	4.9	4.0	5.9	10.8	10.8
Japan	1.0	6.7	9.0	9.3	12.3	0.0	7.0	5.7	12.5	11.8
Korea (DPRK)	20.1	20.1	20.1	20.1	20.1	n.a.	1.0	n.a.	n.a.	0.0
Korea (Republic)[b]	3.0	2.0	4.0	13.0	14.4	n.a.	3.0	6.5	5.6	5.0
Lao People's Democratic Republic	n.a.	9.4	21.2	22.3	25.2	0.0	0.0	n.a.	0.0	11.1
Malaysia	5.0	7.0	14.5	13.1	14.1	0.0	8.0	n.a.	9.1	9.4
Mongolia	25.0	3.9	7.9	6.8	6.6	0.0	0.0	10.0	5.9	20.0
Myanmar/Burma	n.a.	n.a.	n.a.	n.a.	n.a.	n.a.	0.0	n.a.	n.a.	0.0
Nepal	6.0	n.a.	7.9	6.4	17.3	0.0	0.0	14.8	7.4	20.0
Pakistan[b]	9.0	1.6	n.a.	20.6	21.1	0.0	4.0	n.a.	5.6	3.6
Philippines[b]	9.0	9.5	11.8	15.4	20.5	10.0	8.0	n.a.	25.0	9.1
Singapore	4.0	3.7	4.3	16.0	24.5	5.1	0.0	5.7	0.0	0.0
Sri Lanka[b]	2.0	5.3	4.9	4.9	5.8	5.1	13.0	n.a.	10.3	5.7
Thailand	3.0	4.8	6.1	9.3	10.7	0.0	4.0	5.7	7.7	10.0
Timor-Leste	n.a.	n.a.	n.a.	25.3	29.2	n.a.	n.a.	n.a.	22.2	25.0
Viet Nam	18.0	18.5	26.0	27.3	25.8	0.0	7.0	n.a.	11.5	4.2

Sources: Inter-Parliamentary Union (n.d.); United Nations Development Programme (2009d).

Notes

a Data has been compiled for the years 1987, 1995, 2000, 2005 and 2008 from various UNDP *Human Development Reports* available online at: http://hdr.undp.org/en/statistics/data (accessed June 2010).

b A female has been prime minister or president.

or as career politicians. A certain number of women have managed to capture the executive level in diverse portfolios (see Table 3.3). South Asian women ministers occupy, mostly, traditionally perceived "soft" portfolios, i.e. health, women's affairs/development, youth and social welfare. In all countries of the sub-region women ministers are something of a rarity at the very center of political power (an exception being Hina Rabbani Khar, minister of economics in Pakistan). Interestingly though, Southeast Asian countries are generally marked by a larger number of women parliamentarians on average, although falling short of achieving the United Nations suggested critical mass of one-third, and women administer a variety of ministerial portfolios albeit also being significantly small in number. In the Philippines, Patricia Santo Tomas worked as minister for employment, Estrella Alabastro as minister for science and technology and in Malaysia and Indonesia women led the ministries of trade (Fleschenberg and Derichs 2008: 25–31).

The following sub-sections investigate the evolution of patterns, trends and types of women's executive political participation across the sub-regions of South and Southeast Asia.

South Asia

South Asia has seen an extraordinary number of female-headed executives in most of its countries, except for Afghanistan, Nepal and the Maldives. Beyond the top job, however, women's say in executive and legislative matters has been minimal since the countries' independence from colonial rule more than 60 years ago. This has only changed to a certain extent in the last decade and a half, largely due to quota provisions, which led to an increased number of active women politicians at sub-national and national governance levels. In the year 2000, only 7 percent of national legislators and 9 percent of cabinet ministers in South Asia were women. Prevailing gender biases and gender segregation of public and private domains across South Asian countries are two of the root causes. Politics and decision-making in general continue to be regarded as male domains, despite inroads made by women into local and national politics, as civil society activists challenging or engaging with the state over demands for women-friendly legislation, a repeal of discriminatory laws and practices and more female presence in governance structures.

> Decision-making has traditionally been regarded as a male domain in South Asia. Often using customs and traditions as a tool, women have been sidelined from most decision-making processes. ... This lack of liberty is a tradition that is rooted in the home and the community where male members maintain strict control over decision-making and follows through to the highest levels of national legislatures.
>
> (Mahbub ul Haq Development Centre 2000: 136)

Women have administered various portfolios as ministers or secretaries of state or as ministers without portfolio: for instance in Pakistan, Nepal, Sri Lanka and

Table 3.3 Women as cabinet members in Asia: percentage and portfolios, 2008

	Total ministers	Number of women	Percentage of women	Portfolio
Afghanistan	30	1	3.3	Women's Affairs
Bangladesh	25	5	20.0	Agriculture Foreign Affairs Water Resources Home Affairs Prime Minister (also responsible for: Women and Children Affairs, Defense, Electricity, Oil and Mineral Resources, Establishment, Housing and Public Works, Religious Affairs)
Bhutan	11	0	0.0	n.a.
Brunei Darussalam	14	0	0.0	n.a.
Cambodia	35	4	11.4	Permanent Deputy Prime Minister Relations with the National Assembly, Senate and Inspection Water Resources and Meteorology Women's Affairs
China	37	4	10.8	State Councilor Minister in Charge of the State Ethnic Affairs Commission Justice Supervision
India	45	5	11.1	President Housing and Urban Poverty Alleviation (also responsible for Tourism) Information and Broadcasting Railways Minister of State (Independent Charge) for Women and Child Development

continued

Table 3.3 continued

	Total ministers	Number of women	Percentage of women	Portfolio
Indonesia	35	5	14.3	Finance Health National Development Planning Trade Women's Empowerment
Japan	21	3	14.3	Justice State Minister for Consumer Affairs & Food Safety Social Affairs & Gender Equality
Korea (DPRK)	73	4	5.5	Two Members of SPA Presidium Vice Chairwomen of SPA Electronics Industry
Korea (Republic)	18	2	11.1	Gender Equality Health, Welfare and Family Affairs
Lao People's Democratic Republic	31	2	6.4	Labor and Social Welfare Minister to the Prime Minister's Office and Head of Public Admin. and Civil Authority
Malaysia	34	1	2.9	Tourism
Mongolia	16	1	6.3	Social Welfare and Labor
Myanmar/Burma	39	0	0.0	n.a.

Country				Portfolios
Nepal	28	2	7.1	Defense Foreign Affairs
Pakistan	48	2	4.2	Population Welfare Social Welfare and Special Education
Philippines	24	3	12.5	President Science and Technology Social Welfare and Development
Singapore	23	1	4.3	Minister of Prime Minister's Office
Sri Lanka	53	3	5.6	Child Development and Women's Empowerment Housing and Common Amenities Youth Affairs
Thailand	26	n.a.	n.a.	n.a.
Timor-Leste	15	3	20.0	Justice Planning and Finance Social Solidarity
Viet Nam	26	2	7.7	Vice President Labor, War Invalids and Social Welfare

Source: CIA (2008).

India: foreign affairs economics, women's development/affairs, youth affairs, education, population/social welfare, information and broadcasting, railways or urban development. Yet at the turn of the millennium, women's executive presence continued to be negligible: "A problem faced by female ministers all across South Asia is that they are seldom appointed to ministries that are normally considered high powered or influential. Social welfare related ministries are generally assigned to women ministers" (Mahbub ul Haq Development Centre 2000: 139–41). This pattern has also persisted under female heads of state or government.

In Sri Lanka, the first cabinet of Chandrika Kumaratunga assigned two women the posts of women's affairs as well as social services (Mahbub ul Haq Development Centre 2000: 141). In accordance with the constitution, her mother Sirimavo Bandaranaike administered the portfolio of defense and foreign affairs when prime minister. During her first presidential stint, Chandrika Kumaratunga chose to maintain control over the ministries of finance and ethnic affairs and national integration in order to be able to tackle corruption as well as to address the Tamil conflict (Jensen 2008: 187). Extended periods of female political rule in Sri Lanka and the early introduction of universal suffrage in 1931 have not broken open the political *malestream* at the sub-national and national levels, in parties, parliament and government structures. Instead, one finds the "stop-gap syndrome," i.e. the common feature of female appendage and widow politicians in Sri Lankan politics (Attanayake 2008: 260). The elitist character of Sri Lankan politics can be found at sub-national and national governance forums, e.g. all four female ministers under Chandrika Kumaratunga came from political families (Attanayake 2008: 265–6). For a brief period, Kumaratunga even chaired the ministerial portfolios of defense, interior and information in 2003 when she sacked parliament and ended a cohabitation government (Jensen 2008: 218–19).

Similarly, both female prime ministers of Bangladesh, Khaleda Zia and Sheikh Hasina Wajed, retained control over various key ministries such as defense, information, planning, power and energy during their governments, a step criticized as overstretching their capacities and thus failing to deliver. In her 1996–2001 cabinet, Sheikh Hasina Wajed assigned women politicians with a strong background in politics or grassroots engagement the significant ministries of agriculture as well as environment and forest. In her gargantuan 2001–6 cabinet of 62 members, Khaleda Zia assigned the same number of women ministers, but in the "soft" portfolios of women and children's affairs, cultural affairs and in a presidential advisor position for primary and mass education (Ahmed 2008: 284; Jensen 2008: 187; Mahbub ul Haq Development Centre 2000: 141). Critics charge that women politicians from reserved seats are commonly assigned less important ministerial portfolios or deputy ministerial posts without the entitlements of full-fledged cabinet membership in comparison to those colleagues who were directly elected (Chowdhury 2005: 185). The political participation of dynastic politicians like Zia and Wajed, alongside a slowly growing number of other women politicians, materializes in a context in which in the first decades after independence in 1971 women were discouraged by and excluded from political parties and public affairs, not only by Islamist parties, but also by the major political parties (Ahmed 2008: 281–3). This pattern prevails at sub-national and national levels: "So far not a single female member of parliament has been appointed as a Speaker or Deputy Speaker. ... Thus, women leaders in Bangladesh have had very limited access to the highest decision-making bodies" (Ahmed 2008: 284, 278). Since gaining independence in 1971 and until the military takeover in 2006, three executives were headed by women, but the percentage of women ministers peaked in Wajed's first cabinet with only 9.1 percent, while two cabinets were without female ministers and the other three had between 3 and 4 percent women in executive positions. The number of female vice-ministers follows this pattern, ranging from 0 percent under the same Wajed cabinet to a maximum of 6 percent under the first Zia cabinet (1991–6) (Chowdhury 2005: 185). Similar to the Southeast Asian Philippines, the political culture and rules of the game in Bangladesh pose a rather insurmountable barrier for ordinary women with no elite or dynastic background: (black) money politics; a high level of criminalization in politics such as guns, goons and violence; male-dominated patronage and lobby networks – apart from gendered socio-cultural biases and patriarchal gender role prescriptions, often inspired by conservative religious interpretations. Subsequently, few women participate at the various levels of political decision- and policy-making. Those who do are often relegated to deputy posts or dispensable tasks or compartmentalized in women's wings and women's committees instead of breaking with window-dressing and entering the political mainstream with a strong voice and leadership experience (Ahmed 2008: 287–92, Chowdhury 2005: 185–6).

The world's biggest democracy does not shine in terms of gender democracy – the first cabinet of Prime Minister Manmohan Singh included seven women out of 78 cabinet members, a female leader of the ruling party and, recently, India's first female president in a largely ceremonial role as well as the first female speaker of parliament. Even before this premiership, women were marginalized or even excluded from executive positions such as cabinet member or chief minister of a state. So far, only five women ever served as chief ministers in the Union of India (Nanivadekar 2005: 212).

Southeast Asia

In the only Southeast Asian country unmarred by colonial domination and with "seventy-two years (1939–2004) of experience of constitutional democracy," namely Thailand, few women have ever ascended to top executive positions: 16 altogether, but only five as full ministers. They administered portfolios like public health and labor or communication and university affairs (Tonguthai and Putanusorn 2004: 201). In fact, despite the early introduction of female suffrage in 1932 and the first woman elected as member of parliament (MP) in 1949, women's representation remained negligible in the following decades, mostly due to "a complex interaction of structural, institutional and cultural variables that have had the effect of establishing the political realm as a near-male monopoly" (Iwanaga 2008: 175–6).

In Cambodia, the national Millennium Development Goals foresee a significant increase in the number of women in political decision-making positions from 2003 until 2015. Women's share should increase from 12 to 30 percent in parliament; from 8 to 15 percent with regard to women ministers and from 6 to 18 percent with regard to secretary of state and from 0 to 15 percent at the level of provincial governor (Khus 2004: 14). At the same time, women's public engagement is met with socio-cultural resistance. Women are seldom perceived as capable of holding political positions given the political violence and "filthiness" involved, which leads to socially imposed restrictions on women's mobility, along with a societal bias on women's capabilities to cope with the competitiveness, stress and intellectual demands of political office. According to Khus (2004: 17), women therefore often do not enjoy the support of families and communities when they aspire to a political mandate. Women's contributions to post-conflict reconstruction were not able to challenge this societal bias and women's low political status (Jacobsen 2008: 149f.). Quite to the contrary:

> Until 1998, there were no female ministers. Women are expected to fulfill domestic responsibilities in addition to maintaining jobs outside the home ... This contradicts the policies of gender equity that have been espoused by every Cambodian government since 1979.
>
> (Jacobsen 2008: 149)

After the United Nations-sponsored post-conflict founding elections in 1993, five women secured deputy positions as "Under-Secretaries of State in the Secretariat of State for Women's Affairs, the Ministry of Social Action, the Ministry of Justice and the Ministry of Foreign Affairs" while others were only able to achieve "low-ranking jobs in government ministries after the elections" (Jacobsen 2008: 159). After the 1995 Beijing Conference, a full-fledged Ministry for Women's Affairs was established, a special advisor to the prime minister on these matters appointed, female legislators from the Cambodian royal family were selected as chairs of parliamentary committees and as ministers, alongside other women as ministers, secretaries of state and undersecretaries of state. At the end of the 1990s, a women's party was established. However, the number of women in governmental, legislative and party leadership positions at subnational and national levels remained low (Jacobsen 2008: 159–60). So far, women have occupied cabinet positions for women's and veteran's affairs, culture and fine arts, social affairs and vocational training (Khus 2004: 22–3). As reasons for women's few inroads into political decision- and policy-making analysts cite colonial legacies, the resurfacing of highly gendered traditional values, women's lower educational levels and the novelty of women in public/political positions and activities (Jacobsen 2008: 161–3).

Indonesian gender specialists emphasize the "pervasive patriarchal culture and the male-dominated political system" as the reason why "[w]omen members elected to parliament are very rarely found in policy making positions" (Soetjipto 2004: 40, 50). Under the rule of Indonesia's first female president Megawati

Sukarnoputri (2001–4), women's minimal share in political decision-making did not alter. She nominated only two women for her cabinet of 37 members (state minister of women's empowerment and minister of trade and industry), but none for the sub-national decision-making level, e.g. as governor or mayor. In the first government after the end of the autocratic *Orde Baru* regime, women served as minister of housing, settlement and regional development as well as state minister of women's affairs (Soetjipto 2004: 50, 53).

In Malaysia, the post-*Reformasi* period – similar to Indonesia – has also led to a positive change in women's political representation at the legislative level, when women transcended the boundaries of their political activity, previously relegated to supporting tasks in electoral and party politics (Abdullah 2004: 93–9). However, women's share in executive positions does not chronicle a similar rise, rather a minimal regression or stagnation from 10 percent (or three women) in 1990, 7 percent (or two women) in 2000 to 9 percent (or three women) with regard to cabinet ministers. At the lower levels, women's share for deputy minister positions increased slightly from 6 percent in 1995 to 8 percent in 2004 while the biggest jump occurred at the level of parliamentary secretaries from 0 in 1990 to 27 percent (or six women) in 2004 (Abdullah 2004: 96–7).

A mixed picture emerges from the Philippines where women are very active in civil society organizations, legislatures and executives, in a country led by women presidents for nearly three full terms since the end of the sultanist Marcos dictatorship in 1986.[3] Critics stress the fact that the post-1986 democracy is characterized as elitist, clientelist and kinship-oriented/dynastic with regard to male and female politicians alike (Veneracion-Rallonza 2008: 215). Commonly, women are assigned so-called "soft" portfolios, i.e. portfolios perceived to be in line with gender role prescriptions and biased socio-cultural values vis-à-vis women's public activities. Gendered assignments of women can be found at the Senate and presidential cabinet levels, in the latter with common portfolios in the areas of "social welfare and development, budget and management, labor and employment, and environment and natural resources" (Muñez 2004: 165).

An interesting case study is East Timor (or Timor-Leste), Southeast Asia's poorest post-conflict nation, currently undergoing nation- and state-building after centuries of colonial rule and repressive occupation. After the 2007 elections, women occupied 20 out of 65 parliamentary seats and three out of nine cabinet positions (including finance and justice). The national women's machinery includes a parliamentary caucus, a parliamentary committee, a state secretariat for the promotion of equality and a commission for gender equality, the latter two affiliated with the office of Prime Minister Xanana Gusmão (UNIFEM 2009a: 30).

Country cases: Burma and Pakistan

In Pakistan, a number of military rulers – with the exception of Zia-ul-Haq – presented themselves as modernizers and – at least on paper – addressed women's issues and maintained or introduced quota systems for legislative bodies. This is not the case in Burma. The military junta is male-only and few women have a stake in public affairs – most often female relatives of military officers, female appendage politicians alongside the important number of women engaging in the pro-democracy movement inside and outside the country via means of unconventional participation.

Description of the political regimes

Since its independence from British-ruled India in 1947, the Islamic Republic of Pakistan has had a history of military-censored weak civilian governments or military takeovers. The military seems unwilling to share or even transfer substantial power to civilian governments. Besides, civilian governments in the 1990s have been severely constrained by a semi-presidential system, a legacy of Zia-ul-Haq, under which the president (often with military background) holds broad key competencies. In addition, an influential bureaucracy confronts those in executive positions. In reference to Table 3.4, Pakistan is classified as a federal state with a parliamentary, albeit de facto presidential, political system with a mixed multi-party election system which includes constitutional reserved seats provisions for women and non-Muslims in the country's national and subnational legislatures. In this highly personalized political system, in which political parties serve as power vehicles for specific political leaders rather than as fully institutionalized bodies of popular interest aggregation, the president appoints cabinet ministers with the advice of the prime minister. In addition, top executive positions such as head of state and government are elected by electoral colleges, i.e. (sub-)national legislatures, rather than directly, and require for a person to be a Muslim.[4] Women achieved the right to vote and stand for elections with the country's independence from British India and had, with the late Benazir Bhutto, twice a female prime minister in the 1990s.

The Union of Burma is marked by extended and continuous periods of political self-isolation due to its parochial praetorian dictators, with a short record of parliamentary democracy and a decades-long history of continuous inter-ethnic secessionist fighting. Its isolationist authoritarianism has both structural and strategic sources – until 1988 a socialist, and since 1962 a nationalist, ideology which justifies a total state command and control, headed by military appointees, over large sectors of society and the economy. The military regime (SPDC) is ranked as one of the world's most repressive political regimes. The male-only appointed cabinet members are recruited nearly exclusively from the country's domineering military and its activities are overseen by the military junta led by General Than Shwe as head of state and Lt. General Thein Sein as prime minister. The 2010 parliamentary elections, the first since 1990, are supposed to result in the establishment of a two-chamber parliament with constitutional reserved seat provisions (25 percent) for appointed military members under a new constitution, itself contested given the adoption by an internationally regarded flawed referendum in 2008.[5]

Table 3.4 Myanmar/Burma and Pakistan: some selected political, socio-cultural and economic facts

	Myanmar/Burma	*Pakistan*
Political facts		
Nature of state	Unitary	Federal
Nature of political regime	Military junta	Parliamentary (de facto presidential)
Election system	Majoritarian	Mixed
Party system	Multi-party, at the moment no parliament	Multi-party
Voter turnout (%)	73.3 (1990)	44.5 (2008)
Quota regulation	No	Election law quota regulation for national parliament
Socio-cultural and economic facts (2007)		
Human Development Index (Nb=182) Rank/Value	138/0.586	141/0.572
Gender Development Index (Nb=155) Rank/Value	n.a.	124/0.532
Gender Empowerment Measure (Nb=182) Rank/Value	n.a.	99/0.386
Adult literacy rate (%)	89.9	54.2
Enrolment ratio (%)	56.3	39.3
Birth rate (%)	2.3	4.0
Female professional and technical workers (%)	n.a.	25.0
Female economic activity (%)	n.a.	n.a.
Estimated ratio of female to male earned income	0.61	0.18
Gross Domestic Product (GDP) per capita (US$)	904	2,496
Public expenses on healthcare (%)[a]	1.8	1.3
Public expenses on education (%)[b]	18.1	11.2
Urbanization rate (%)	33.9	37.0

Sources: CIA (2010a); Germany (2010); International IDEA (2010); United Nations Development Programme (2009b, 2009c).

Notes
a 2007: in percentage of government spending, 1995–2005: in percentage of GDP.
b In percentage of government spending.

Evolution of women's presence in the executive

In the less developed countries of South and Southeast Asia, women generally have less access to education, employment and resources compared to men from the same status group. On the one hand, this leads to fewer opportunities for an active political engagement at the various governance levels. As shown in Table 3.4, in the cases of Pakistan and Burma, both countries rank low with regard to (gendered) human development, also in regional comparison. Pakistan ranks in the lowest quarter of the human and gender development indices, given its low rates of literacy, enrollment, female managers, female skilled workers as well as overall formal female economic activity and a high male–female income disparity. Similarly, human development levels in Burma are equally ranked low with the United Nations Human Development Index although statistics are scarce so that no value could be calculated for the gendered dimensions. But it is important to note that rates of adult literacy or enrollment are significantly higher and the male–female income disparity is significantly lower than in Pakistan. On the other hand, women's participation in South and Southeast Asian politics is thus often intimately linked to a feudal factor: female mobility and agency correlate with social descent so that class trumps gender and opens up public agency options in a rather misogynist, segregated socio-political environment. As a consequence, the political arena is dominated by elitist women who bring along the necessary support system (e.g. education, money), "a dominance also supported by their privileged location in pre-existing social and political hierarchies" (Tambiah 2002: 8).

In this regard, Pakistan is an exemplary case in point. The country has seen a few women ministers in the various civilian as well as military governments, for instance responsible for women's development and youth affairs, education, information and broadcasting or population welfare (Zahab 2005: 279–80; Mahbub ul Haq Development Centre 2000: 139–41). An interesting exception has been the former Pakistani minister of economics, Hina Rabbani Khar, who briefly occupied this office under the military government of General Pervez Musharraf.

Nevertheless an outstanding achievement, the emergence of two-time Prime Minister Benazir Bhutto, fits perfectly into the general pattern of women in Pakistani top politics so far – a politics dominated by a few elite families, including the occasional woman.[6] Other prominent examples of appendage politicians in their own right are the 1965 presidential woman candidate Fatima Jinnah, sister of the country's founding father; Jahan Ara Shahnawaz, member of the constituent assembly (who was particularly devoted to codifying women's rights); Nusrat Rana, the first woman ever to contest a general seat; Nasim Wali Kahn, a politician and party leader in the conservative Khyber Pakhtunkhwa; and Syeda Abida Hussain, the first woman to win on a general seat.

Furthermore, women enter high level politics – mainly temporarily – when their husbands are jailed or assassinated, as was the case with Benazir Bhutto's mother Nusrat (Zulfikar Ali Bhutto) and sister-in-law Ghinwa (Murtaza Bhutto), Tehmina Durrani (Mustafa Khar, former Punjab Chief Minister) and Kulsoom Nawaz (Nawaz Sharif, former prime minister and exiled after 1999 until 2007). As Mehnaz Rafi, an exception to the overall general female participatory pattern, explains, "the public becomes sympathetic with widows and orphans which is a convenient political capital for a party to give leadership to female relatives."[7]

In Burma, very few women entered the male domain of politics throughout the country's modern history; indeed, Burma is the only country of Southeast

Asia were women are absent from political decision-making at most levels given a male-exclusive military regime. But the post-colonial period started off differently as women received the right to vote under British colonial rule[8] in 1935, and the right to stand for elections in 1946, shortly before the country's independence, with women being elected straight into Burma's first democratic parliament in 1947. The first woman to contest elections was Daw Hnin Mya in 1936, who won a seat in Burma's first Legislative Assembly in the first elections that granted women political citizenship (Mi Mi 1984: 157). In the short period of parliamentary democracy from 1948 to 1962, an overall number of 18 women contested national parliamentary elections, but only one woman so far, Ba Maung Chein, held the rank of a minister in the cabinet of Prime Minister U Nu for a short period (1953–4), as responsible for Karen Affairs (Silverstein 1990: 1009; Mi Mi 1984: 159).

Like in most South and Southeast Asian countries, we also find a pattern of dynastic pathways to female political involvement. For example, in 1947, after the assassination of the post-independence shadow cabinet under the founding father Aung San, wives of the deceased independence leaders were appointed as temporary members of parliament, like Daw Khin Kyi, wife of Aung San and mother of Aung San Suu Kyi (Silverstein 1990: 1009; Mi Mi 1984: 159). Such a co-option of women into politics via familial ties existed already during British colonialism and continued under various military regimes since 1962, where the generals' wives occupy important posts as brokers in the political patron–client wicker-work/pyramid and in their leadership of corporatist or social organizations.[9] This pattern of political recruitment permeates many South and Southeast Asian political cultures and systems.

Factors explaining women's access to the executive

Pakistan and Burma are Asian nations where military rule and religion have mediated and often restricted female opportunities for political participation and women's access to political decision-making, among other factors. In both cases, the male-exclusive institution of military regimes has had a part in shaping women's public roles, as has religion. Interestingly though, conservative religious forces and their scriptural interpretations have posed an obstacle to women's acceptance as political leaders and public figures in both countries. However, the role of military rulers/regimes with regard to granting or denying women a stake in public decision- and policy-making is more ambiguous, as previously mentioned.

Although women constitute 22.5 percent of seats in the parliament of Pakistan – given the quota regulation introduced in 2002 by the military regime under General Musharraf – the gender-sensitive societal picture worsens when it comes to female administrators and managers or female professional and technical workers or female literacy and educational enrollment. Through the concept of *purdah*, which permeates all spheres of women's lives in Pakistan, many women are discouraged from active participation in public places, such as decision-making and the exercise of active and passive voting rights, resulting in a rather limited female political representation, except for the periods in which quota regulations are in place (Shaheed *et al.* 1998: 3, 16, 22; Zia and Bari 1999: 23–6). Consequently, female political representation and participation follow the principle of co-opting women through reserved seats and are characterized by an elite-oriented "appendage" phenomenon. Women in rural as well as urban lower to low middle classes make up the most marginalized and disadvantaged group. Moreover, politics is dominated "by few interest groups, an alliance of bureaucracy, military, feudal or tribal class" in a cultural setting where "women are not seen separate from the family due to social patriarchal structure"[10] and therefore few enter politics based on their own merit.[11] Nevertheless, political socializing remains difficult for all women politicians, who are constrained by lack of critical mass and the weight of religion in their interpersonal relations and acceptance.[12] Since *nizam-e-Mustafa*, the Islamization of law and society introduced by Zia-ul-Haq over three decades ago, the misogynist-oriented "political pendulum has by no means been reversed" (Rouse 2004: 102). To this day, "the socio-economic and cultural factors constricting women's operative framework remain largely untouched" (Shaheed *et al.* 1998: 1).

In present-day Burma, we find three major socio-political players or power holders, who all draw the terminology of their political values and traditions primarily from Burmese culture, most of all Theravada Buddhism. First, the military *junta*, including its extensive vertical crony system across the territory; second, the *sangha* (Buddhist clergy), who are also deeply embedded and influential in Burmese society across the country; and, third, the pro-democracy movement under the leadership of Aung San Suu Kyi, which is the less visible one in terms of physical and institutional presence under the authoritarian circumstances, and hence represents rather a symbolic power and counter-weight based on a mixed set of universal and Buddhist democratic values.

When one travels through Burma, women's overall presence in public life, especially in the economic sector of everyday commodities, is striking in a country where society's life and fate is exclusively dominated by male decision-makers, in the form of the military in the political field (with the key exception of Aung San Suu Kyi or *The Lady*) and Buddhist authorities (the *sangha*) in the spiritual arena.

> Traditionally political power was a male preserve and membership of the Buddhist monk-hood an exclusively male privilege. Cultural concepts ensured official power gravitated to the male while Buddhist ideologies reaffirmed men's superior status in the hierarchy of rebirth. Despite this, women played critical roles in society, the economy and the household and in many areas enjoyed equality with men.
>
> (Mills 2000: 265)

The exclusively male military regimes[13] of nearly half a century had a severe impact on the status of Burmese women: the state was profoundly militarized and thus became more masculine, which had a "detrimental impact on women's lives as their customary independence and status was eroded" (Mills 2000: 266). Given this context, the exceptional challenge to the regime and its legitimacy through pro-democracy opposition leader Aung San Suu Kyi's leadership and socio-political vision becomes even more evident and significant: "As the 'space' ascribed for women in Burma was reduced, it was a woman leader who demanded an equal 'space' not only for women but for all members of the community that is modern Burma" (Mills 2000: 266). As one of Aung San Suu Kyi's advisors put it: "Although women have equal rights, there are nearly no important women in politics. The only important woman is under arrest."[14]

According to opinions gathered inside Burma and among the exiled community in Thailand, there is a general belief that women are not discriminated against and are equal to men. Women can have all kinds of professions and positions if they wish to, although, in reality, men are regarded as the legitimate householders, and women are represented neither above middle management level, nor in leadership and decision-making positions in politics, society and economics.[15] The female under-representation in decision-making bodies derives from cultural Buddhism-based beliefs, which generate the thinking that women do not have the capacity to speak in public and, instead, occupy the prime role of family caretaker.[16]

However, the nature of the decades-long military regime[17] and a general societal male bias, which endows women with less (or no) leadership competencies and which includes a gender-specific socialization along the values of passivity, nurturing support and "to take the back seat," are identified as the main obstacles for women's political leadership.[18] With the public–private split still very much in place and due to the nature of the political regime, it appears that only certain women can access public and political arenas. Only those women, who are "politically correct" (for the regime), can be successful and hence have the right connections at their disposal, which means women from privileged descent – this applies to the economy, to government service as well as to social organizations.[19] So far in Burma, very few women have entered the male domain of politics throughout the country's modern history. Although Burmese women have engaged in politics, under British colonialism and in different post-independence regimes (since 1948), by means of both conventional and unconventional political participation, the number of women ministers is negligible.

Do women executives represent women?

Given the low numbers of women in executive office in the post-colonial period since 1945, it is nearly impossible to know whether women in executives can and do represent women if they have to operate in a nearly male-exclusive, often misogynist socio-political system as can be found in the case studies under review. This question comes too early to be answered in the case of Burma with only one female cabinet minister in the 1950s. However, Aung San Suu Kyi is an outspoken leader for women's rights, participation and development and she certainly serves as a role model for her female followers in the pro-democracy movement. But her concerns are so far only on paper and communicated in speeches and they lack the test of implementation as when in elected or appointed political office.

With regard to Pakistan, a similar picture can be drawn for the quantitative dimensions of female executives. One also has to acknowledge the nature of the Pakistani state and its regulatory quality with regard to the implementation of laws and the impact of quota provisions. The state lacks a functional and sectoral outreach and Pakistani society is marred by legal pluralism and a restricted access of women to political and judicial institutions, not only to the public arena as such. Consequently, several initiatives by women ministers in the field of anti-discrimination laws as well as protective legislation (e.g. sexual harassment, domestic violence), for example by Sherry Rehman of the government of Benazir Bhutto's widower Asif Ali Zardari, definitely represent and consider women's concerns and interests. But these policy-making efforts face an uphill battle for implementation and thus daily significance for the "average" woman in Pakistan. While Benazir Bhutto is referred to as a role model for women politicians and female political aspirants across the political spectrum, her gender policy regime has been criticized for achieving too little. In addition, it is questioned whether elite women politicians or appendage politicians from the country's influential families can really represent the majority of women in a highly stratified society where little inter-class mobility and interaction occurs and the women's movement is also criticized for lacking grassroots participation and agenda-setting. However, it remains to be seen what those women politicians, who entered the political system through reserved seats at the grassroots levels, will be able to achieve in the coming years when climbing up the political ladder.

Conclusion

"Instead, gender equality is neither a sufficient nor a necessary condition for shattering the executive glass ceiling. Moreover, a country with a woman leader does not signify the end of gender discrimination" (Jalalzai 2008: 229). Asian top executives such as Corazon Aquino, Benazir Bhutto, Indira Gandhi, Khaleda Zia, Sheikh Hasina Wajed or Chandrika Kumaratunga did not opt for the way of Chilean reform president Michelle Bachelet with her parity government and female ministers for economy and defense, Angela Merkel of Germany or Ellen Johnson Sirleaf of Liberia with a critical mass of women in cabinet positions. Instead, many appointed long-standing or new political allies and loyalists to executive posts and considered few other women, sometimes only female family members as in the case of Khaleda Zia (elder sister) and Benazir Bhutto (mother) (Jensen 2008: 179–88, 226).

It is somewhat surprising that those women who have risen to the top have not included more women in their governments. ... In selecting members to serve in their cabinets, political leaders must take into account a number of considerations that have worked against the inclusion of women. First, a leader, if she is prudent, will reward those who backed her candidacy. Second, a leader is likely to appoint some with extensive experience, especially if she herself is a newcomer to high-level office, and, finally, she must include representatives of the various interests in her political party or coalition of parties as she is dependent on their support.

(Jensen 2008: 174)

A rather negative case in point is Megawati Sukarnoputri with not a single woman in her large 33-member cabinet and no female advisor to her presidency, because, as she explained in an interview, "it's very hard and tough work. I am doing it, yes, but that is why I think I am rather unique" (as quoted in Jensen 2008: 186). In contrast, Gloria Macapagal-Arroyo appointed seven women to her presidential cabinet in order to increase female political participation (Jensen 2008: 185). Others point to the fact that most female heads of state or government gained political power in volatile circumstances, for instance directly after a political transition, in a political power stalemate or in a post-conflict scenario marked by low levels of political institutionalization and/or high(er) levels of political contestation. At the same time, an elite background does not necessarily translate into a genuine concern and progressive understanding of women's interests and welfare (Jalalzai 2008: 207ff.).

During the last decades, women have been assigned soft portfolios or subministerial positions in Asian executives. This picture is changing with women assuming nearly the whole range of cabinet tasks: from agriculture, foreign affairs, home affairs, urban planning/infrastructure, finance, trade, justice, defense to social welfare related topics such as labor, social/population welfare, education or women's affairs/development in 2008.

When reviewing the literature, it became evident that most of the studies assess women's political representation and participation at the national and subnational legislative levels or quota regulations and their impact on representation and political performance rather than evaluating women's inroads and performance in national cabinets. Another literature focuses on women prime ministers and presidents, as outlined above. Take, for example, Veneracion-Rallonza's statement on male and female presidents, governing since the Philippine democratic transition in 1986:

it is interesting to point out that the term of Fidel Ramos (1992–8) saw the most number of pro-women laws enacted, with a major concentration on women in development and economic empowerment. ... Corazon Aquino comes in second for the enactment of women-related laws. ... As a woman political leader, she [Gloria Macapagal-Arroyo] has been governing with the framework of *realpolitik* or politics of power and thus, has not shown any counter-pattern to her male predecessors.

(Veneracion-Rallonza 2008: 236, 245)

Little information can be found on what impact women ministers had on legislative policy-making and on serving as role models for other female political aspirants. Two examples from Southeast and South Asia illustrate certain symptomatic concerns as well as of a research desideratum to be addressed. First, with regard to Thailand's female ministers:

> None of them has made a point to explicitly promote women's issues, even as women's groups pressure them to do so, probably believing that, as female cabinet ministers, if they can show their capabilities in their jobs and show them comprehensively, they will become role models for other women as well as make it easier for men to accept women in higher decision-making positions.
>
> (Tonguthai and Putanusorn 2004: 201)

Second, in their report for the United Nations Human Development Reports Program, researchers concluded with regard to South Asia: "The tragedy of the female parliamentarian or cabinet minister is that even women in influential positions have tended to focus on 'national' rather than women-specific issues" (Mahbub ul Haq Development Centre 2000: 141).

This finding is not entirely surprising given their novelty factor and the continuously low number of women in cabinet and parliamentary positions as well as the pervasive androcentric institutional environment, socio-cultural values and features of political culture in most countries. Women have just started to tremble the various glass ceilings and glass walls in many political arenas in order to overcome their political and socioeconomic marginalization. In a number of countries, women politicians tend(ed) to have an elitist background and are thus not serving as role models for their fellow female citizens from different social strata.

Notes

1 This comparative analysis does not consider in depth, due to editorial constraints, East Asia and Australasia (e.g. Australia, New Zealand) or countries such as Iran, which certain indices classify as Asian or Asian-Pacific countries. Australasia is considered in the next chapter.
2 The country is referred throughout the text with the name of Burma, in full acknowledgement of the political dispute. In the various tables of the chapter, however, the country is referenced as Myanmar/Burma to allow easier identification in international statistics.
3 Roces highlights another pattern of female political participation at the higher levels of Filipino political power, namely, that of the wives and even mistresses of powerful male politicians in a system marked by kinship politics and puissant patronage networks:

> Philippine politics is not male-dominated but gendered. In the gendering of power and politics, men exercise official power as senators, congressmen, mayors, and councilors. Women are ascribed unofficial power and traditionally expected to occupy the space behind the scenes wielding power as part of the support system of the kinship group.
>
> (Roces 2000: 115; see also Veneracion-Rallonza 2008: 241)

4 CIA (2010c).
5 CIA (2010b, 2009a).

6   Pakistan is a very class-conscientious society where one needs good connections
      in society (even advantage compared to men without it) and needs to speak
      English which is the language of power – Benazir Bhutto had all three, plus a
      better public image than her brothers. Nobody thought of the gender issue when
      she rose to power – after a certain class status, a person becomes nearly gender-
      less as class protects to a certain extent.
           (Beena Sawar, journalist and filmmaker, interviewed in Karachi, April 2004)

7 Interview in Lahore, April 2004.
8 Burma experienced female reigns in the fifteenth and nineteenth centuries. Women
   were involved politically in very limited numbers during British colonialism as
   members of Rangoon City Corporation, Legislative Council, Student Union of
   Rangoon University and, probably the most prominent, Daw Mya Sein who represented Burmese women at the Round Table Conference in London where the country's fate was discussed (Silverstein 1990: 1008–9).
9 Interview with an advisor of Aung San Suu Kyi, Rangoon, March 2004. According
   to Yi Yi Myint's report on Burma's gender profile – written from a pro-regime
   perspective – few women head government departments in the position of director
   general or managing director (the highest rank available to a woman as several
   interview partners confirmed), but there are no current or long-time official statistics available (Yi Yi 2000: 38). In the country report to the 1995 Beijing Conference, it is written that although women hold 40 percent of public service posts in
   state organs and ministries, only a meagre 0.4 percent hold high level posts, resulting in 0.11 percent of women employed in the public sector (Yi Yi 2000: 39). Yi
   Yi Myint comments: "Just as men are heads of households, it is perhaps considered
   more appropriate for men to be the public figures of authority and power" (Yi Yi
   2000: 39).
10 Anis Haroon, interviewed in Karachi, April 2004. By contrast, women are perceived
   as a pacifying and unifying force by natural instinct, which is extended to public life
   and population, as Senator Farhatullah Babar, Press Speaker of the Pakistan People's
   Party (PPP) and Benazir Bhutto outlined during the interview in Islamabad, April
   2004.
11 "Ironically, it was a military dictator who brought so many women into politics. Class
   trumps gender so only high class people can become patrons – they haven't earned it,
   it is the reward of their ancestors" (Sabeen Jatoi, lawyer, interviewed in Karachi,
   April 2004).
12 According to Asma Jahangir, Salma Waheed and Mehnaz Rafi, interviewed in Lahore,
   April 2004, Senator Farhatullah Babar, Press Speaker of the PPP, interviewed in
   Islamabad, April 2004, and Sherry Rehman, former close aide of Benazir Bhutto,
   former minister of information under President Zardari and leading PPP woman
   parliamentarian, interviewed in London, July 2004.
13 According to Mills (2000: 274), women constitute less than 1 percent of military
   members, largely in medical and clerical duties and with no combat roles.
14 Interview conducted in Rangoon, March 2004.
15 However, there exist more than just subtle gender barriers for professional women,
   given that long working hours, business dinners or business travels are not considered appropriate for married women (Ma Thanegi, interviewed in Rangoon,
   March 2004). Even in the opposition party National League for Democracy (NLD)
   women are mainly active in supportive roles such as petition-makers, organizers of
   signature lists and office staff, rather than in executive positions in the executive
   council of the NLD or in the different bodies of the exiled movement, which are
   nearly all taken by male colleagues.

16 Interviews conducted in Thailand in March and April 2004 with members of the pro-democracy opposition movement and women's rights activists (e.g. Nang Hseng Noung, Women League of Burma; Zipporah, Karen Women Organisation or Dr. Cynthia Maung, prominent medical doctor and head of a refugee clinic). Exemplary is a middle-aged male interviewee, a former government servant turned artist, who defined the ideal woman as a housewife, fond of children, educated, supportive of his lifestyle and demands. According to him, women cannot be leaders, as they always need a helping hand (interview conducted in Mandalay, March 2004).

17 As one former government servant pointed out, women hardly reach leadership positions (above assistant management director) as those posts are provided for retired military who are then transferred into government service (interview conducted in Rangoon, March 2004).

18 Opinion gathered among various women interviewed who themselves occupy leadership positions, mainly in social life. One female interviewee (of Kachin origin) pointed out that a strong female leader always encounters harsh criticism: mistakes are attributed to her family life and personality – which seems also to be true in the case of Aung San Suu Kyi, who would not be criticized so severely if she were a man. Men might accept the leadership quality of white women, but they still have to prove that they accept women as leaders in their own ethnicity (interview conducted in Rangoon, March 2004).

19 This opinion was prevalent among NGO workers as well as businessmen. The issue of political correctness in regard to gender discrimination can be seen, according to one of Aung San Suu Kyi's friends, that "she" remains under arrest and is not allowed to achieve the power she is entitled to (interviewed in Rangoon, March 2004).

4 Oceania

Jennifer Curtin and Marian Sawer[1]

Introduction

Oceania is a highly diverse region, made up of Australia, New Zealand and a large number of Pacific Island states and territories. Basically, it includes two sub-regions – Australasia and the Pacific Islands, that is Melanesia, Micronesia and Polynesia. Australasia consists of Australia (and associated dependencies) and New Zealand. Melanesia includes the independent states of Papua New Guinea (PNG) and Fiji and parts of Indonesia, among others, while Micronesia and Polynesia each encompass a few independent island states as well as dependencies such as New Caledonia (France), unincorporated or special territories such as Guam (United States) and Easter Island (Chile), or islands that form part of another sovereign nation such as Hawaii (United States). Nearly every part of Oceania was at some point annexed by a foreign power, though there was little European settlement – the two major exceptions being Australia and New Zealand. The British established colonies in the region beginning with Australia in the late eighteenth century, followed by New Zealand and Fiji in the nineteenth century, with much of the region eventually forming part of the British Empire. Other colonial powers in the region included France, Germany and the United States. Oceania's indigenous population is very diverse. During the nineteenth century the number of indigenous inhabitants decreased dramatically as a result of European settlement, beginning to recover only during the twentieth century (Caldwell *et al.* 2001: 9–11). In the aftermath of World War II many Pacific islands won their independence, usually peacefully, though a large number remained territories of European, Asian and American powers.

This chapter focuses on women's experience of executive positions in Australia and New Zealand. We argue that while an inclusive political culture and institutional design matter to women's executive presence, women's activism inside and outside political parties remains the key to increasing the numbers of women both in parliament and in cabinet. First, this chapter describes the Australian and New Zealand political regimes; second, it examines the evolution of women in the political executives; third, it reviews some of the factors explaining women's presence in cabinet; and fourth, it assesses whether women cabinet ministers make a difference for women. At the outset, however, this chapter provides a regional overview of women's participation in executives in Oceania.

Regional overview

Table 4.1 shows the percentage of women in Australasia and the Pacific Island parliaments and cabinets in January 2010. A first observation is that a clear gap exists between Australasia and the Pacific Islands as far as the proportion of women parliamentarians and cabinet ministers is concerned: women are much more numerous in the legislative and executive branches of the former than in those of the latter. Indeed, the average proportion of women in Australasian parliaments and cabinets is 31.3 percent and 25.9 percent, respectively, while the Pacific Island numbers are 2.5 percent and 7.3 percent, respectively. As this chapter will show, women have occupied positions of executive leadership in Australia and New Zealand. By contrast, in the sub-regions of Melanesia, Micronesia and Polynesia no woman has ever been appointed or elected president or prime minister, and as of January 2010 three countries (Nauru, Solomon Islands and Tuvalu) had no women at all in either parliament or cabinet. In Tonga, no women were elected in the 2008 election, but one woman was appointed to cabinet, automatically making her a member of parliament. Samoa (with Fiji[2]) has historically had the highest representation of women in its legislative and executive branches among the independent states in the region. In January 2010, Samoa had four women in parliament (8.2 percent) and three women in cabinet.[3] In Papua New Guinea, the sole woman in the 109-member parliament was Australian-born Dame Carol Kidu, also a member of cabinet since 2002.

A second observation drawn from Table 4.1 is that for all Pacific Island states (except Vanuatu), the percentage of women in ministerial positions is higher or equal to the proportion of seats they occupy in parliament. By contrast, the ministerial/parliamentary difference is negative in Australasia, meaning that women are proportionately less numerous in cabinets than in parliament. It may be hypothesized that in the Pacific Islands women reach political power more easily thanks to the discretionary capacity of some chief executives to appoint non-elected cabinet members, a phenomenon observed in other countries such as France (Murray 2009).

Given the absence of women from public decision-making in many South Pacific states, there has been considerable interest in the possibility of temporary special measures such as reserved seats for women in parliament. This would bring women into the pool for appointment to cabinet in the largely Westminster-style political systems. An existing example is the Autonomous Region of Bougainville, so far the only place in the Pacific to reserve seats for women in parliament (excluding the parity system in place for the French territories). The 2004 Constitution of the Autonomous Region of Bougainville provides for three reserved seats for women in its House of Representatives, with members elected to represent the interests of women in three separate geographical regions (s. 55 (1)). The constitution also guarantees women a place in cabinet, the woman

Table 4.1 Percentage of women in parliament and ministerial positions in selected countries of Oceania, January 1, 2010

Sub-regions/countries	...parliament	...ministerial positions	Difference ministry/ parliament
Australasia			
Australia	27.3 (41/150)	23.3 (7/30)	–4.0
New Zealand	33.6 (41/122)	28.6 (8/28)	–5.0
Mean	30.1 (82/272)	25.9 (15/58)	–4.2
Pacific Islands			
Melanesia			
Fiji	Parlt dissolved by 2006 coup	9.1 (1/11)	–
Papua New Guinea	0.9 (1/109)	3.7 (1/27)	+2.8
Solomon Islands	0.0 (0/50)	0.0 (0/23)	0.0
Vanuatu	3.8 (2/52)	0.0 (0/13)	–3.8
Micronesia			
Federal States of Micronesia	0.0 (0/14)	16.7 (1/6)	+16.7
Kiribati	4.3 (2/46)	7.7 (1/13)	+3.4
Marshall Islands	3.0 (1/33)	10.0 (1/10)	+7.0
Nauru	0.0 (0/18)	0.0 (0/6)	0.0
Palau	0.0 (0/16)	25.0 (2/8)	+25.0
Polynesia			
Samoa	8.2 (4/49)	23.1 (3/13)	+14.9
Tonga	3.1 (1/32)	8.3 (1/12)	+5.2
Tuvalu	0.0 (0/15)	0.0 (0/8)	0.0
Mean	2.5 (11/434)	7.3 (11/150)	+4.8

Source: Inter-Parliamentary Union (2010d).

minister being elected by and from women in the House of Representatives.[4] These constitutional provisions, part of a settlement following from civil war, illustrate the progress being made by women in many post-conflict situations around the world (Sawer 2010: 235–6). While Bougainville is a sub-national region, in 2010 the Papua New Guinea government was bringing forward a bill to establish 22 reserved seats before the 2012 national elections.

Interestingly, some still-dependent territories in the Pacific have significantly higher proportions of women in their assemblies. In 2008, the French *collectivités d'outre-mer* of French Polynesia and New Caledonia had 53 and 46 percent women in their legislatures, respectively. These generous percentages are attributable to the French "parity law" which states that the difference between the number of female and male candidates cannot be more than one, and that women and men candidates must alternate from the beginning to the end of the list.[5] However, the parity law does not extend to the cabinet. In 2008, the Cook Islands and Niue, both territories that are self-governing in free association with New Zealand, had 20 and 12.5 percent women in their legislatures, respectively.

By contrast with the other independent states in the region, politics in Australia and New Zealand looked relatively feminized in 2009. Julia Gillard[6] was deputy prime minister and Julie Bishop was deputy leader of the federal opposition, while Quentin Bryce was Australia's first woman governor general. At the state level, there were women premiers (and governors) in New South Wales and Queensland and a woman opposition leader in South Australia. In New Zealand, long-standing woman Prime Minister Helen Clark had lost office in 2008 after being Labour leader for 15 years, nine as prime minister. However, there was still a visible presence of women political leaders in 2009: the Green and Maori parties each had a woman co-leader, and the opposition Labour Party had a woman deputy leader. Looking at executive government more broadly, while in 2009 men in dark suits still dominated swearing-in ceremonies, 20 percent of cabinet positions were held by women at the federal level in Australia, and 30 percent in New Zealand. Because the pattern of women's participation in executive government in Australasia is very different to that of the rest of the Oceania, this chapter will focus on Australia and New Zealand rather than on the more recently independent states in the region.

Country cases: Australia and New Zealand

Description of the political regimes

Australia and New Zealand share a common political inheritance as former British colonies on the other side of the world to the "mother country." By the end of the nineteenth century they had gained a reputation as advanced democracies, with votes for all women in New Zealand in 1893 and in South Australia in 1894. By 1902 most women (*c.*99 percent) became eligible to vote and stand for parliament nationally in Australia – there had been slippage in relation to Indigenous voters in the 1902 Commonwealth Franchise Act.

While having much in common, politically and culturally, the traditional Westminster system evolved in different ways in the two countries: New Zealand has a classic unitary system and a unicameral parliament while Australia has a federal system of government and bicameralism both at the federal level and in five of its six states. Australia began experimenting with proportional representation (PR) in the nineteenth century and all of its bicameral parliaments use PR for the election of one of their chambers. New Zealand stayed with single-member constituencies until 1996, when it moved to a mixed-member proportional system (MMP) and multi-party governments. Historically, the basic political cleavage in both countries has been between Labour[7] and conservative parties. Inherited party loyalties have been strong until relatively recently, when there has been a weakening of party identification in both countries and increased volatility and drift among young voters to parties such as the Greens. Despite increased fragmentation of the party system, particularly in New Zealand, long-standing Labour and non-Labour parties are still the major players in government formation. In New Zealand the dominant conservative party is the National

Party, while in Australia it is the Liberal Party of Australia, which at the federal level is usually in coalition with the rural-based Nationals.

In the Westminster tradition, all ministers must be elected members of parliament. Where there are upper houses, as in Australia, governments are formed in the lower house but ministers also come from the upper house. For example, at the federal level about one-third of the ministry generally come from the Senate. By convention, political parties control the method of cabinet selection and this may differ across parties. On the conservative side, party leaders appoint all ministers (or shadow ministers) and allocate their portfolios. However, where conservative parties are in coalition, the leader of the junior party or parties will nominate who is to fill their positions. Labour parliamentary parties in both countries have been notable for electing their front bench, although the leader allocates portfolios. From 2007 the Australian Labor Party (ALP) started moving away from the principle of election of the ministry by the parliamentary party, but Australian prime ministers still need to accommodate factional preferences as well as the concerns with geographical representation that are usually a factor both in federal and in unitary systems. Gender became a significant consideration from the 1970s and in New Zealand the inclusion of Maori became salient at the same time. In New Zealand Labor leaders could issue "guiding principles" to influence the choices of the parliamentary party (McLeay 1995: 62).

In Australia, at the federal level there has generally been a two-tier ministry since 1956, with not all ministers in cabinet. Usually there will be about 20 ministers in cabinet, with another ten outside. Women are consistently better represented in the ministry as a whole than in cabinet, although the difference is usually slight (for example, 23 percent versus 20 percent after the 2007 election). At the state level all ministers are still included in cabinet. In New Zealand, the use of outer-ministries took hold in the mid-1980s and while several women began their executive careers in this way, the process has been complicated with the adoption of MMP, with outer-ministries being allocated to minor-party members of parliament (MPs) as an aspect of the coalition formation process. As at the federal level in Australia, in New Zealand there are generally about 20 ministers in cabinet and a maximum of six outside.

Evolution of women's presence in the executive

It took a long time in both Australia and New Zealand before the absence of women from parliament and from executive government became widely regarded as a "democratic deficit." Despite the mobilization of women during World War II, when many gained leadership experience, the post-war period saw a reaffirmation of the priority of domestic roles. When women did start entering cabinets in the 1940s the pattern differed in Australia and New Zealand and these histories will be dealt with separately here.

In Australia the first women to gain ministerial office were all from the conservative side of politics and there were only eight of them in the whole period from 1947–79. The first was Florence Cardell-Oliver, appointed to the Western

Australian cabinet in 1947 in an honorary capacity but given a full ministerial portfolio after two years. She had been involved in a free milk campaign and as Minister for Health introduced free milk for Western Australian school children. The next was Dame Enid Lyons, appointed to federal cabinet in 1949, also in an honorary capacity. She was the widow of a former Labor premier who had become a conservative prime minister. She had won a party room battle to extend childhood endowment policy to first children, a popular election policy that assisted the conservatives to present themselves as the party of the family (Lyons 1972: 107, 109). When appointed as a cabinet minister, Lyons remarked that, in the absence of a portfolio, she was in cabinet "to pour the tea."

The pattern of conservative pre-eminence in bringing women into govern-ment changed dramatically in the 1980s, a decade in which the mobilization of women in the 1970s made its mark in the Labor Party and Labor women started to enter parliament in a more permanent way. Between 1980 and 1989, 28 women were appointed as ministers in contrast to the eight women appointed in the previous 30 years (Black 1996: 39). Of the 28 appointed in the 1980s, the vast majority (25) were from the Labor Party.

The consciousness-raising of the 1970s and the increased presence of women in parliaments in the 1980s began to make all-male cabinets look odd and unrep-resentative. One effect of this raised consciousness was that women became "over-represented" in cabinets relative to their parliamentary representation. Moon and Fountain, in their pioneering study of women as ministers in Aus-tralia, calculated that women constituted 14 percent of parliamentarians but 20 percent of ministers at the state level in 1992 (Moon and Fountain 1997: 458). Such over-representation no longer existed in 2009, when women were under-represented in ministerial positions overall, despite some exceptions (see Table 4.2). Table 4.2 presents data on women in the ministry as a whole rather than just in cabinet, in the interests of comparability with the earlier study.

In 2009 women parliamentarians were under-represented in the ministry in six of the nine jurisdictions and significantly under-represented in one (Western Australia). If we look more closely at the latter case, however, we find that women make up only 17.5 percent of the parliamentary Liberal Party, the domi-nant partner in the coalition government (as against 17.6 percent of the minis-try). This reminds us that in parliamentary systems the pool of eligibles for appointment to the ministry consists in members of the governing party or parties, not members of parliament as a whole. The reason for the great disparity between parliamentary presence and presence in the ministry in Western Aus-tralia is that the parties with comparatively high representation of women (the ALP and the Greens) are not in government.

There has been a great increase in the numbers of women in parliament, largely due to the quotas adopted by the ALP in 1994. The Labor Party has also been responsible for the entry of Indigenous women both into parliaments and into cabinets. The first Indigenous women were only elected to parliament in 2001, but by 2008 they had entered cabinet in both New South Wales (NSW) and the Northern Territory and in the Northern Territory an Indigenous woman

Table 4.2 Women as a percentage of Australian parliamentarians and ministers, November 1, 2009

Parliament	Women as percentage of MPs[a] (and as percentage of Labor MPs)	Women as percentage of ministers[b] (and as percentage of Labor Shadow Ministers)
Commonwealth[c]	29.6 (35.7)	23.3
New South Wales	28.1 (32.9)	31.8
Victoria	31.3 (36.5)	25.0
Queensland	36.0 (49.0)	33.3
Western Australia	29.5 (35.1)	17.6 (38.8)
South Australia	31.9 (41.7)	26.6
Tasmania	27.5 (27.8)	40.0
Australian Capital Territory	41.2 (42.9)	40.0
Northern Territory	32.0 (41.7)	25.0

Notes
a Numbers are aggregated for both houses where the parliaments are bicameral as the ministry is drawn from both.
b Both cabinet ministers and ministers outside cabinet are included here, but not parliamentary secretaries. All ministries were Labor in 2009 except for Western Australia.
c Commonwealth is the term for the federal level of government in Australia.

(Marion Scrymgour) was deputy chief minister. In terms of other forms of diversity, women from non-English-speaking backgrounds have been elected for both Labor and non-Labor parties, although it was the federal Labor government elected in 2007 that made another breakthrough. It included a woman cabinet member (Senator Penny Wong) who combined two "firsts," being both an Asian-Australian and an 'out' lesbian.

Because the conservative parties in Australia have been putting fewer women into parliament, a conservative coalition government, such as that elected in Western Australia in 2008, will have fewer women in its parliamentary party to draw on for its ministry. At the same time, if we compare the presence of women in Labor ministries to their presence in the pool from which such ministries are drawn, rather than to their presence in parliament as a whole, the degree of under-representation is even more significant (see Table 4.2). While quotas oblige the party factions to preselect women for parliament, they do not apply to the selection of the ministry, a process still largely controlled by the factions.

In New Zealand there was also a slow start to the entry of women into executive government. Only three women ministers were appointed during the period up to 1979, but unlike in Australia, where all ministers appointed in this period were from the conservative side of politics, in New Zealand two out of three were Labour. For example, Mabel Howard became New Zealand's first woman cabinet minister in 1947, after only four years in parliament. She was Minister of Health and Child Welfare until Labour lost the election in 1949. When Labour returned to power in 1957 Mabel Howard was still a parliamentarian, and was made Minister of Social Security and Minister in Charge of the Welfare of Women and Children. Meanwhile, Hilda Ross, a National Party MP, had become New Zealand's second woman cabinet minister in 1949, also after only four years in parliament and, like Howard, was given responsibility for the welfare of women and children, and, later, social security. In 1972, the first Maori woman minister, Whetu Tirikatene-Sullivan, was made Minister of Tourism, Associate Minister of Social Welfare and Minister for the Environment in the Labour government. She remains the longest-serving woman parliamentarian, with 29 years in parliament from 1967 to 1996.

Despite the rise of the women's movement in the 1970s, the National prime minister, Robert Muldoon, maintained an all-male cabinet throughout National's nine-year period in government (1975–84). It was not until the election of a Labour government in 1984 that any further women ministers were appointed. Since 1984, 32 women have served as ministers in New Zealand.

Political scientists Davis (1997: 76) and Siaroff (2000: 198) argue that women's best chance of being in cabinet is immediately following an election. The data in Table 4.3 reflects this approach: only post-election cabinet appointments have been counted, with the results of reshuffles between elections excluded. And, in contrast to the Australian data, these figures represent only women in cabinet and do not include ministers outside cabinet.

Just as there has been a steady increase in women's parliamentary representation over the past 25 years in New Zealand, so too can we see an increase in proportion of women in cabinet over the same period. And, just as Labour is credited with driving the increase in the former, so too have they been responsible for pushing up the percentage of women ministers. The first significant rise occurred in 1984 with the election of the fourth Labour government, and the proportion increased further with Labour's re-election in 1987. The National government elected in 1990 included two women in its cabinet, one of whom was Finance Minister. But it is not until Labour became the government in 1999 that we see another significant increase in women's ministerial presence.

Table 4.3 Women as a percentage of New Zealand parliamentarians and ministers, 1981–2009

Election year/government	Women as percentage of MPs	Women as percentage of cabinet ministers
1981 National	8.7	0.0
1984 Labour	11.6	10.0
1987 Labour	14.4	15.0
1990 National	16.5	10.0
1993 National	21.2	5.0
1996 National	28.3	11.0
1999 Labour	29.2	35.0
2002 Labour	28.3	30.0
2005 Labour	33.1	30.0
2008 National	34.0	30.0

The "over-representation" of women ministers evident in Australia in the earlier period is not a feature of the New Zealand executive. Only in 1999 and 2002 do we see a higher proportion of women in cabinet than the proportion of women in parliament. This outcome has two likely explanations. First, women in the Labour Party have, since the late 1970s, sought to ensure that women candidates are selected for safe seats to enable them a chance to build a political career. This progress was augmented by the introduction of MMP, which enabled more Labour women to enter parliament via the party's list. These women provided the incoming Labour government in 1999 with a core group of experienced women able to take up positions in cabinet.

Second, Davis (1997: 19–20) finds that there is a correlation between women prime ministers and the proportion of women cabinet ministers. However, to date there have been too few women leaders at the cross-national level to test whether this is a causal relationship (but see Chapter 7 on Latin America).[8] For example, Norway's Gro Harlem Brundtland was known for her commitment to the appointment of women (as was Chile's Michelle Bachelet more recently), but United Kingdom Prime Minister Margaret Thatcher, by contrast, was the only woman in her cabinet. In New Zealand, Helen Clark's first cabinet included seven women, but Jenny Shipley's included only one other woman. Yet, given Shipley could choose her cabinet, while Clark could not, what does this tell us about women leaders selecting women ministers? Certainly it is the case that the Labour Party's "participatory" convention meant Helen Clark could not select her own cabinet. However, her support of women's representation was well known by women in caucus, and Labour's "representative" convention of ensuring Maori and women be elected to cabinet was upheld during her term in office. In addition, the norm of Labour leaders making their caucus colleagues aware of their ministerial preferences, through informal channels, meant Clark no doubt had some indirect influence on cabinet selection.

Since 2002, the proportion of women in the New Zealand cabinet has plateaued at 30 percent, while the proportion of women in parliament has continued to increase, once again leading to an "under-representation" of women in the executive compared to the legislature. One interesting feature is that with the election of the National government, the proportion of women in cabinet has not declined (unlike past years). This suggests that a contagion effect between Labour and National in terms of women's representation, the beginnings of which emerged in the 1990s, has continued into the twenty-first century.

A question which inspires several studies of women's participation in the executive concerns the portfolios women hold. What of the other major finding of Moon and Fountain (1997) – that women tend to be over-represented in welfare portfolios? We shall follow the categorization of portfolios used by Moon and Fountain to compare the situation in 1997 and today. They use a categorization based on that used by Rose (1976) to differentiate three types of government activity. The first is *defining* activity, which includes defense of territorial integrity, maintenance of internal order and the mobilization of finance (to which we would add the coordinating of government). The second is the mobilization of *physical resources* (such as roads, railways and communications). The third is *social* portfolios attending to the well-being of citizens (including education, labor, health, welfare and culture).

It should be noted, though, that this categorization is unavoidably approximate. Many portfolios encompass more than one of Rose's general types of government activity.[9] In addition, many ministers, especially in the smaller Australian states and territories, hold multiple portfolios. We have classed these ministers according to their first-listed portfolio, which has led to a slight over-emphasis on the number of state-defining portfolios. For instance, Katy Gallagher, the Australian Capital Territory (ACT) treasurer, also holds the portfolio of Health and Industrial Relations (from November 2009), but is counted only as "state-defining."

Moon and Fountain show that over a span of 26 years (1970–96) women held a disproportionate share of the social portfolios, most markedly at the Commonwealth level. So while governments became relatively keen to have some female presence in their ministries, this was still largely confined to the nurturing portfolios as was the case around the world as women first entered executive government. In 2009 women held the education portfolios in five of the nine Australian jurisdictions and their experience at Commonwealth/state ministerial meetings could approximate that of an Irish Minister of Education at intergovernmental meetings in the European Union: "I can go to a European Council meeting now, and all the education ministers are women. It's a kind of branding almost" (quoted in Sykes 2009: 40). Women have also been disproportionately allocated health portfolios in Australia, and in 2009 held such portfolios in five of the nine jurisdictions (although not the same five where they held the education portfolio). As we shall see below, however, holding social portfolios has not necessarily been a barrier to high office. In 2009 two women deputy premiers and one woman deputy chief minister held health portfolios, an indication of the political sensitivity of this portfolio with its "hot button" issues such as waiting times for surgery.

What is interesting is the extent to which this gender stereotyping of portfolios persists and how it corresponds to gender differences in issue priorities expressed by women voters. We have already seen that there has been a substantial increase in the number of women in the "pool" from which Labor ministries are drawn. Increasingly women also come from similar backgrounds to their male colleagues, most manifestly coming from backgrounds in paid political work whether for Labor politicians or unions and often having law degrees.

Despite these increased similarities in occupational backgrounds women are still unlikely to be allocated the same kinds of portfolios as their male colleagues. The evidence is that women are still disproportionately represented in the social portfolios. In 2009 well-being or social portfolios made up 34 percent of all portfolios in Commonwealth, state and territory governments, but 59 percent of the portfolios held by women (see Figure 4.1). As in the earlier period, in 2009 women were significantly more over-represented in social portfolios at the Commonwealth level than at the state level.

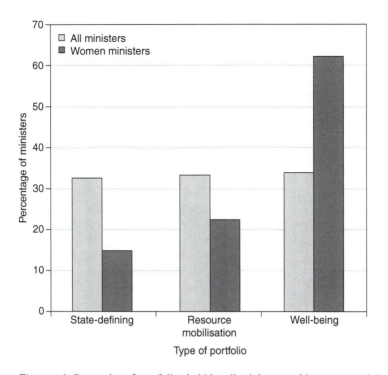

Figure 4.1 Categories of portfolios held by all ministers and by women ministers in Commonwealth, state and territory governments, Australia, November 1, 2009.

One of the issues for women has been the way their entry into executive government and responsibility for "big-spending" departments has coincided with discursive shifts in the English-speaking democracies toward neo-liberalism and demands for cuts in public expenditure (Sykes 2009). Although allocated "nurturing" portfolios women have had to take responsibility for such cuts or else lose favor with their colleagues. In Australia Senator Susan Ryan's resistance to budget cuts while she was education minister in the 1980s speeded her political demise. Still, one study of several advanced industrial democracies found that the allocation of social portfolios to women has generally resulted in more women-friendly social policy (Atchison and Down 2009: 17).

While over-represented in social portfolios, women remain particularly under-represented in "defining" (security, defense, economic) portfolios. These portfolios made up 29 percent of all portfolios in Australia but 14 percent of those held by women. At the Commonwealth level the disparity was even greater in 2009, with no women holding "defining" portfolios. It should be noted that at this level of government it has been the conservative parties that have been somewhat more inclined to appoint women to economic portfolios (for example,

Senator Margaret Guilfoyle, Minister for Finance 1980–3, Senator Helen Coonan, Minister for Revenue and Assistant Treasurer, 2001–4). The reason may be a combination of the professional backgrounds of the women concerned and their pursuit of such portfolios. In terms of the third category of portfolios, resource mobilization, there was slightly more gender balance. This category is more important at the state than at the Commonwealth level, and makes up 38 percent of all portfolios and 28 percent of those held by women.

Despite assumptions that social portfolios are "soft" and of low prestige, the holding of such portfolios has not necessarily posed a barrier to women becoming head of government. The first woman to become a head of government in Australia was Rosemary Follett in the Australian Capital Territory in 1989, at the first election after the achievement of self-government. She held the non-traditional positions of treasurer and attorney general in addition to that of chief minister and was the first woman to attend a premiers' conference, after 88 years of federation. However, the next women to become heads of government were Dr. Carmen Lawrence in Western Australia in 1990 and Joan Kirner in Victoria in the same year. They held the more traditional education portfolios at the time they became premier. They both inherited governments that were in deep trouble and in urgent need of a new look. Both women lost their first election as premier, thanks to the political damage their governments had sustained before they took office, for example, financial mismanagement in Victoria and serious corruption scandals in Western Australia.

The first woman to be elected as a state premier was Anna Bligh in Queensland, who became premier in 2007 and won the state election of 2009. She had held the education portfolio for almost five years before taking on economic portfolios when she became deputy premier. Women chief ministers had successfully contested elections in the two territories, including Clare Martin who led the Labor Party to victory for the first time in 23 years of self-government in the Northern Territory. All women heads of government in Australia have led Labor governments, with one exception in the Australian Capital Territory. In 2009 Kristina Keneally became Labor premier in NSW in similar circumstances to her predecessors in Western Australia and Victoria – a Labor government that was in deep trouble due to mismanagement and corruption scandals.

In New Zealand, as in Australia, women have always been more likely to hold social rather than defining portfolios (see Figure 4.2), and they almost never hold resource portfolios. It does appear that as the number of women in cabinet increases, so does the range of portfolio allocations (although this has not been the case with the most recent National government, with five of the six portfolios held by women defined as social). And, over the past 25 years a smattering of women have held key defining portfolios: Ann Hercus was Labour minister for police as well as welfare between 1984 and 1987, Ruth Richardson was National's finance minister between 1990 and 1993 and, in the National government in 2010, Judith Collins was ranked sixth in the cabinet line-up as Minister of Police.

Moreover, just as is the case in Australia, being responsible for social portfolios does not preclude women becoming head of government. In 1997 Jenny

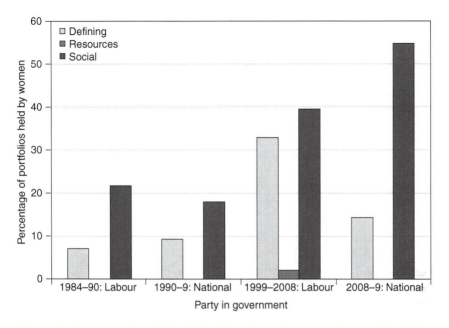

Figure 4.2 Categories of portfolios held by New Zealand women ministers, 1984–2009.

Shipley took over the leadership of the governing conservative National Party to become New Zealand's first woman prime minister, even though her ministerial experience was in health and women's affairs. Helen Clark's rise as leader was more incremental; she became a minister in 1987, deputy prime minister in 1989 and Labour leader in 1993. During this time her portfolio responsibilities were also predominantly social: labor, housing and health. In 1999, New Zealand experienced an internationally unusual election campaign where the two major parties were both led by women. Most media reported that the "gender factor" had been neutralized as a consequence – that is, because both leaders were women there was little media focus on their gender during the campaign (Curtin 1997). Helen Clark won the 1999 election and went on to become New Zealand's longest-serving Labour leader.

While categorization of portfolios is a useful means for analyzing the position of women in executives, it is also the case that cabinet positions are informally ranked, with portfolios such as finance, national security and foreign affairs having significantly more weight and prestige than what are often considered softer or more traditionally "women's" portfolios, such as health and welfare. But portfolio ranking also depends on the national context, the particular government's agenda, the size of the budget allocation, and the personalities involved. Certainly finance would always be central to a government's platform, but in New Zealand, defense ranks lower than trade and police while the health portfolio always ranks in the top six. Over the past 10 years the attorney general and

Treaty of Waitangi portfolio has been ranked as high as fifth and was a portfolio held by Margaret Wilson before she went on to become New Zealand's first woman speaker of the House.

Formally, the head of executive government in both Australia and New Zealand is the governor general (representing the Queen) and, at the state level in Australia, the governor. The first woman governor general, Quentin Bryce, did not take office in Australia until 2008, 18 years after Dame Catherine Tizard had become New Zealand governor general. New Zealand's second woman governor general, Dame Silvia Cartwright, was appointed in 2001. Up until now, it has been Labour governments in both New Zealand and Australia that have been responsible for all appointments of women as governors, with one exception in South Australia.

Factors explaining women's access to the executive

In both Australia and New Zealand political parties are the key to access to executive positions and we would expect parties of the left to have a greater commitment to all forms of social equality, including gender equality, than parties on the right. However an "in principle" commitment to equality may be complicated by industrial unionism and religious ideology. In both countries Labour parties were created as the political arm of the trade unions and focused on the achievement and protection of a family wage, sufficient for a male breadwinner to be able to support a wife and children at home. While the focus on the male breadwinner created obstacles to women's equality, these obstacles were overcome more readily in New Zealand than in Australia, where Catholic family ideology resulted in barriers for women such as the marriage bar in public sector employment, lasting for much longer. New Zealand Labour lacked the Irish Catholic "machine" politics and strongly institutionalized factional system found in the Australian labor movement and was historically more open to standing women as candidates. While only six women were elected to parliament between 1933 and 1946, four were from the Labour Party and at no time since 1946 has the number of National women elected exceeded the number of Labour women politicians (Curtin 2008a).

In both countries it was women's movement mobilizations in the 1970s that brought about major changes and it was the Labour parties that were more responsive to the new social movements than their conservative counterparts. In both countries Labour women campaigned for party reform in the wake of crushing electoral defeats and Labour women's organizations were reinvigorated and/ or new ones created. In New Zealand the women-only branches established at the time of the party's founding are still a feature of the party today (Devere and Curtin 2009). The relative absence of strongly institutionalized factions in the New Zealand Labour Party meant that progress was smoother and the Labour Women's Council began to play a significant role in party policy-making (Curtin 2008b). It provided the leverage that enabled the feminization of the party: three different women held the position of party president from 1984 and by the late

1990s women formed a majority of party membership (Grey and Sawer 2005: 180).

In Australia Labor women had to contend with strongly entrenched factional power structures; careers in the party depended on factional support. The factions were largely controlled by men, although women relatives of factional leaders sometimes played trusted roles. Long-established and vigorous women's organizations in the party could fall victim to factional warfare, as when the left-dominated NSW Labor Women's Committee was abolished by a right-dominated state executive, after existing for more than 80 years. However, although women were divided by factional loyalties, they did develop cross-factional campaigns for quotas that would apply both to the party organization and to party pre-selections. Quotas were first achieved on a voluntary basis in 1981 but progress was very patchy; there was another campaign resulting, in 1994, in mandatory quotas: pre-selections would be nullified and reopened by the national executive if quotas were not fulfilled. As a result of these gains by Labor women, reinforced by the creation of the feminist "ginger" group, EMILY's List (see below), the ALP now puts far more women into parliament and into ministries than does the conservative side of politics. However, as we have seen, there is a shortfall of women in Labor ministries as quotas do not extend to this level.

Another variable affecting the entry of women into parliament and hence into the pool for ministerial positions is the electoral system. In Australia women have generally been better represented in houses of parliament elected by PR than those elected from single-member electorates, as clearly seen in the contrast between women's representation in the Senate (elected by PR) and in the House of Representatives. Women have always been better represented in the Senate and it has provided the same number of women cabinet ministers as the House of Representatives, despite being the smaller house from which only one-third of the ministry is usually appointed. Hence PR in the Senate has been an important pathway for women into the executive. In general, it can be argued that bicameralism and federalism provide additional pathways to executive office; it should be noted that in Australia women have held a higher proportion of ministries at the sub-national than at the national level, including the position of head of government.

The picture in New Zealand is somewhat more complex. In classical Westminster mode, New Zealand had a first-past-the-post electoral system until 1996. However, despite the first-past-the-post electoral system being renowned for constraining women's electoral opportunities, New Zealand was exceptional in electing comparatively high numbers of women. Prior to the first MMP election in 1996, women's representation had already reached 21 percent without the adoption of party gender quotas. With the adoption of MMP in 1996, the representation of women in parliament increased to 28.3 percent and in 2008 reached a high of 34 percent. The entry of large numbers of women did not require party quotas, as in Australia, but rather owed much to the feminization of the New Zealand Labour Party. However, the rise in women's parliamentary presence in

1996 did not have an immediate impact on women's representation in cabinet. The latter increased significantly only after the election of a Labour-led government in 1999. This reflects Siaroff's (2000: 209) and Davis' (1997: 88) findings that while increasing the number of women in parliament matters to women's access to cabinet, the relationship is also influenced by which party is in government.

It is also worth noting that New Zealand's parliament has been more open to its Indigenous people than its Australian counterpart. Four electorates reserved for Maori were established in 1867 and when women were granted the vote in 1893, this right applied to all women, including Maori. The first Maori woman MP, Iriana Ratana, was elected in 1947 to represent one of the four Maori electorates. Since then, Maori women have increased their presence in parliament, representing both general and Maori electorates and, with the advent of MMP, have pursued political representation through a wider range of parties, including the newly established Maori Party (2005). In 2009 there was one Maori woman in the New Zealand cabinet and one, the co-leader of the Maori Party, in the outer ministry. By contrast there has never been an Indigenous woman in the Australian federal parliament or ministry, although there have been Indigenous women in the Northern Territory cabinet since 2003 and one in the NSW cabinet since 2007.

Do women executives represent women?

It can be argued that "the ladder to power is a triangle, and the closer you are to the top the less room there is to move" (Dowse 2009: 4). Often women ministers have little room to move, due to government commitments, cabinet solidarity and the constraints imposed by financial markets and public opinion. Nonetheless, feminist ministers and heads of government in Australia and New Zealand have been identified as critical actors who introduced measures to promote gender equality. Following are some examples only – more systematic work is required to assess the relative significance of ministerial gender and contextual factors such as party ideology and an organized women's movement.

The first woman head of government in Australia, Rosemary Follett, chief minister of the ACT, shocked the local newspaper by her commitment to the appointment of women to 50 percent of positions on government advisory bodies; she sent back lists submitted by ministers if they did not contain enough women's names (Sawer and Simms 1993: 154). A senior federal Labor minister in the 1980s, Senator Susan Ryan, was responsible for the Commonwealth Sex Discrimination Act 1984 as well as the Affirmative Action (Equal Opportunity for Women) Act 1986 – both of which were highly controversial at the time, although strongly supported by women within the Labor Party as well as within the broader women's movement. Joan Kirner, as Minister for Conservation, Forests and Lands in the Victorian government, initiated the highly successful Rural Women's Network as well as being one of the women ministers who advocated for the capital endowment of the Victorian Women's Trust, making it both financially viable and independent of government. After losing office as premier, and with the support of another woman ex-premier, Dr. Carmen Lawrence, Kirner went on to establish EMILY's List, a significant source of support for Labor women candidates who have made pro-choice and gender equity commitments.

Another way in which women ministers can express gender equity commitments is through their selection of departmental heads and ministerial staff. Susan Ryan, as federal education minister, was responsible for the appointment of the first woman to head a federal department. At the state level, Kirner and Lawrence also appointed the first women to head departments.[10] Generally women ministers have also been more likely to appoint women to their staff, including in senior positions. For example, in 2009 women formed a majority (55 percent) of the 412 ministerial staff at the federal level in Australia, but many were in traditionally female positions such as receptionist, diary secretary or office manager. However, women ministers were disproportionately likely to appoint women to the position of chief of staff – 71 percent of women ministers had female chiefs of staff, compared with 40 percent of ministers as a whole.[11]

In New Zealand, there has been some increase in the number of women selected for government-nominated positions over the same period that there were more women ministers in cabinet. In 1998, women accounted for just over 200 of the (re-)appointments to Crown company boards; by 2002 there were just under 400 (although the total number of appointments also increased over this period, meaning the proportion of women did not change significantly) (MWA 2002). By 2006, the percentage of women who were ministerial appointments on state sector boards and committees stood at 42 percent (HRC 2008).[12] Small increases are also evident in the proportion of women chief executives appointed to head government departments. In 1999, prior to the arrival of the Clark government, there were six women chief executives (16 percent) and, by 2008, this had increased to nine (23 percent), seven of whom were heading "social" departments, and only one of whom was head of a large department (in terms of staff and budget). So while some progress has been made in female ministerial appointments, it hardly represents a significant change over ten years, and more analysis is needed before we can claim that this increase is a result of there being more women in cabinet.

As already mentioned, we cannot assume that increasing the numbers of women in the cabinet will necessarily lead to the substantive representation of women. The cabinet, in Westminster systems at least, is protected by the convention of collective responsibility, whereby secrecy and confidentiality around the processes of executive deliberation make it difficult to reveal the extent to which women ministers have represented, acted or spoken for women. Moreover, the ideological profile of the party in government will impact on the influence of women ministers, whether or not they are feminist in orientation.

In the case of New Zealand, Labour women ministers have been more active than their National counterparts in advancing women's "interests" if measured in terms of policy outputs. Women ministers in the fourth Labour government

(1984–90) were critical to the passage of pay equity legislation, increasing expenditure on child care, implementing rape law reform and unpaid parental leave, and ensuring family benefits were not abolished during a period of neo-liberal economic reform. Between 1999 and 2008, women ministers again made an impact through their support for paid parental leave, increasing entitlements for working families, reinstating the role of trade unions, raising the minimum wage and renewing New Zealand's commitment to its reporting obligations under the Convention on the Elimination of All Forms of Discrimination Against Women (CEDAW) (Curtin 2008b; Curtin and Devere 2006). By contrast, the two most high-profile National women ministers of the 1990s (Ruth Richardson, Minister of Finance, and Jenny Shipley, Minister of Social Welfare), oversaw a radical overhaul of the welfare state and labor market in New Zealand. Family payments were cut, targeting was introduced and individual work contracts became the norm, decimating trade unions and stalling any progression on the minimum wage – all of which had a negative impact on women and children (McClelland and St John 2006). However, analysis of Jenny Shipley's work as Minister of Women's Affairs suggests that she attempted to advance other policies for women, but was constrained by the overarching strategic direction of the National government (Curtin and Teghtsoonian 2010).

Finally, understanding the impact of women ministers in New Zealand is complicated by the introduction of MMP in 1996. This change has led to the formation of coalition or minority governments with support arrangements involving minor parties. As a consequence, (minor) ministerial portfolios or government spokesperson positions are often given to members of smaller parties. There have been several recent examples where women have used their position as outer ministers or government representatives to leverage policy outcomes favorable to women. For example the advent of paid parental leave was due in no small part to the work of an Alliance MP, Laila Harre, who was Minister of Women's Affairs (1999–2002) (Curtin and Teghtsoonian 2010). Similarly, three member's bills introduced by Greens MP Sue Bradford were supported (and passed) under the Labour government, all of which could be seen as of benefit to women. These included removing the defense of "reasonable force" when smacking children (Crimes Amendment Act 2007), allowing mothers in jail to keep their babies for longer, and applying the adult minimum wage to 16- and 17-year-olds (see McLeay 2009). Thus, it appears there are several interrelated factors, both institutional and political, that need further exploration if we are to explain when women ministers will act for women.

Conclusion

Although Australia and New Zealand were pioneers of women's political rights, in both countries it took many decades before the arrival of second-wave feminism made women's absence from parliament and public decision-making into a political issue. Women's movement mobilization has achieved progress in both countries, although it has been somewhat slower in Australia than in New

Zealand. In both countries reform of the Labour Party has been crucial in increasing access by women to parliament and hence to the pool for ministerial office. The reforms took different routes in the two countries, requiring the introduction of party quotas in Australia, where factional barriers to women were stronger, but not in New Zealand where the Women's Council took on an increasingly important role. The factional structure of the Australian Labor Party remains a barrier to increasing the proportion of women selected for cabinet, although the first woman premier, Dr. Carmen Lawrence, succeeded in having women make up one-third of her cabinet in 1990 and this figure was later matched by Queensland Premier Anna Bligh. While Labor's electoral quota, the election of Labor governments and women premiers have enhanced women's executive presence in Australia, this success is still contingent on factional support, which in turn inhibits cross-factional "sisterhood." And even a highly successful woman deputy prime minister, Julia Gillard, has been subject to gendered criticism for remaining "deliberately barren" and hence out of touch with the experiences of ordinary "mums and dads" (Sawer 2009: 171).

In New Zealand, women's activism within the Labour Party has been particularly effective, resulting in the election of Labour women to influential positions in the party hierarchy and their selection for safe electorate seats. Safe seats have enabled women to position themselves for ministerial office, and ultimately the party leadership. Under Helen Clark's leadership as prime minister there was a significant increase in women's executive presence with a record-setting 33 percent of women elected to her first cabinet, and with three women (out of three) ministers outside cabinet.

As we have seen, proportional electoral systems bolster the proportion of women in parliament and expand the pool of potential women ministers in both countries. Although the adoption of a proportional representation system in 1996 led to an increase of women in the New Zealand parliament, thereby increasing the pool of female talent, this is only part of the story. Women prime ministers and a sustained presence of high profile women ministers over the past decade appears to have resulted in a "normalization" of women's presence in executive politics. That the center-right National government has maintained the same proportion of women in cabinet as its Labour predecessor suggests as much. Similarly in Australia, conservative governments now have difficulty resisting expectations of female presence in the ministry. While the previous conservative prime minister, John Howard, said that to worry about the sums was "patronizing" and "old-fashioned" (when the number of women in his cabinet dropped), clearly he was whistling in the wind.

Whether this upward trajectory in both countries can be sustained over time will depend on a range of factors: a continuing supply of experienced women MPs; a continuing recognition by parties on both the right and left of the need for inclusive executive representation; and, continuing pressure from organized women to ensure such recognition.

Notes

1 We would like to thank Gillian Evans, Norm Kelly and Kirsty McLaren for help in preparing the data and Janet Wilson of the Parliamentary Library, Parliament of Australia.

2 Fiji has been under military rule since 2006, however, and was suspended from the Commonwealth of Nations in 2009.

3 This includes Fiame Naomi Mata'afa who has been a cabinet minister since 1991 and is the daughter of Samoa's first prime minister, a paramount chief.

4 Section 80, 1), c) of the Constitution of the Autonomous region of Bougainville 2004 states that the membership of the

> Executive Council shall consist of ... a woman member of the House of Representatives appointed by the President, being the woman member nominated by the women members (both those elected to represent the interests of women and any women members for single member constituencies).
> (see Constitution of the Autonomous Region of Bougainville 2004 at www.paclii. org/pg/legis/consol_act/cotarob2004558 (retrieved April 2010))

5 See *Loi organique n°2000–612 du 4 juillet 2000 tendant à favoriser l'égal accès des femmes et des hommes aux mandats de membre des assemblées de province et du congrès de la Nouvelle-Calédonie, de l'assemblée de la Polynésie française et de l'assemblée territoriale des îles Wallis-et-Futuna* (www.legifrance.gouv.fr/affich-Texte.do;jsessionid=24944587CD75A506FA915713B496AEC6.tpdjo06v_2?cidText e=JORFTEXT000000216538&idArticle=&dateTexte=20100403#LEGIART I000006386396 (retrieved April 2010)).

6 On 24 June 2010 Julia Gillard became Australia's first woman Prime Minister. After a subsequent election she headed a minority government.

7 The spelling of "Labor" differs in the two countries, with the Australian Labor Party dropping the "u" while the New Zealand Labour Party has retained it. Where the parties are referred to collectively, the original spelling is used for the sake of convenience.

8 Bochel and Bochel (2008: 431) find a statistically significant relationship between the sex of the council leader and the proportion of council cabinets who are women. However, not all council leaders have the power to choose their cabinet, so it remains unclear whether the sex of the leader is the determining factor.

9 We have been guided by Moon and Fountain's decisions on difficult cases, but have made different decisions where the focus of activity or the boundaries between portfolios have changed. Thus, while Moon and Fountain designated the environment a "resources" area, we have classified the current federal portfolio of Environment, Heritage and the Arts as "well-being."

10 Ryan appointed Helen Williams to head the federal Education Department in 1985, the first woman to be the head of a department at the federal level. Kirner appointed Ann Morrow to head the Victorian Education Department in 1988 and Lawrence appointed Marcelle Anderson to head the Western Australian Department of Cabinet in 1990.

11 See the Parliament House Occupants' Directory, December 21, 2009.

12 The category of state sector boards and committees is more encompassing than the previous mentioned category of Crown company boards and so these two periods are not comparable.

5   Central and Eastern Europe

Maxime Forest

Introduction

The recent history of the Central and Eastern European countries (CEECs)[1] makes clear that commonly shared historical experiences have shaped the institutional, political and social conditions for women's access to – or not – executive positions in those countries. During World War II, Central and Eastern Europe (CEE), not to mention Russia, faced brutal Nazi occupation. From 1945 onwards, the region underwent a process of Sovietization, defined as the nationalization of most sectors of the domestic economy and the elimination of political opposition to the benefit of communist parties. Although at different paces and with much differentiated levels of political contention the social and economic crisis of the Soviet model erupted from the late 1960s onwards, affecting each of these countries. The unexpected collapse of communism not only hit the CEECs simultaneously, but opened a rather peaceful process of transition to liberal democracy and market economy, with the exception of former Yugoslavia which had opted for a homemade socialism (and had not belonged to the Soviet area). This process resulted in an ever greater integration of the CEECs into the western world, crowned by the eastern enlargement of the European Union (EU).

Drawing on an historical-institutionalist, path-dependent perspective (Bruszt and Stark 1998: 15–48), this chapter attempts to provide a differentiated overview, which emphasizes the impacts of diverse domestic paths of Sovietization, transitions to democracy and EU accession on women's access to executive positions since World War II. In order to prevent any generalizations regarding the state-socialist period, common patterns will be counterbalanced by differentiating features with regard to women's participation in decision-making. As the masculinization of power during the first stages of democratic transition and the recently observed advent of state women might generate contradictory, but similarly unbalanced analyses, this chapter will opt for the same confrontation of empirical evidences[2] with regard to the post-communist era and the impact of EU accession.

The first section of this chapter describes the major trends in electing/ nominating women to executive positions across the region since World War II.

It pays special attention to the effects of the different stages of state-socialism, emphasizing the contradictions of the social engineering carried out by the former political regimes. The chapter further distinguishes between the two major processes of the post-communist era – transition to democracy and EU accession – with regard to their potential impact on the feminization of governments. The second section introduces the country cases – Croatia, Lithuania and the Czech Republic – through a comparison of the major institutional features of their respective political systems, which enables a better understanding of the key developments in women's access to executive office. These developments are detailed both for the state-socialist and the post-communist periods, stressing context-specific variables that may explain the differential impact of Sovietization, transition and EU accession processes on executive women. The second section also explores generic variables usually considered by the literature (cultural values, electoral rules, party alignment), and the role potentially assumed by external variables, in the form of policy transfers or norms diffusion, especially in the context of Europeanization. Finally, the last section assesses the potential effect of executive women on the advancement of women's interests and gender rights and suggests a few medium-range conclusions.

Regional overview

Devastating for Central Europe, World War II brought the eradication of national elites, including first-wave women's movement leaders, but also some strong resistance movements encouraging female involvement (Jancar 1990: 45–9).[3] Anti-occupation uprisings and/or liberation by Soviet forces paved the way for post-war Sovietization[4] which not only fostered fast industrialization thanks to the inclusion of millions of women into the labor force, but also aimed at shaping new gender references (Attwood 1999; Cîrstocea 2002). As part of this process, women were granted active political rights where those had not been gained during the interwar period, and political mobilization through women's mass organizations opened new channels to access political representation and executive positions.

By preventing pre-war right-wing parties from reintegrating into the political spectrum, in favor of leftist parties historically more committed toward women's emancipation, the immediate post-war period permitted the access of an unprecedented number of women into executive positions. Between 1945 and 1950, 15 women were appointed to governmental offices (11 with the rank of minister) in Bulgaria, Czechoslovakia, Hungary and Romania, in the Slovenian and Croatian provinces of Yugoslavia, and the Soviet Republic of Estonia. By comparison, no woman had achieved similar positions before 1945 and the female population had remained disenfranchised in Bulgaria, Romania and Yugoslavia. In most cases, however, women leaders were ascribed to the area of care, with the exceptions of Estonian Olga Lauristin (cinema), Bulgarian Tsola Dragoycheva, "awarded" the ministry of posts, and Czech social-democrat Ludmila Jankovcová (light industry).[5]

As indicated in Table 5.1, the most intensive stage of Sovietization, during the 1950s,[6] was even more favorable in terms of women's access to executives, with about 30 women appointed to governmental offices throughout the decade. Only a few of them, however, actively contributed to the "construction of socialism" while being in charge of light industry (Czechoslovakia, Hungary, Bulgaria), food industry (Latvia, Czechoslovakia) or chemical industry (Czechoslovakia). The early 1950s also inaugurated a disempowerment of executive offices to the benefit of central planning and the highest party structures, which included only a few women veterans of the resistance against Nazism and of the hidden activities of communist parties.[7]

Yet, as the economic growth brought by fast-track industrialization was coming to an end, the gendered consequences of the Soviet model – limited access to contraception, spare-time devices and social facilities for working women (Heitlinger 1985; Kligman 1998) – contributed to worsen the effects of women's "double burden" (for a discussion of this aspect of women's situation under communism see Jancar 1978: 12–37). The "women's issue" was by then considered solved, however, and most women's organizations were dismantled, thus limiting their participation in public activities. Consequently during the 1960s, women's access to executive positions was more limited at the same time that their representation in some legislatures was decreasing as well.[8] But the rampant crisis of the Soviet model – be it in its most dramatic manifestations as

Table 5.1 Governmental positions held by women in Central and Eastern Europe, 1949–2009[a]

	1949–59	1959–69	1969–79	1979–89	1989–99	1999–2009
Bulgaria	2 (2)[b]	3 (4)	4 (7)	3 (5)	11 (27)	14 (53)
Croatia	2 (–)	– (2)	– (1)	1 (–)	4 (3)	18 (18)
Czech Republic[c]	4 (3)	1 (–)	1 (2)	3 (3)	7 (21)	14 (33)
Estonia	3 (n.a.)	2 (n.a.)	– (n.a.)	2 (n.a.)	10 (n.a.)	11 (n.a.)
Hungary	4 (1)	1 (–)	2 (1)	3 (1)	4 (12)	12 (14)
Latvia	– (–)	2 (–)	2 (–)	3 (1)	8 (5)	21 (7)
Lithuania	– (–)	3 (1)	2 (–)	1 (–)	7 (8)	8 (13)
Poland	1 (1)	– (–)	1 (–)	4 (–)	10 (9)	20 (27)
Romania	3 (–)	3 (–)	2 (1)	14 (7)	2 (12)	18 (49)
Slovakia[d]	– (–)	– (–)	1 (1)	1 (3)	12 (19)	6 (12)
Slovenia	1 (1)	– (1)	– (–)	– (1)	5 (16)	15 (40)
Per decade	20 (8)	15 (7)	13 (13)	35 (21)	80 (132)	157 (266)

Source: author's calculation.

Notes

a Table 5.1 shows offices held by women. Individuals have been counted more than once if they have held more than one portfolio or if they have been appointed several times across different decades.

b Numbers outside parentheses are for minister, and numbers within parentheses are for state secretary and deputy minister.

c Figures from 1949 to 1999 are for the Czech lands *and* the federal level of Czechoslovakia.

d Figures are for Slovakia only, be it as part of federal Czechoslovakia (1969–92) or an independent state.

in Budapest (1956) and Prague (1968) or through a decade of protest as in 1970s Poland – led the CEECs to reshape their social contracts. Preventing a decline in birth rates, reducing the female labor force due to limited available work positions and maintaining the illusion of women's access to political power were thus among the main objectives of the new policies carried out from the early 1970s onwards.[9]

In the field of political activity, quotas for women were progressively established in state legislatures. Whereas female representation had not exceeded 12 percent in Poland or 18.4 percent in Czechoslovakia by 1965 (but had reached over 30 percent in the Baltic Soviet republics) a complex social engineering progressively increased female representation above 25 percent. Similar efforts were undertaken to recruit more women into communist parties,[10] with limited results for party leaderships. Women did not exceed 10 percent in party central committees and practically did not feature in politburos. And if the absolute number of women in executive positions almost tripled between 1970 and 1989, women only rarely assumed significant positions, while their presence often portrayed the most hated features of the *nomenklatura*.

The transition to democracy resulted in a sharp drop in women's representation in state legislatures due to the end of the quotas, achieving an average (bottom) level of 8.9 percent in 1992. In contrast to their active participation in the civic mobilizations that precipitated the fall of communism, women were under-represented among the "strategic actors" negotiating the transitions.[11] Female leadership was then only to be found in Lithuania, with Kazimiera Prunskienė as prime minister in 1990–1, in Poland, with Hana Suchoka as chief of government in 1992–3, and in Bulgaria, with the cabinet led by Reneta Indzhova in 1994–5.[12] Yet, the picture is much more balanced if we consider that 68 women were granted 80 ministries and at least 122 others held 132 executive positions during the first ten years of post-socialist transformation, corresponding to the restructuring of the state, the marketization of the economy and the building of statehood in the case of Slovenia, Croatia and the Baltic states. Although this is to be weighted with respect to the much greater cabinet instability and the specialization of policy-making[13] under democracy, it is still twice as many executive positions as during the two previous decades. Unlike their predecessors, female executives have also enjoyed greater access to ministries such as economy, finance, defense or interior, with 28 portfolios in the aforementioned domains and a similar proportion related to care and the environment.[14]

An even more pronounced tendency is to be reported for the decade 1999–2009, characterized by the legislative and policy transfers of the EU accession, including the politicization of gender equality issues. In a context where female presence in state legislatures significantly increased, progressively closing the gap with the EU-15 average,[15] nearly 400 women held governmental offices, 134 of them holding 157 portfolios. The same decade saw the first two elected women heads of state in CEE: Latvian Vaira Vîke-Freiberga (1999–2007), and Dalia Grybauskaité, elected President of Lithuania in 2009. Additionally, in a few countries such as Bulgaria or Croatia, efforts have been made toward feminizing executives, although with some populist undertones.[16] Last but not least, EU membership has introduced a new avenue for women to access executive positions.[17]

At this point, however, it seems necessary to pay closer attention to social, political and institutional contexts, as well as to the different opportunity structures available to women for achieving executive positions in CEE. These objectives can be tackled through the comparison of Croatia, Lithuania and the Czech Republic, which can be distinguished from three points of view: *geopolitical*, as these countries can be attached to three categories of post-socialist states – a former province of federal, non-aligned, Yugoslavia, a post-Soviet republic and a "popular democracy" under Soviet influence; *cultural*, as the secular, urban and industrious Czech Republic could be opposed to more Catholic and rural Croatia and Lithuania; and *institutional*, as two of these three young democracies rank among the 55 semi-presidential countries identified by Elgie and Moestrup (2008: 5), while the Czech Republic revived its parliamentary practice from the interwar period. Different paths of extrication from state socialism, as well as different statuses with respect to EU membership, also contribute to make especially valuable the comparison of three countries which best encompass the complexity of post-war Central and Eastern Europe.

Country cases: Croatia, Lithuania and the Czech Republic

Description of the political regimes

Croatia: from Tudjman authoritarianism to the redefinition of executive powers

Soon after Croatia emancipated from the Yugoslav Federation, the first war in former Yugoslavia broke out and shaped the functioning of its democratic institutions for at least a decade. As a state at war, Croatia was ruled by the nationalist Croatian Democratic Union (HDZ) and its founder, first-elected president Franjo Tudjman (1990–2000) who prioritized patriotic mobilization over pluralism. During two five-year mandates, one in war and one in peacetime, Franjo Tudjman revealed himself to be the undisputed chief executive, due to the competencies formally granted by the 1990 constitution but also to the close control exerted over a cabinet exclusively constituted of members designated by the HDZ. If, according to Article 111, the government was responsible both to the president and to the House of Representatives, in practice, 202 members of the cabinet were nominated/dismissed, including six prime ministers, by presidential decision between 1990 and 1999. As a consequence, as noted by Kasapović (2008: 54), "the Croatian government was a typical 'presidential cabinet' that practically behaved as the president's executive service." Tudjman's past as a high-ranking officer for Tito and member of the Yugoslav communist league, but also as an ideologist of Croatian statehood, was decisive in the presidentialization of the executive.

This situation, characterized by strong presidential features and limited democracy, changed dramatically after Tudjman's death in late 1999 and the opposition's victory in 2000. The HDZ was ousted from power by a six-party coalition, and the reform undertaken by the new government modified the balance of power, substantially limiting the prerogatives of the president. Major changes also resulted from the transforming political culture of the HDZ, less favorable to a strong executive leadership in peace conditions (also under the pressure of public opinion), and from the building of a culture of compromise between coalition parties which enabled long-lasting cabinets. The recent evolutions of executive power in Croatia are also significant when considering peaceful cohabitations between HDZ prime ministers Ivo Sanader (2003–6) and Jadranka Kosor (2009–), and independent and social-democrat presidents Stipe Mesić (2000–10) and Ivo Josipović (2010–).

Lithuania: weakening the presidential institution from inside

In the Lithuanian case, the short-lived interwar experience of independence and democracy is critical to understanding the disputed choice of semi-presidentialism by the early 1990s. Although reformed communists who then enjoyed strong voting preferences initially rejected re-establishing the presidential institution, which had progressively confiscated executive and legislative powers between 1927 and 1940, a compromise was found among the main forces represented at the constituent *Seimas* (by which presidents de facto ruled the country between 1989 and 1992). The example of neighboring Poland and personal interests surely contributed to shape the 1992 constitution. Yet, it is mainly to emphasize institutional continuity with the two political experimentations of pre-war Lithuania that, along with a single house elected with a mixed system and a 4 (later 5) percent threshold, a directly elected president was also established, but with limited powers, except for nomination (Krupavičius 2008: 69).

Far from being a proxy for political stability, however, semi-presidentialism has generated unexpected conflict at the executive level. Since the members of the cabinet are mainly responsible to the Seimas, the first two elected presidents, Algirdas Brazauskas (1993–8) and Valdas Adamkus (1998–2003), adopted rather low institutional profiles, only dismissing and nominating prime ministers (eight in the first eight years of independence) as the result of changing majorities or major financial scandals. Populist Rolandas Paksas repeatedly overstepped the spirit of the constitution, attempting to interfere in the prerogatives of the prime minister and the parliament. Major controversies, however, arose from alleged corruption and ties with the Russian mafia during the 2003 presidential campaign. As a result, Paksas was the first elected president in post-communist Europe to be removed from office by an impeachment procedure, in 2004 (Krupavičius 2008: 75–7). Whereas successful impeachment can be understood either as a sign of political instability or consolidated institutions, it can also be argued that the complex electoral and executive architecture of Lithuania did not produce much greater instability than in the neighboring Baltic republics, which do not present such semi-presidential features.

The Czech Republic: blurred parliamentarism

If the functioning of contemporary political regimes in Croatia and Lithuania has been strongly influenced by the role assigned to the head of state, the Czech Republic seemingly features as a "pure" parliamentary democracy. The 1992 constitution adopted after the dissolution of Czechoslovakia established an asymmetric bicameralism, with a lower house (Poslanecká Sněmovna) and a Senate (first elected in 1996), which is almost a copycat of the pre-war institutional architecture that once made Czechoslovakia the only functioning democracy in Central Europe (Elster 1995). Despite a 5 percent threshold, proportional representation and the survival of an orthodox communist party which has so far been excluded from any coalition at the national level (Perrotino 2000) have complicated the constitution of stable majorities. If the right-wing Civic Democratic Party (ODS) founded by Václav Klaus could initially secure sufficient support, the rise of social democrats (ČSSD) from the mid 1990s onwards, the resilience of the Communist Party and internal divisions within the ODS and among its "natural" small allies have limited the support to "winning" parties to around 30 percent since 1998. However, instead of anticipated elections, Czech parties usually opted for caretaker governments such as the one led by Jan Fischer in 2009–2010, or "gentlemen's agreements" obtained after hectic bargaining between the ODS and the ČSSD.

While placing major prerogatives in the hands of the lower house and the government that stem from the ruling majority, the constitution, nonetheless, maintained a president of the republic. Due to the vivid memory of the praised two first Czechoslovak presidents, socialist Czechoslovakia was the only popular democracy which had not abolished the office. The office's symbolic meaning, attached to state continuity and moral authority, thus constituted a strong argument in favor of a mainly representative function, granted with a suspensive veto and limited prerogatives for the designation of the cabinet. First post-communist Czechoslovak (1990–2) and Czech President (1993–2003) Václav Havel not only restored the image of the function, but also made the most of constitutional competencies in the name of the civic virtues he promoted as a dissident. His successor, former prime minister Václav Klaus, proved even more controversial for using his suspensive veto on many occasions, especially to counter the process of ratification of the Lisbon Treaty and to prevent the extension of gender rights.[18] Despite unreachable majorities and controversial use of the president's competences, Czech executives can also be described as internally stable. Unlike in most of the CEECs, the number of governmental offices proved to be relatively stable and usually met the area of competences of the respective parliamentary committees (Crowther and Olson 2002), thus facilitating a more balanced legislative initiative between the government (50 percent) and the chamber (30 percent). Additionally, although several governments have lost the trust of a relative majority of the parliament during the course of the scheduled term, changing coalitions do not always mean a radical change in the composition of cabinets. Moreover, if unstable majorities strongly undermine the ability of cabinet members to develop their own agendas, ministers representing small coalition parties such as the Christian Democrats, the Freedom's Union or the Greens enjoy greater autonomy vis-à-vis the head of the government.

In the light of these three case studies, it can be argued that post-communist institutional contexts regarding the structure and the practice of executive power have been largely path-dependent toward pre-socialist institutional legacies, the paths of extrication from state-socialism, and the building of statehood (through independence and war-making). These variables, as well as other differentiation patterns, are also critical to analyzing the presence of women in executive positions since World War II.

Evolution of women's presence in the executive

At the beginning of the 2010s, a brief overview of women in executives in our three case studies indicates differentiated situations that suggest rather ambivalent trends. In Croatia, HDZ Jadranka Kosor was designated prime minister in 2009 of a coalition cabinet in a context of cohabitation. She obtained the support of the Sabor elected in 2006 with about 21 percent female deputies. The same year, Dalia Grybauskaité was the first ever elected female president of Lithuania, easily gathering an absolute majority on the first round of election, whereas the share of women in the Seimas decreased from 22 to 18 percent. In the Czech Republic, the proportion of women in the Chamber dropped from 17.5 to 15 percent in 2006, and the caretaker government appointed in 2009 included three women, two fewer than in the previous one. Taken separately, long-term trends to be observed since World War II do not explain the current levels of women's representation in executives, but they surely provide useful insights into understanding the differentiated situations of the CEECs.

Yugoslavia/Croatia: former Yugoslavia: short-lived feminization in troubled times

In Yugoslavia, a number of women entered active politics in the ranks of the communist league in the immediate aftermath of the Nazi occupation. Yet, only a few were nominated to governmental positions, such as Anka Berus who simultaneously entered the executive committee (top executive) of Croatia and assumed the ministry of finance from 1947. Similarly, only a few female war veterans made their way through state and party institutions during the 1950s and 1960s, assuming non-ministerial offices in the domain of care. However, incipient liberalization during the "Croatian spring" of 1968–70 coincided with Savka Dabecević-Kućar being designated president of the executive committee (1967) and later first secretary of the Croatian communist league (1969). As liberalization was intertwined with the claim for greater autonomy inside

Yugoslavia, she was soon dismissed upon Tito's decision. Another woman, Milka Planinc, was designated from among hard-liners to replace her (1971). Yet, her nomination suppressed only for a short period Croatian aspirations (at least until Tito's death, in 1979), and did not put a stop to the political and intellectual mobilization that simmered in Slovenia, Croatia and even Serbia. For instance, the re-thinking of the "self-management" model included a reflection on the role of women in the public sphere, and academic and literary circles became increasingly open to western feminism (Jancar 1985). It is in this context that in 1982, at a time when Margaret Thatcher was the only woman ruling in the western world, Milka Planinc was nominated prime minister of Yugoslavia, becoming the only female leader among socialist states. A decade of growing ethnic tensions throughout the federation, the 1980s made the competition for executive offices of vital importance in the hidden fight between the Serbian communist league and its Croatian and Slovenian counterparts. In this context, no woman occupied a significant executive position in Croatia between 1980 and the dissolution of Yugoslavia, largely anticipating the (re)masculinization of power after 1990.

Independent Croatia: the advent of new female leaders

Of the 202 ministers nominated by Franjo Tudjman between 1990 and 1999, only four were women who occupied seven governmental offices (3 percent), mainly related to environmental and care issues. At the same time, in 1992, only 5 percent of members of the lower house of the Croatian Sabor were women, partly due to an unfavorable electoral system and to the designation of a similarly low proportion of female candidates by the winning HDZ. Despite a few "women-friendly" changes being introduced in the electoral law, less than 8 percent were elected in 1995 (Glaurdic 2003: 285). In 2000, however, mainly due to the designation of about 25 percent female candidates, mostly to winnable positions, by the winning Social Democrat Party (SDP, ex-communists), the proportion of women in the Sabor rose to 20 percent. At the same time, feminizing cabinet positions was considered a symbolic means to end the Tudjman era of authoritarianism and ethno-nationalist rhetoric: eight women entered the coalition government – four at the rank of minister, with SDP Zeljka Antunović briefly holding the portfolio of defense. As Croatia initiated its rapprochement with the EU, feminizing executive elites became a matter of political consent between major parties, being used as a sign of greater commitment toward democratic values by the HDZ. While other parties such as the SDP and the Croation Social Liberal Party (HSLS) had established women's sections back in the early 1990s, the HDZ "Katarina Zrinska"[19] organization was founded in 1998 in order to appeal to the female vote and improve women's intra-party position. In 2003, her president Jadranka Kosor entered the new coalition cabinet as minister of family, later of foreign affairs. At the same time, two other women were nominated as ministers of justice and European integration, and eight women as state secretaries. And if after the 2009 elections the share of women in executive positions remained unchanged, two of them have been designated prime minister and vice prime minister, 40 years after the succession of Savka Dabcević-Kućar and Milka Planinc to the highest executive positions.

Lithuania: Soviet Lithuania: between record quotas and nomenklatura selection

Briefly annexed to the Union of Soviet Socialist Republics (USSR) as a result of the Molotov–Ribbentrop Pact in June 1940, Lithuania was re-established as a Soviet republic in 1944, being prey to anti-communist guerrilla activity until the early 1950s. As in other Baltic republics, Sovietization was performed through the mass deportation of native populations, the abolition of the symbols of Lithuanian nationhood (to begin with the use of native language) and, to a lesser extent, through Russian colonization. Lithuanian women, who had been granted active political rights soon after state independence in 1918 but never represented more than 4.7 percent of the Seimas in the interwar period (Krupavičius and Matonyté 2003), were brought into politics by the communist party (Misiunas and Taagepera 1993: 359–60), thus providing human resources for the designation of – fake – female representatives to the Lithuanian Supreme Soviet. Between 1947 and 1951, the proportion of women delegates increased from 22 to 29 percent. Due to the tense post-war conditions, however, women did not obtain significant executive positions until the late 1950s. In 1959, Leokadija Diržinskaité-Piliušenko, formerly a local executive, was appointed vice prime minister and from 1961 to 1976 also served as a minister of foreign affairs, a purely honorific function maintained in order to preserve the illusion of Lithuanian statehood toward the western world. While scrupulously implemented quotas progressively increased women's legislative representation up to 35.7 percent by 1980 – an absolute record in the USSR – only three other women accessed executive positions between 1961 and 1990.

Women executives in post-communist Lithuania: one step forward, two steps backward?

In 1988, the Sąjūdis Initiative Group emerged from the political contest initiated in the wake of perestroika. Sąjūdis, initially a 35-member group (of which only three were women), soon coordinated mass demonstrations that eventually led to free elections being held in February 1990. After gaining 101 out of the 141 seats in the Lithuanian Supreme Council, the Sąjūdis majority proclaimed independence from the Soviet Union in March and nominated Kazimiera Prunskienié, a former member of the communist party but one of the three female members of its initial committee, as a prime minister. After she resigned from office in 1991, Prunskienié joined the Farmers' Party (center-right). But in 1992, female representation in the Seimas dropped to its lowest at 7.1 percent although with a left-wing majority, which appointed only three female deputy ministers. In 1995, Prunskienié co-founded the Lithuanian's Women's Party as a way of capturing public attention. Her initiative helped to put pressure on major parties to nominate more female candidates. During the 1996 elections, wooed by conservative Homeland Union and Christian Democrats, the share of women in the Seimas increased to 18.3 percent, at that time the highest level in CEE, and seven women joined the government, including Laima Andrikiené in charge of initiating the accession negotiations with the EU. If legislative representation dropped to 10.6 percent in 2000, women maintained a relatively strong position within the cabinet, with three ministers (including finance) and eight deputy ministers during the term. Women's access to executive positions remained quite unchanged even after their representation at the Seimas hit a record high of 22 percent in 2004. Since the 2008 elections, with only 18 percent women in the legislature and only one female minister within the conservative cabinet designated, women's presence in Lithuanian politics can hardly be described as a bed of roses.

Meanwhile, however, women's position has been reinforced by the growing credibility of female presidential candidates, in the context of the destabilization of the presidency. Kazimiera Prunskienié passed the second round of the election in 2004 after the impeachment of President Rolandas Paksas, and was defeated by former President Adamkus by a decent 47.4 to 52.6 percent of votes. In 2009, Dalia Grybauskaité, a diplomat who served twice as a deputy minister (foreign affairs and finance), once as minister of finance (2001–4) and as the first Lithuanian EU Commissioner (2004–9), was brilliantly elected in the first round of the presidential elections.

Czechoslovakia/the Czech Republic: post-war Czechoslovakia: resilient feminism vs. fake representation

After its liberation by Soviet *and* United States troops in April–May 1945, a plural democracy was restored in Czechoslovakia, from which were banned right-wing parties compromised by German occupants. President Beneš, heir of the first Czechoslovak President Tomáš Garrigue Masaryk, returned from exile and left-wing parties joined into a "National Front," undertaking the expulsion of the German population and a huge program of nationalization. Through local executive committees and thanks to strong voting preference, communists progressively gained control over the main sectors of society. Barely a month after the liberation, communist women established Slovak and Czech Women's Unions, and female representatives of the National Front (communists, social-democrats and socialist-nationals) – many of whom had hid or were sent to concentration camps during the war – established a National Front of Women (NFW). At the same time, former leaders of the strong women's organizations of the First Republic (1918–38), following recently released deputy Monika Horáková, founded a Council of Czechoslovak Women (CCW). Although being prey to the attempts of communist women to take control of women's mobilization, the NFW and the CCW coordinated their efforts with intra-party women's sections to promote better access for women to executive and legislative positions

(Feinberg 2006: 195–205; Uhrová 2005).[20] If this strategy failed to significantly improve parliamentary representation (6.7 percent in 1946 free elections), it confirmed women's position in state and party executives, with social-democrat Ludmila Jankovcová being nominated Minister of Light Industry.

In February 1948, the Communist Party assumed undisputed control over the government. In the immediate aftermath of the "Prague Coup," communists and pro-communist social democrats took control of the NFW and the CCW, ousting former women's movement leaders. In May, almost uncompetitive elections gave 89 percent of the ballots to the communist-led National Front and in September, feminists and dissident socialist-national party leaders Horáková and Zemínová were placed under arrest. In April 1950, all women's organizations were dismantled or merged into the Czechoslovak Women's Union, and in May, the two aforementioned feminists leaders featured among the eight convicted in the first "Prague trial." Zemínová was condemned to a 30-year sentence in a labor camp and Horáková entered history as the only woman sentenced to death during the 1950s political trials in CEE.

Only three women were appointed to executive positions, and 11 percent elected to parliament after the 1948 elections. Yet, the "women's issue" that had gained an unprecedented relevance since the early years of the first Czechoslovak republic, was considered to be solved, as the new constitution ensured full equal rights. In 1953, whereas Czechoslovak women were granted full access to abortion, the Women's Union was dismantled, inaugurating more than a decade of low political mobilization and weak influence inside the party and executive structures. By that time, Czechoslovakia perfectly illustrated the situation in most of the Soviet area. Nevertheless, it briefly distinguished itself from other socialist countries, due to the resilience of the grassroots feminism inherited from the interwar period. Indeed, local sections of the Women's Union were progressively reactivated during the 1960s, in order to palliate the lack of social facilities for working mothers. By 1967, in the early moments of the Prague Spring, these largely self-organized groups became part of a nationwide organization with free membership. In its Action Programme of June 1968, a copycat of the one adopted by the Communist Party, the new Women's Union placed the access of women to executive positions at the top of its priorities.[21] A strong supporter of reformist party leadership even after the Soviet invasion of August 1968, this 150,000-member organization was soon converted into a fake mass organization by pro-Soviet hard-liners. During the last two decades of the regime, only four Czech women accessed executive positions both at the federal and the Czech level, with one of them, Women's Union leader Marie Kabrhelová, featuring among the most hated representatives of the nomenklatura.

Post-communist politics and women in the Czech Republic: (self-) killing hopes?

In the immediate aftermath of the Velvet Revolution, its main coordinating actor, the Civic Forum (CF), argued on the basis of its open and democratic nature to place a few women in legislative and executive positions, first by nominating them to replace some of the communist deputies removed from office by late 1989. But its leaders soon faced resistance from local civic forums throughout the country when trying to secure winnable positions for women in the first free elections (1990). At the executive level, political bargaining between the different streams of this composite political actor eventually prevented CF leaders from obtaining more than two portfolios for women. Moreover, the dissolution of the CF and the rise of professional political parties soon favored classic intra-party selection and party politics over civic mobilization. The advent of a male democracy, evident in the election of 90 and 93 percent male lower houses in 1990 and 1992, respectively, was accompanied by the withdrawal of some of the main female actors from democratic transition. Former dissidents and members of the CF thus opted for the continuation of their civic commitment to civil society organizations, in line with the anti-politics values of the Czechoslovak dissidence.

Consequently, the reign of the civic Democratic Party ODS, (1992–8) cemented the exclusion of women, with only five female deputy ministers appointed during this period. However, its progressive weakening did not entail major changes. After the 1996 elections, the increase in female legislative representation from 7.3 to 15 percent was mainly due to communist and far-right lists, and had no effect on women's access to executive positions. Anticipated elections of 1998[22] confirmed the rise of the Social Democrat Party. But the first left-wing government appointed since the dissolution of Czechoslovakia outraged critics from among feminist insiders, after women's access to the executive was limited to non-ministerial positions.[23] From 1998 onwards, the issue of women's participation in politics has drawn growing public attention, with polls showing an overwhelming support for women's increased representation. This surely helped former dissident Hana Marvanová to be designated the first chairwoman of a major Czech party, the Freedom Union, and women candidates to gain an unprecedented 17 percent of seats in the Chamber of Deputies in 2002. Despite her party joining the new coalition cabinet, Hana Marvanová soon resigned from all her mandates after receiving personal, deeply gendered attacks from the media. And the only major social-democrat female minister in office between 2002 and 2006, ČSSD vice president and president of the social democrat women's union Petra Buzková met a similar fate three years later.[24] In 2006, the comeback of the ODS did not have the expected (negative) impact in terms of access to the executive. If the first government appointed did not count any woman as a minister, the second cabinet designated in 2007 with the support of the Greens and the Christian Democratic Party was the most feminized in Czech history, with five women out of 24 ministers (21 percent), among them the respected Christian Democrat Vlasta Parkanová in charge of defense. The care-taker government appointed in 2009 did not repeat such a "record," with only three women out of 17 members of the cabinet (17.6 percent).

Factors explaining women's access to the executive

Paying attention to much differentiated historical and political contexts does not prevent consideration of more generic variables as well. Although they are likely to interact, these variables can be grouped in different clusters, whether they result from cultural values (religion, conception of gender roles), institutional arrangements (voting system, form of the state and form of the regime, party system) or rather exogenous processes (policy transfers, notably under the influence of EU accession, norms diffusion).

Cultural values and "gender regimes"

Since the very beginning of post-communist transformations in Central and Eastern Europe, this level of analysis has drawn a considerable amount of scholarly attention (see the contributions to Funk and Mueller 1993, for instance Šiklová: 84–93 and Goven: 224–240; see also Corrin 1999: 1–7 and Watson 1997: 21–9). As a lecture on the impact of democratic and economic transition in terms of backlash pointed out, the emergence – or the revival – of conservative discourses about gender social roles, variables such as the influence of religious beliefs, in relation to the urban/rural cleavage and the sexual division of labor, were considered of specific relevance. In Poland, for instance, the construction of gender roles – including under state-socialism – has much to do with the role of the church as a social and political actor (Heinen and Matuchniak-Krasuska 2002), and there is strong evidence that traditionalist and Christian Democratic parties (re-)established in CEE after 1989 have often attempted to question or even suppress women's sexual, reproductive and social rights.

In Croatia, where nearly 88 percent of citizens declared themselves to be Catholics in 2001, the public expression of faith has played a central role in the reactivation of national identity during the 1980s, and the justification of the "homeland war" against Serbian minorities supported by Belgrade. With regard to women's role in politics, the context of ethnic war intertwined with traditionalist values through the feminization/embodiment of the nation (Jalušić 2004: 145–67) contributed both to sacralizing women's bodily integrity and, ultimately, to legitimating sexual assault against "others' women" as a means of war.[25] The evolution of Croatian politics since 2000 proved to be more favorable to women's access to executives also because of the marginalization of the ultranationalist Croatian Party of Rights (HSP) and the growing secularization and pacification of the HDZ's rhetoric, whose conservatism was reoriented toward the issue of same-sex unions, against which a HDZ MP claimed in 2005 that "85 percent of the population considers itself Catholic and the Church is against heterosexual and homosexual equality" (Kuhar 2008).

In Lithuania, which claims to be almost 80 percent Catholic, the church has recovered a considerable influence, especially considering that it was heavily persecuted. The expression of faith also played a symbolic role in the preservation of nationhood and the opposition to communism. Yet, the church did not shape political discourses to the same extent as in neighboring Poland. For instance the Christian Democratic Party, which has been less likely to nominate female candidates, has lost most of its influence, while women insiders came to favor the adoption of intra-party quotas. If Croatia and Lithuania seem to credit the decreasing influence of religious beliefs with the willingness/support for women to enter active politics, the highly secularized Czech Republic illustrates that weak religiosity and a consistent support for the feminization of high politics combined with a relative support to the extension of gender rights[26] do not result in better access to executive positions. Despite constituting a differentiating pattern, the incidence of cultural and religious values does not provide any macro-level explanation for women's access to the executive in these case studies.

Institutional arrangements and party politics

Literature on women's access to politics in contemporary democracies has demonstrated the relevance of institutional arrangements in providing the opportunity for women to access political mandates. Initially, the voting system has been considered the main variable, but now tends to be intertwined with secondary variables such as the vote counting method, the size of the district, the number of allocated seats, and intra-party selection procedures. But in CEE, where proportional representation (PR) is the rule, and mixed systems the exception, thorough analyses have shown the voting and the vote counting methods to have a relatively marginal influence on women's presence in politics, at least if considered in isolation from other potential explanations (Matland 2003). And party and/or district magnitude have been somewhat predictive only in a few cases, such as Hungary or Slovenia (Antić 2003; Ilonszki and Montgomery 2003). Instead, analysts have shown that, following Norris and Lovenduski's insights (1995: 21–32), intra-party recruitment procedures (including voluntary intra-party quotas) are of great relevance to explain women's trajectories in party politics (see, for example, Antić 1999). The role of women's sections inside major political parties has also been pointed out as a means of fostering more competitive and transparent recruitment and nomination processes (Saxonberg 2000).

In these three cases, it is likely that relatively unstable procedures have amplified the discretionary nature of cabinet designations. The impact of party women's sections and of the attempts to establish women's parties on the constitution of party lists and the designation of women to executive offices tends to validate this argument. In Croatia, the rise of Jadranka Kosor is strongly related to the lobbying of party structures by the HDZ's women's section, while in Lithuania, both women's sections established according to the Scandinavian model and the women's party founded by Kazimiera Prunskienié had some impact on the feminization of parliamentary and executive politics. By contrast, in the Czech Republic, the lack of real progress can also be attributed to the weakness (or absence, as in the case of the ODS) of party women's sections. The failure of popular Petra Buzková to expand the recruitment of female candidates among social democrats illustrates this situation.

Political alignment is usually considered a key element to analyze levels of women's representation in state legislatures and, to a lesser extent, in party memberships. As for the likeliness to be designated in a winnable position, political alignment proved itself to be highly relevant in CEECs, pointing out the importance of intra-party organization and procedures (including the adoption of intra-party quotas). Left-wing parties have been considered more prone to nominate female candidates, and this has been clearly the case in Croatia and the Czech Republic. By contrast, it is worth noting that *all* female prime ministers and heads of state elected or designated since 1989 have been recruited by the center-right, as well as 41 out of 52 (79 percent) of the women who held major ministries (finance, economy, defense, interior or foreign affairs) during the two past decades.

Additionally, whereas the effects of semi-presidential systems remain understudied, and therefore unclear as far as women's access to executive positions, the three case studies from this chapter provide useful insights. In Croatia, strong semi-presidential features during Franjo Tudjman's terms coincided with the locking of nomination procedures and the virtual exclusion of women. Instead, downsizing presidential prerogatives resulted in a larger access to executive positions. In Lithuania, the influence of the semi-presidential system is difficult to establish, as the narrow access of women to governmental offices is balanced by their credibility both as prime minister and head of state, in this case as a remedy for a troubled institution.

External variables

Regarding women's access to politics, analysis of the role of external variables has mostly addressed debates about the possible institutionalization of voluntary and legal quotas for party lists, and the strong resistance those kept generating in post-communist Europe (see, for example, Goven 1993 and some of the contributions to Matland and Montgomery 2003). In this regard, the role of international agencies, women's networks, international party alliances (such as the Socialist International), and western party women's sections, have been mentioned. Meanwhile, the "domestic impact of Europe" (Börzel and Risse 2003) through EU accession has been mainly investigated from a top-down perspective, mostly focusing on the implementation of gender equality policies in CEE (Falkner and Treib 2008). Nevertheless, some sociological approaches have shown that the Europeanization of gender and equality issues has gone far beyond norm implementation and institutional transfers, also including cognitive side effects in the form of the diffusion of concepts, policy paradigms and social learning (Forest 2006a; Krizsan 2009).

Although this would deserve its own chapter, I argue that Europeanization largely affected the framing of the issue of women's access to political power. Since the opening of accession negotiations with eight CEECs in 1998, the number of executive women has more than doubled, and in Croatia, the greater agreement of major parties about EU accession coincided with the feminization of institutional politics. Beyond coincidence, two kinds of phenomena deserve mention:

1   Europeanization has placed gender equality issues on the legislative agenda, through the adoption of laws and newly created institutions; and

2   in some countries, feminizing politics has been understood as an evidence of greater commitment toward European values. This can be seen since 2000 in Bulgaria, Romania, but also in Croatia and Lithuania, where electing or designating women to executive offices – one of them a former EU commissioner – served as a proxy for transparency.

Do women executives represent women?

From a more substantive – and normative – point of view, the question remains whether the relatively weak, but improving, access of women to executives in CEE resulted in specific endeavors regarding gender equality and women's interests. This is a contentious issue, since the contribution of women to the adoption of new legislation is better evaluated through legislative process tracking and the study of legislative voting preferences. With the exception of a few countries, namely the Czech Republic, most of the CEECs meet the "90 percent rule" (executives initiate 90 percent of bills and obtain 90 percent of what they want, Olson 1980: 174); even in this case, the law-making process nevertheless involves parliamentary committees and MPs in the ranks of the ruling majority. Therefore, the actual contribution of individual members of the cabinet can hardly be isolated. For instance, in our analysis of voting in the Czech lower house from 1996 to 2008, we found only two examples of "female votes:" one to oppose a parliamentary bill proposing a ban on abortion, another to adopt a bill introduced by the cabinet that recognized same-sex partnerships. In the latter situation, both female executives and women MPs had a major influence on the whole legislative process.

But it can be argued that being often in charge of social affairs or health, female ministers in office, at least during the first decade of the transformation, share some responsibility for the elimination of many of the women-friendly aspects of social policies carried out under state socialism. Moreover, executive women cannot be solely credited with the most far-reaching legislative changes introduced in favor of gender equality in the past ten years, as those mostly originated in the context of conditional EU accession (Forest 2006b). Even if these modifications were passed in the form of cabinet bills, thus mobilizing highly feminized ministries of social affairs, they often returned to male politics when provoking major contestation, as in the Czech Anti-discrimination Law during its hectic adoption process.

Conclusion

Women's access to executive power in Central and Eastern Europe cannot be analyzed only through the lenses of institutional arrangements and party politics. Since World War II, CEECs have undergone three major institutional and political transformations – Sovietization, transition to democracy and EU accession (be it completed or not) that prevent any classic analysis in terms of polarization or institutional legacies. But at the same time, no "methodological exceptionalism" should any longer prevail to interpret each of these transformation processes in the light of women's access to executive functions, since those are strongly interlinked by the resilience of some political, social and institutional structures. In this part of Europe, women were granted far-reaching social rights and accessed superior education and paid work before many of their western counterparts, but were only occasionally admitted to real executive positions during four decades of state socialism. That is why their access to political power cannot be interpreted as a consequence of their improving social position. Instead of isolated variables or one-sided interpretation, we have thus proposed a complex, path-dependent, analysis of three case studies. Our analysis tends to put the main variables usually invoked by the literature, such as electoral rules, political alignment (and party system), the form of the regime, and cultural values opposing women's participation in the public sphere, into the broader perspective of transforming societies, where none of these variables can be taken for granted once and for all.

On the one hand, our positioning encapsulates the structural complexity of this part of Europe since World War II, but on the other hand, it is necessarily limited to medium-range conclusions. Regarding the state-socialist period, it is clear that women's access to executives was conceived as the least important part of a politics of fake representativeness, thus leaving women out of real power positions. Only on a few occasions of greater political contention, such as the short-lived liberalization movements in Czechoslovakia and Croatia in 1967–70, did it become a relevant issue, with a potential impact on women's presence. With regard to post-communist politics, we emphasized two contradictory processes: the masculinization of power during the transition to democracy, and the window of opportunity opened by EU accession. In this context, we argue that the contribution of executive women to the promotion of women's interests in Central and Eastern Europe is mainly to be found in the breach they have progressively opened, both in quantitative and qualitative terms, by accessing responsibilities that fall beyond the area of care to which they have been traditionally ascribed. In that sense, executive women have surely contributed to undermine the gendered division of political work that still prevails in this part of the continent.

Notes

1 For the purpose of this study, CEECs under consideration are the following: Bulgaria, Croatia, the Czech Republic, Estonia, Hungary, Latvia, Lithuania, Poland, Romania, Slovakia and Slovenia.
2 This chapter is based upon my PhD dissertation defended in 2009 at the Institut d'Etudes Politiques de Paris, *A Gendered Analysis of Political Change in Parliamentary Politics. The Chamber of Deputies of the Czech Republic* (738pp.). For the purpose of my research, a comparative analysis of women's access to decision-making in Eastern Europe was carried out, largely drawing on first-hand sources:

parliamentary archives, archives of former women organizations under the socialist era, interviews with former female executives. As for the Lithuanian and Croatian cases, my data have been completed by secondary sources and benefited from useful insights by Prof. Irmina Matonyte, Kaunas University, and Roman Kuhar, Peace Institute, Ljubljana.

3 In Yugoslavia, about two million women were involved in supporting homeland and communist movements, of which about 100,000 joined Tito's liberation army, according to Wiesinger (2008: 32).

4 Be it rampant, as in Hungary, legitimized in polls, as in Czechoslovakia, or the result of Soviet occupation, as in the Baltic states.

5 Nomination to the Ministry of Light Industry sounded like a reward for her servile contribution to the dissolution of her own party. She was later nominated vice prime minister, "the highest post held by any woman behind the Iron Curtain," as stated in *Time Magazine*, December 27, 1954.

6 To be characterized by strong ideological mobilization and the massive access of women to paid work.

7 For example, Ana Pauker, born Rabinsohn (1893–1960), one of the founders of the Romanian Communist Party.

8 For instance, in Czechoslovakia, female representation to the local and national assemblies dropped by 25 and 14 percent, respectively, between 1954 and 1964, according to a report of the Czechoslovak Women's Union issued in 1966 and quoted in *Zpravodaj Česko-slovenský Svaz Žen* (1968).

9 Following the 1956 uprising, Hungary was the first country to implement new policies to ensure women's mobilization, re-establishing a mass women's organization and fostering political recruitment and intra-party promotion (Fodor 2002). On women's policies in CEE during the quota era, see Wolchik and Meyer (1985: 189–300).

10 For state legislatures, the final objective was around 30 percent. Outside of the USSR, this was only reached in Czechoslovakia by the end of the 1980s. As for party membership, in 1966, the Czechoslovak communist party was the most feminized in the Soviet bloc, with barely 28 percent female members. But by the beginning of 1970s, this proportion did not even reach 25 percent in any party in the region, with the Yugoslav communist league having the lowest figure, at 16 percent (Jancar 1985).

11 Only a few women thus joined the roundtable negotiations in Poland, Czechoslovakia, Hungary and Bulgaria.

12 In the Polish case, this is to be put into the context of the strong presidency of Lech Walesa.

13 Through the multiplication of intermediate positions such as state or under-state secretary and chief of department.

14 The proportion was almost strictly the same at the level of state secretaries (47/49).

15 In 2008, the average in the ten new member states plus Croatia was 17.1 percent.

16 In Bulgaria, feminization was used as an electoral argument by the party of former King Simeon II in 2001 and later promoted as a means to overcome widespread corruption and meet European values by the Party of Citizens for the European Development of Bulgaria, which is not exempt from accusations of nepotism and corruption, as shown by the rejected nomination of Rumiana Jeleva as a EU Commissioner in January 2010.

17 Between 2004 and 2009, three women from post-socialist Europe were nominated to the charge of EU Commissioners. Simultaneously, new member states from CEE have been represented at the European Parliament by delegations feminized over 30 percent, close to the EU-15 average of 33 percent.

18 President Klaus repeatedly vetoed the Anti-discrimination Act, adopted under EU-pressure in 2009. The same year, his posture over the ratification of the Lisbon Treaty contributed to the fall of the government led by his successor to the presidency of the ODS.

19 From the name of a patriot noble woman of the seventeenth century.
20 Unlike during the pre-war period, when feminists mostly intended to enfranchise the women's movement from party politics, they attempted to reinforce their respective positions inside political parties.
21 The document states that it aims at: "obtaining the largest number of qualified and educated women to be represented in every State, political and economic organs, from the local to the central level," *Programme of Action of the Czecho-slovak Women's Union*, June 1968, p. 3.
22 Convoked after a schism within the ODS due to a major financial scandal.
23 A shadow cabinet of women was established by female MPs of the majority, drawing public attention including from overseas: "Czech Women Battering Stone Wall of Politics," *New York Times*, February 27, 1997.
24 Both female leaders returned to their original vocation as lawyers.
25 Although sexual assault was systematically used as a means of war only during the conflict in Bosnia and mostly by Serbian militias, cases were also reported during the re-occupation of the Krajina region by the Croatian Army in 1995.
26 According to the Czech Public Polls Institute, in 2008, the registered partnership for same-sex couples adopted in 2006 enjoyed a 75 percent approval, and a similar proportion claimed to be pro-choice. In 2003, according to the Czech Statistical Office, barely 32 percent claimed to be believers.

6   Sub-Saharan Africa

Gretchen Bauer[1]

Introduction

This chapter considers women's presence in the executive branch in sub-Saharan Africa, the 47 countries south of the Sahara Desert. While several African countries have climbed to the top of world rankings in women's legislative representation in recent years – Rwanda is the current world leader with more women than men in its Chamber of Deputies – women have not made similar advances into the pinnacle of executive power in Africa. In mid 2010 only one woman held a top executive position in an African country – Ellen Johnson Sirleaf, who became president of Liberia in early 2006. In sub-Saharan Africa women have been slow to gain access to cabinet level positions; however as with legislative representation that appears to be changing. Part of the explanation for this executive-power deficit lies in sub-Saharan Africa's post-colonial trajectory of single-party rule and military regimes that precluded women's independent organizing and denied free and fair elections to women or men candidates.

Liberia and Rwanda are two recent exceptions to the lack of women executives in sub-Saharan Africa and they are the focus of this chapter. Both cases reveal the political opportunities that have been seized by women activists and women's organizations in post-conflict or post-transition settings in Africa in the last two decades. These cases demonstrate that despite very poor social and economic indicators women have been able to attain the highest offices in the land in some African countries. Moreover, preliminary research suggests that women executives and their allies are working to represent the interests of women in some sub-Sahara African countries. Before turning to the two cases, an overview of the region is provided.

Regional overview

Only a handful of women have ever served in the top executive positions in Africa in the twentieth or twenty-first centuries, usually as prime minister. Mostly in the early years of the twenty-first century, a few African women have also served as vice president or deputy president (see Table 6.1). In recent years, more African women are standing for executive office though their chances of winning

Table 6.1 Women heads of state in Sub-Saharan Africa, 1960–2010

President	Prime Minister	Vice President	Deputy President	Other
Ellen Johnson Sirleaf *Liberia* 2006–present	Elisabeth Domitien *Central African Republic* 1975–6	Wandira Speciosa *Uganda* 1994–2003	Kadidja Adeba *Djibouti* 1992	Carmen Pereira *Guinea* Acting Head of State 1984
	Sylvie Kinigi *Burundi* 1993–4	Aisatou N'Jie Saidy *Gambia* 1997	Phumzile Mlambo-Ngcuka *South Africa* 2005–8	Ruth Sando Perry *Liberia* Chairwoman of the Council of State 1996–7
	Agathe Uwilingiyimana *Rwanda* 1993–4	Joyce Mujuru *Zimbabwe* 2004	Baleka Mbete *South Africa* 2008	
	Mame Madior Boye *Senegal* 2001–2	Alice Nzomukunda *Burundi* 2005–6		
	Maria das Neves Ceita Batista de Sousa *São Tomé e Príncipe* 2002–3 and 2003–4	Marina Barampana *Burundi* 2006–7		
	Luisa Dias Diogo *Mozambique* 2004–10			
	Maria do Carmo Silveira *São Tomé e Príncipe* 2005–7			

Source: Worldwide Guide to Women in Leadership (2009g).

are slim. Adams (2008: 476) reports that between 1997 and 2007, 23 different women ran for president in 19 different elections in 14 different countries in Africa. Most of the 27 women who ran for president received less than 1 percent of the vote. Adams (2008: 477) attributes the low vote for women to strong incumbents, weak party systems and a high number of candidates in most cases. In contrast to many parts of Asia and Latin America, African women presidential aspirants (and other modern African women leaders) have not been related to powerful men or political families (Adams 2008: 477; Jalalzai 2008: 224).

Cabinet posts have also eluded African women though less so in recent years in some countries. In 1996 about half of African countries were below the world average for women in cabinets of 6.8 percent and half above (with a range of 0 to 33.3 percent); in 2010 about half of African countries were below the world average for women in cabinets of 16.9 percent and about half above (with a range of 0 to 53.3 percent) (Russell and DeLancey 2002: 148; Inter-Parliamentary Union 2010d). Russell and DeLancey (2002: 154) identify two periods of significant increase in women's access to cabinets in Africa, beginning around 1975 and then again around 1990. These coincide with dramatic moments in Africa and the world, namely the start of the United Nations Decade for Women and first United Nations Conference on Women in 1975 and the onset of political transitions across Africa in the 1990s. In mid 2010 eight African countries were among the top 30 countries worldwide with 30 percent women or more in ministerial positions. In the late 2000s, as Table 6.2 reveals,

Table 6.2 Numbers of ministries headed by women in sub-Saharan Africa, 2007–9

	Numbers of ministries/numbers of different countries
Defense	11 ministries/10 countries
Education; Training; Science and Technology	30/18
Family; Children; Women; Seniors; Disabled	43/25
Finance	6/6
Foreign Affairs	12/10
Health; AIDS	21/13
Housing; Urbanism	7/5
Human Rights	4/3
Information; Communication; Transportation	16/13
Interior, Home, Security	8/7
Justice; Keeper of the Seals	17/13
Labor; Employment	7/7
Natural Resources; Environment; Agriculture	34/17
Public Works; Infrastructure	5/5
Social Affairs	7/7
Tourism; Culture	15/11
Trade; Commerce; Industry; Economics	30/20
Youth; Sports; Recreation	7/6
Other	40/22

Source: Worldwide Guide to Women in Leadership (n.d.).

African women were finding significant representation in "hard" as well as "soft" portfolios, including foreign affairs, justice and trade and industry. Further, it should be noted that while education and health are typically considered "soft" portfolios, they are usually among the ministries which receive the greatest allocation of national resources in an African country.

Adams (2008: 478) suggests that "an historical tradition of women leaders in Africa" may explain why few women leaders in Africa have gained power through family ties. Indeed, the small number of women leaders in the modern period contrasts sharply with the, according to one source, more than 200 women who have been political leaders in Africa since the early seventeenth century.[2] This includes a wide range of positions, peoples and places around the African continent. For example, in the pre-colonial period, Queen Nzinga M'Bandi of N'Dongo and Matamba ruled for 40 years in the seventeenth century, even serving for three years as the Governor of Luanda on behalf of the Portuguese. Queen mothers of the Asante in Ghana routinely held the second highest political position in the state. Women from many societies in Africa, in areas as diverse as contemporary Ethiopia, Cameroon, Tanzania, Botswana and South Africa, served as regents, ruling until their sons came of age to take over political leadership. Women served as chiefs and paramount chiefs, queens and sultans all over Africa, in the pre-colonial and colonial periods, with the numbers appearing to diminish in the post-colonial period, though women do still serve as traditional leaders in Africa today (see Becker 2006; Matemba 2005; Steegstra 2009; Stoeltje 2003).

There are good reasons why so very few African women have reached the pinnacle of formal political power in the years since World War II. Most African countries only gained their independence beginning in the early 1960s. In the 80 years before independence, the entire continent, save for Liberia and Ethiopia, was under colonial rule by, primarily, the British, French and Portuguese. Many scholars suggest that colonial rule brought about an overall decline in the position of women, in particular, relative to that of men (Berger and White 1999; Parpart 1988; Staudt 1987). As Parpart (1988: 210) writes:

> For most African women (with the exception of some urban women) the colonial period was characterized by significant losses in both power and authority. Colonial officials accepted Western gender stereotypes which assigned women to the domestic domain, leaving economic and political matters to men. As a result, although many African men suffered under colonialism, new opportunities eventually appeared for them, while women's economic and political rights often diminished. Colonial officials ignored potential female candidates for chiefships, scholarships and other benefits. Many female institutions were destroyed.

For the most part, political independence did not restore women's power and authority. While at independence most African countries adopted the democratic political systems practiced by the departing colonial powers in the metropole (but not in Africa), those systems remained in place for very little time. Instead, within the first decade of independence most African countries reverted to the authoritarian rule of the colonial period – turning to single-party rule, military rule or some combination thereof. Political power was highly centralized in the executive and removed from the legislature, judiciary, political parties and civil society. Constitutions were abandoned, legislatures dissolved, judiciaries ignored, political parties proscribed and independent organizing outlawed. Single-party rule was often marked by personal rule, rule by "big men" and presidents-for-life. In many countries there were no elections or, at best, elections that served as referenda on a single candidate – thus preventing women and men from seeking political office. Military regimes precluded women from leadership positions as most, if not all, African militaries excluded women from participation at any level. In any of these centralized regimes the most senior political position for a woman was usually held by the leader's wife – what Jibrin (2004) refers to for Nigeria and Ghana as the "First Lady Syndrome."[3] In addition, state-created national women's associations typically occupied all of the space allowed for organized political activity by women – aside from participation in the women's wings of ruling parties – as Fallon (2008) persuasively shows for Ghana. All of this began to change in the early 1990s with Africa's "second independence."

Beginning in the late 1980s and continuing throughout the 1990s regime change swept across Africa. In many instances pressure for political liberalization led to transitions to multi-party political systems and the holding of free and fair elections. Today a range of regimes exists in Africa; whereas autocratic regimes dominated the continent by the late 1980s, a diversity of regimes characterizes Africa today. Posner and Young (2007: 127) note another important difference in Africa since 1990, namely that formal institutional rules have come to matter much more than in the past. Whereas in the first decades of independence most African rulers left office through violent means, since 1990, the majority have left through institutionalized means – by resigning at the end of a term or losing an election. Critical for this study, Posner and Young (2007: 127) assert that: "Elections are also becoming more important as a mechanism for selecting leaders in Africa, as reflected in the large increase in both their number and their competitiveness." This has provided new opportunities for African women activists and politicians.

Tripp (2001: 142–4) was the first to point out the important role that women played in the transitions that commenced in Africa in the early 1990s. She noted that: "Like student organizations, labor unions, and human rights activists, women's organizations openly opposed corrupt and repressive regimes through public demonstrations and other militant actions." In other cases, women took advantage of early political openings "to make bolder strides in the political arena." Among other things, women consolidated independent women's organizations, demanded women's expanded participation in politics, including through affirmative action policies if necessary, and even formed their own political parties in countries as diverse as Zambia, Zimbabwe, Lesotho and Kenya. Women's most visible political gains came in their increased representation in national legislatures. In mid 2010, eight of the top 35 countries worldwide in terms of women's representation in a single or lower house or parliament were in Africa, with 26 to 56 percent women members.[4]

Many of these transitions in sub-Saharan Africa took place in the aftermath of conflicts. These conflicts included wars of liberation, civil wars, guerilla wars, genocide and its aftermath, among others. As in other parts of the world, post-conflict transitions in Africa have, perversely perhaps, provided opportunities for women to become more involved in formal politics (Bauer and Britton 2006; Tripp *et al.* 2006; Tripp *et al.* 2009). Writing about Uganda, Pankhurst (2002: 127) observed that violent conflict, which results in major disruptions to gender relations, can also provide "new opportunities to articulate debate about gender politics as well as for individual women to live in a different way." Of the eight African countries among the top 35 worldwide in women's legislative representation in mid 2010, all but one (Tanzania) was a post-conflict country.[5]

Country cases: Liberia and Rwanda

Description of the political regimes

Liberia in West Africa and Rwanda in East Africa have been chosen as the case studies featured in this chapter – given the relatively large number of women in the executive branch in both countries. Neither of them may be considered typical African countries but then one cannot really find *any* country in sub-Saharan Africa that is representative of other sub-Saharan African countries. That said, they are not unlike many other countries in Africa and the world in which women have come to power during or following periods of political instability, conflict or turmoil. Liberia has been selected because Ellen Johnson Sirleaf, the current president, is the first elected woman head of state in Africa. Moreover, about one-third of the members of Liberia's cabinet are women[6]. Rwanda has been selected because about one-third of the members of its Council of Ministers are women. In addition, Rwanda's lower house of parliament, the Chamber of Deputies, from which the cabinet members are *not drawn*, has 56 percent women members – the highest in the world and the first time that women outnumber men in a national legislature. Rwanda's constitution forbids sitting members of parliament from serving as ministers. While ministers are some-times named from members of parliament, they must resign their posts to serve in the government. The women in cabinet come mostly from two other places – civil society and the ruling Rwandan Patriotic Front, including some women who have served as governors or in other posts.[7] Similarly, members of cabinet in Liberia are also not drawn from the legislature; Article 3 of the Liberian constitution forbids a person holding office in one branch of government from simultaneously holding office in another branch.[8]

The two cases represent two different types of government and electoral system. Liberia is a republic in which the president, directly elected for a six-year term (with a two-term limit), is both the chief of state and head of government. The cabinet is appointed by the president and approved by the Senate. A bicameral legislature consists of a 30-member Senate (serving nine-year terms) and a 64-member House of Representatives (serving six-year terms). Senators and representatives are directly elected in a simple majority system with two seats from each constituency or county. Rwanda is a presidential republic. The chief of state is the president who is directly elected for a seven-year term (with a two-term limit); head of government is the prime minister. A Council of Ministers, or cabinet, is appointed by the president. A bicameral parliament consists of a 26-member Senate (serving eight-year terms) and an 80-member Chamber of Deputies (serving five-year terms). Fourteen members of the Senate are indirectly elected by the 12 provinces, the city of Kigali and universities and institutions of higher education; eight members are appointed by the president and four by the Forum of Political Organizations. At least 30 percent of members of the Senate must be women, according to the constitution. Fifty-three members of the Chamber of Deputies are directly elected through a closed list proportional representation electoral system; 24 members occupy "women's seats," with two selected from each province. The remaining three members are selected by youth and disability organizations.[9]

Evolution of women's presence in the executive[10]

Liberia is unique in Africa for not having been colonized by Europeans. Rather, the territory was settled by freed American slaves, under the auspices of the American Colonisation Society, beginning in 1847. These settlers, who came to be known as Americo-Liberians or, later, Congos, dominated the country and its indigenous population for more than a century.[11] In particular, the Americo-Liberian True Whig party was in power from 1883 until 1980 when the last True Whig president was ousted in a military coup. True Whig president William Tubman was in power from 1944 until 1971; when he died in 1971 he was replaced by his vice president William Tolbert who served as president until he was overthrown and executed during the 1980 coup. Master Sergeant Samuel Doe, who perpetrated the 1980 coup, was the first indigenous Liberian to lead the country; his ascent to power prompted an exodus of Americo-Liberians from the country. In 1985 he "won" an election widely considered to be fraudulent prompting the outbreak of civil war in 1989 and a second coup in 1990 in which he was deposed from power and killed. There followed nearly a dozen attempts to resolve the conflict in Liberia, including one that brought Ruth Sando Perry to power as Chairwoman of the Council of State in 1996–7. An election in 1997 brought warlord Charles Taylor to power; during his rule atrocities and war continued with fighting spilling over into neighboring Sierra Leone. Taylor was finally ousted and exiled to Nigeria in 2003 by which time the country had been embroiled in gruesome conflict for 14 years, with more than 300,000 people killed, more than half a million people internally displaced, and many more forming a Liberian diaspora in neighboring countries and overseas. A Comprehensive Peace Agreement in 2003 brought the conflict to an end; a two-year

National Transitional Government of Liberia (NTGL) brought together two rebel forces, the former government and members of civil society. National elections were held in October 2005 under the watchful gaze of 15,000 United Nations peacekeeping troops, with a presidential runoff in November 2005 (Bauer 2009: 194–6; Harris 2006). In January 2006 Ellen Johnson Sirleaf was inaugurated as president.

In the post-World War II period it has not been unusual for women to be included in cabinets in Liberia. President William Tubman (1944–71) had no women as cabinet secretaries, though women did serve at junior levels, as assistant and deputy secretaries.[12] Under President William Tolbert (1971–80), women served for a time as Agriculture Minister, Health and Social Welfare Minister (three different women), Posts and Telecommunications Minister and Finance Minister (Ellen Johnson Sirleaf from 1979–80). Samuel Doe (1980–90) appointed two different women as Minister of Health and Social Welfare, one as Minister of Postal Affairs, and one as Minister of Commerce, Industry and Transportation. Finally, Charles Taylor (1997–2003) named two different women as Minister of Planning and Economic Affairs, and other women as Minister of Education, Minister of Commerce and Industry, Minister of Post and Telecommunication, and Minister of Gender Development. Moreover, several women served as ministers in transitional governments in Liberia from 1990–7 and 2003–5.

When Ellen Johnson Sirleaf became president in 2006, she named many more women to cabinet, including her first Minister of Finance (2006–8), and Ministers of Agriculture, Commerce, Foreign Affairs, Gender and Development, Justice, and Youth and Sports. This represented six out of 21 ministers in late 2009.[13] In addition, President Johnson Sirleaf has appointed no fewer than 27 deputy ministers and assistant ministers (some ministries have more than one assistant or deputy minister) in the first years of her administration.[14] According to Otieno (2008: 31), these are 40 percent of Liberia's deputy and assistant ministers, the highest percentage of women at this rank in Africa. The very high number of women cabinet secretaries or ministers in Liberia in the latter half of the twentieth and early twenty-first centuries – and the broad range of their portfolios – is remarkable for an African country, indeed any country in the world. Similarly, Ellen Johnson Sirleaf's election to the office of president is unprecedented in Africa.

Rwanda, like most of the rest of Africa, was formally colonized by a European power – one of Germany's few African colonies – in the late nineteenth century. When Germany lost World War I, it also lost its colonies in Africa; Rwanda was handed over to Belgium as a League of Nations Mandate, becoming a United Nations Trust Territory after World War II. In Rwanda the colonial powers retained the highly centralized Tutsi dominated monarchy that ruled before the colonial period, in the process transforming "what had been a hierarchical but flexible system into a more rigid, bureaucratic colonial state, and one that intensified ethnic divisions [between the minority Tutsi and majority Hutu]" (Newbury 1992: 196). In the prelude to independence, a Hutu-led revolution in 1959 overthrew the Tutsi-dominated monarchy. By the time of independence in

1962, "the monarchy had been abolished and Tutsi authorities had been expelled from power; many had fled the country" (Newbury 1992: 197).

At independence Rwanda was led by Hutu President Gregoire Kayibanda and an elected National Assembly. In just over a decade, however, Kayibanda was ousted in a military coup led by Major General Juvenal Habyarimana. The 1973 coup was prompted, in part, by lingering tension over privileged access among Tutsi, but also reflected significant regional and class rivalries among Hutus. Habyarimana quickly consolidated his power, establishing single-party rule in 1975 and subsuming all political and social activity, including women's organizations, under the party. In 1989 civil society organizations, with women at the forefront, began to demand political liberalization; in June 1991 the ruling party gave up its monopoly on political power and in April 1992 a first multi-party or coalition government was formed (Longman 1998). Habyarimana remained in power in the new government, until he was killed in an airplane crash in April 1994 – the crash that sparked the genocide that killed nearly one million Rwandans. Longman (2006: 136) describes the genocide as "organized by a group of powerful government officials, military officers, and businesspeople from the Hutu majority group who sought to use violence to reverse the political reforms of the preceding years and reassert their political power." Moderate Hutus, deemed to be part of the political opposition, as well as Tutsis considered accomplices of the Rwandan Patriotic Front (RPF), who had invaded from Uganda in 1990, were targeted. The genocide was ended after three months by the RPF, led by Paul Kagame, who then installed a transitional government of national unity. This transitional government was in place in Rwanda from 1994 until 2003 when a new constitution was adopted and the first post-genocide presidential and National Assembly elections were held.

Until the RPF came to power in 1994 women hardly participated at all in government in Rwanda. According to Longman (2006: 134), the government of Gregoire Kayibanda "took little interest in women's empowerment, and women were unrepresented in government." According to Women for Women International (2004: 8–9), though a Ministry for Women was established in 1965, "neither this nor the launch of the [United Nations] decade of women in 1975 had a significant impact in addressing women's legal, cultural, social and educational marginalization." It appears that only one woman served in cabinet in that period – the Minister of Social Affairs and Public Health during 1964–5.[15] The ascent to power of Juvenal Habyarimana in 1973 "had little impact on the position of women in Rwanda, as the new president also advanced a conservative social agenda that did nothing to improve women's specific economic, social and political power" (Longman 2006: 135). Indeed, by 1985 "politics was still dominated by men ... Not one woman participated in the national government, or the local administration at prefecture [provincial] and commune [district] levels. Women constituted only 12 percent of parliamentarians and 2 percent in the diplomatic service" (Women for Women International 2004: 9).

When a multi-party government was introduced in Rwanda in 1992 the first few women began to enter the executive. Three women served varying terms from 1992 to 1994, as Minister of Education, Minister of Commerce, Industry, Mines and Artisans, Minister of Justice and Minister of the Family and the Promotion of Women (a ministry only created in 1992). Agathe Uwilingiyimana, who was the Minister of Education for one year, also served as prime minister until her assassination in 1994, in the wake of Habyarimana's death. By contrast, once the RPF came to power, women began to hold cabinet posts in significant numbers. During the transitional government from 1994 to 2003, ten women served in ten ministerial posts: as Minister of Family and Women's Affairs, Minister of Transport, Minister of Justice, Minister of State for Interior, Communal Development and Resettlement, Minister of Gender and Women's Development, Minister of State for Lands, Human Resettlements and Environmental Protection, Minister of State for Social Affairs, Minister of State for Environmental Protection, Minister of State for Forestry and Minister in the President's Office. The first presidential and National Assembly elections were held in 2003, retaining Paul Kagame (who had become president of the transitional government in 2000) and electing a Chamber of Deputies that was 49 percent women, catapulting Rwanda to world leader in women's parliamentary representation. A second set of post-genocide legislative elections was held in 2008, electing a Chamber of Deputies with more women than men. Kagame's first cabinet had 11 women, including as Minister of State for Skills Development, Vocational Training and Labour, Minister of Lands, the Environment, Forestry, Water and Natural Resources, Minister of Justice, Minister in the Office of the Prime Minister, Minister of State of Community Development and Social Affairs, Minister of State of Primary and Secondary Education, Minister of Education, Minister or State of Lands and Environment, Minister of State of Economic Planning, Minister of State of Agriculture and Minister of State of Cooperation. In mid 2009 Rwanda's cabinet had nine women members (out of 25), including the Minister of Information, Minister of Gender and Family Promotion, Minister of the East African Community, Minister of Education, Minister of Foreign Affairs, Minister of Infrastructure and Minister of State for Social Affairs and Community Development.[16] The outstanding presence of women in cabinet *and* parliament in Rwanda is rivaled only by South Africa and some Nordic countries.[17]

Factors explaining women's access to the executive

This section examines to what extent social, economic and political variables may have influenced women's access to executive positions in Liberia and Rwanda. It appears that both cases conform to Jalalzai's (2008: 223) finding, based on a survey of women presidents and prime ministers from 1960 to 2007, that women's status in society and politics varies considerably throughout the world in those places where women are in executives, with several women being leaders in countries where women's status is low. So, for example, most social and economic indicators for Liberia and Rwanda reveal very poor countries with a low status for women.[18] Liberia is a country of 3.5 million people, 60 percent of whom live in urban areas. By contrast, Rwanda, the most densely populated country in Africa, has a population of around 10.5 million people, only 18 percent of whom live in urban areas. Most Rwandans survive as subsistence farmers in the rural areas. Liberia contains a mix of religions with 40 percent of the population Christian, 20 percent Muslim and 40 percent adherents of traditional beliefs, while in Rwanda 95 percent of the population is Christian (more than half are Catholics) and 5 percent Muslim. In 2007 Rwanda was ranked 167 out of 182 countries with a Human Development Index (HDI) of 0.460; Liberia was ranked 169 with an HDI of 0.442. Both countries had very high fertility rates in 2009 – six for Liberia and five for Rwanda. Similarly, in 2009 infant mortality rates in both countries were very high – 138/1,000 in Liberia and 82/1,000 in Rwanda. Life expectancy at birth in both countries was extremely low in 2009: 41 for men and 43 for women in Liberia and 49 for men and 52 for women in Rwanda. In Liberia, according to 2003 estimates, only 42 percent of adult women and 73 percent of adult men were literate. In 2000 females attended school for eight years and males for 11. In Rwanda in 2003, 65 percent of adult women and 76 percent of adult men were literate. In 2005 it was estimated that females attended school for nine years and males for eight. Both countries are also ranked extremely low on the Gender-related Development Index: out of 155 countries in 2007, Liberia was ranked 142 and Rwanda was ranked 139.

Both economies are also at the bottom of world rankings. Liberia is richly endowed with natural resources including water, minerals and forests, but much of its infrastructure, especially in and around the capital Monrovia, was destroyed by the conflict of the last few decades. The per capita gross domestic product (GDP) at purchasing power parity (PPP) estimated for Liberia in 2008 was US$500. By contrast, landlocked Rwanda has few natural resources and has relied primarily on the cultivation of coffee and tea. As in Liberia, conflict – the 1994 genocide – severely impacted the country's fragile economic base and temporarily set back its ability to attract investment. Per capita GDP at PPP estimated for Rwanda in 2008 was US$900. In both countries it is assumed that women are nearly as economically active as men, though figures are scarce. The ratio of estimated female to male income stood at 0.50 in Liberia and 0.79 in Rwanda in 2007.

This review suggests that, as with women's legislative representation, there appear to be no simple correlations between, say, type of religion and whether women are elected (or selected) to executive office, or women's high or low socioeconomic status and women's access to executive office.[19] Indeed, in the mid 1990s Russell and DeLancey (2002: 156–7) failed to find a positive correlation between high life expectancy, high literacy and high GNP per capita and number of women cabinet members in 41 African countries, finding only a positive correlation between high life expectancy and more women in cabinet. In both Liberia and Rwanda *some elite* women have made great strides despite the low status of women overall. This confirms another of Jalalzai's (2008: 207) findings, namely, that women frequently rise to power as members of privileged groups. Though women's overall status may be low some women from elite backgrounds, particularly in terms of income and education, are nonetheless able to gain access to significant political offices. The many women in cabinet in Liberia (and other distinguished positions) from the middle of the twentieth century onward illustrate this point well.[20] Fuest (2008: 207) relates that in Liberia from the start of settler rule, settler women had certain privileges:

> From the nineteenth century female settlers in Liberia could buy and sell land, enter into contracts, bring legal suits and initiate divorces, appeal to the legislature and exercise similar forms of agency. Americo-Liberian women were not legal equals with men but the rights affecting the women of the Republic were among the most progressive in the world at the time.

She notes that women were granted the right to vote with men in 1946 and began to occupy executive and legislative positions in government from the 1950s. Interestingly, Fuest (2008: 208) asserts this was part of a strategy of settler rule meant to exclude the indigenous population:

> In order to secure their ruling position the Americo-Liberians excluded aspiring, educated Afro-Liberian men from high-level positions. Families of the ruling oligarchy preferred to see their female members in political posi- tions and had them educated accordingly when the education system expanded in response to economic growth in the 1950s and 1960s.[21]

Thus, in these cases, women's elite status trumped their gender status; just as importantly, elite women were being used to exclude another group from access to power.

In terms of political factors affecting women's access to executive office, women and men (property owners) in Liberia gained the right to vote and to stand for election in 1946 – much earlier than most other Africans still living as subjects in colonies at the time.[22] In Rwanda women and men gained the right to vote and to stand for election in 1961, one year before independence. Access to the vote with men at independence does not seem to have helped women in Rwanda, however, with the first women elected to the national legislature only in 1981: four of 64 deputies elected in 1981 were women, nine of 70 elected in 1983 were women, and 12 of 58 elected in 1988 were women, the last time elec- tions were held before the 2003 election.[23] The Inter-Parliamentary Union has no gender disaggregated data for elections in Liberia prior to the 2005 election.

Elections for president are held somewhat differently in Liberia and Rwanda. In Liberia, following the Comprehensive Peace Agreement of 2003, the presid- ent is directly elected by secret universal ballot. According to the country's 2004 Electoral Reform Law the winning presidential candidate must achieve a major- ity of votes and if there is no such winning candidate the first time voters go to the polls then there will be a second round of voting. In the 2005 election there were 22 candidates in the first round with no candidate achieving a majority. The highest vote getters were George Weah and Ellen Johnson Sirleaf who achieved 28 and 20 percent of the vote, respectively. A second round of voting was therefore held in which Ellen Johnson Sirleaf achieved 59.6 percent of the vote to George Weah's 40.4 percent. Since a new constitution was adopted in Rwanda in May 2003 the president is directly elected by secret universal ballot. In the first pluralistic presidential elections in Rwanda's history in August 2003, Paul Kagame was elected with 95 percent of the vote; two other contenders split the remaining 5 percent of the vote.

None of these political factors seems to have particularly helped women gain access to political office in Liberia or Rwanda. Elite women in Liberia were able to be appointed to the executive earlier than other African women due to circumstances peculiar to Liberia's history. Women in Rwanda had to wait two decades to gain access to parliament and three to gain access to cabinet, after being granted the right to vote and stand for office in the year before independence. What holds much more explanatory power for both countries and the women executives in them is the shared conflict experience. In this respect Liberia and Rwanda are entirely consistent with the literature that suggests that all over the world women have often ascended to executive office in times of political instability or transition. Indeed, this and associated factors probably account in large part for the advances that women have made in the executive in both countries. This comes into play in a number of ways.

As with women's increased legislative representation in Africa, opportunities created by a post-conflict situation and the ability of a mobilized women's movement to take advantage of those opportunities go a long way toward explaining women's executive successes in these two countries. During conflict and its aftermath women take on new roles – as household heads, combatants and civil society leaders, among others. Conflicts help to weaken patriarchal structures and shift gender roles, while post-conflict transitional governments draft new constitutions and establish new institutions (Adams 2008: 479; Bauer 2009: 207). A very important aspect of first post-conflict elections is that women (and men) are likely *not* to be contending with "entrenched male incumbents" (Tripp *et al.* 2006: 118). In Liberia, Harris (2006: 376) found that the lack of an incumbent in the 2005 presidential election – with vastly superior resources at his disposal – meant that "the political field remained remarkably open." Moreover, the conflict experience can also mean that there are women candidates available who might otherwise not be. In Liberia, according to Fuest (2008: 218), many Liberian women (including Ellen Johnson Sirleaf) spent years of exile overseas, benefiting from critical education or training opportunities, often supported by international organizations. But without women's organizations or a mobilized women's movement, the female gains of devastating conflicts may instead be dwarfed by female losses (Fuest 2008: 202).

So, for example, many analyses of Ellen Johnson Sirleaf's election in Liberia attribute a pivotal role to women's organizations and women voters (Adams 2008; Fuest 2008; Bauer 2009).[24] The candidates for president were many – 20 men and two women – with the two strongest contenders being George Weah, an international soccer star from the slums of Monrovia and Ellen Johnson Sirleaf, a Harvard-educated economist and political exile who had participated in some earlier Liberian governments. Ellen Johnson Sirleaf's successful elect-oral strategy was to hold Weah to less than 50 percent of the vote in the first round of voting and hope that she would be the second highest vote getter and face him in a runoff. At that point, "to the extent that women might vote together for a well qualified fellow woman, eliminating these competing loyalties could help consolidate women's support for Sirleaf" (Bauer 2009: 197). While no one has yet proven that women were responsible for Johnson Sirleaf's victory, Bauer (2009: 209–10) shows that women's organization activity remained consistent from the first round to the runoff election, while that of other civil society groups tapered off. She suggests that this may have had a "profound effect" on voters in Johnson Sirleaf's favor. Adams (2008: 481–2) relates that women activists and women's organizations, spurred on by the woman Minister of Gender and Devel-opment from the transitional government, played a critical role in registering large numbers of women voters and mobilizing them and others to vote for Johnson Sirleaf in the second round of elections. On numerous occasions, Ellen Johnson Sirleaf herself has credited women with electing her to the highest office in Liberia. Indeed, in her memoir, Johnson Sirleaf (2009: 264) calls the women of Liberia her "secret weapon" in the election: "More than anything, it was the women of Liberia who turned this election, for me and for themselves."

It should be noted that, as in other parts of Africa, women's organizations in Liberia had played an important role in bringing about peace to the war-torn country. Organizations such as the Liberian Women's Initiative, Women in Peace Building Network, the Association of Female Lawyers in Liberia and the Mano River Union Women Peace Network "raised awareness about the conflict and its effects on civilians, pressured ruling factions to participate in peace talks, advocated for the inclusion of women in peace negotiations, and provided support to those displaced by the conflict" (Adams 2008: 481; see also Bauer 2009; Bekoe and Parajon 2007; Fuest 2008). Once peace was established these same organizations focused their attention on Liberian women's political repre-sentation, lobbying to have gender quotas included in the new electoral laws. Though no gender quotas were included, the National Electoral Commission adopted guidelines that called upon political parties to include at least 30 percent women among their candidates. One of the groups that backed this call was Liberia's 50–50 movement. Sawyer (2008: 187–8) suggests that: "While women's organizations did not endorse the Sirleaf campaign officially, support for her candidacy was an unspoken objective of the 50–50 movement."

As in Liberia, so in Rwanda have some unique historical factors contributed to women's increased presence in government today. Pearson and Powley (2008: 20) report that

a progressive perspective on gender is not necessarily entirely new to Rwanda; many Rwandans refer to pre-colonial cultural practices of gender equality when explaining the factors behind women's contemporary status, and cultural attitude is a strong factor in women's level of political participation.

By and large, however, women's increased presence in the executive in Rwanda is attributable to the country's post-conflict status and women's mobilization – just as in Liberia. In the immediate aftermath of the conflict women constituted a majority of Rwanda's population; this meant that they were immediately forced to take on multiple, often new, roles. It also meant, according to Powley (2004: 5), that women had to be "central to the process of governing, reconciling, and rebuilding the country." Indeed, Powley notes that in Rwanda there was a recognition that since the conflict was "gendered," the recovery should also be gendered. Moreover, Powley's research found that ordinary Rwandans felt women could better lead that recovery in that they were perceived to be better disposed to forgiveness, reconciliation and post-conflict peace building (2004: 6–7).

Also as in Liberia, the exile experiences of some women positioned them well for posts in government. Women are and have been in influential positions within the RPF party hierarchy and many have been appointed to strategic positions in the transitional and post-transition governments (Powley 2004; Longman 2006). The RPF, according to Longman (2006: 139), "has consistently articulated its support for women's rights, including the right for women to hold public office." Longman (2006: 140) and Pearson and Powley (2008: 20) attribute the RPF's support for women's rights to the exile experience of many members in neighboring Uganda where the women's movement has been particularly strong and where quotas have boosted women's participation in parliament (a "contagion effect"). These authors argue that RPF leader Paul Kagame, in particular, has been a staunch advocate of women's involvement in government and of gender sensitive policy initiatives. Indeed, Kagame (and the RPF) have received many accolades for their "revolutionary steps to increase female representation in governance" (Burnet 2008: 369).

Women's organizations have contributed significantly to women's increased political participation in Rwanda. Several groups such as Duterembere, Haguruka and Reseau des Femmes had been formed in the pre-genocide period as part of the movement for political reform. In the aftermath of the genocide they expanded their roles while other organizations such as the umbrella organization Pro-Femmes were formed. Longman (2006: 138–9) suggests that the extensive involvement of women in Rwandan civil society has been a major reason for women's increased political participation. For one thing, activism in women's organizations has provided much needed experience from which to enter politics – with the mixed result that "the best women in civil society keep being drawn into government, named to commissions or ministries or the parliament." For another, women's groups have actively promoted the legitimacy and importance of women holding office (Longman 2006: 138–9). They have done this by promoting government policies that reserve positions for women and by encouraging the candidacies of individual women.

Many scholars have identified a direct link between the United Nations Conferences on Women held in 1975, 1980, 1985 and 1995 and progress in several African countries in terms of women's increased mobilization and organization, the establishment of national machineries for women, and the appointment or election of more women into political office (see Tripp *et al.* 2009). For example, Fuest (2008: 219) notes the important impact on Liberian women of their participation in the Beijing conference in 1995: "In activists' narratives, this seminal experience in particular motivated the participants to push for women's rights and provided symbolic resources, such as recourse to international resolutions … to back up demands for affirmative action." Indeed, regional, continental and international organizations have played a significant role in seeking to pressure governments to respond to women's demands for greater access to political power. In 1997 a Southern African Development Community (SADC) Declaration on Gender and Development called upon member states to meet a goal of 30 percent women in decision-making positions by 2005; in 2008 the SADC Gender Protocol upped the ante to 50 percent women by 2015. On a broader scale, the African Union (AU), successor body to the Organization of African States in 2002, has set a global precedent for gender equality by adopting the principle of gender parity in decision-making and electing five female and five male commissioners to lead the organization. While these targets often go unmet the pressure generated by such declarations and protocols assists women's movements in making demands upon their own governments.[25]

Do women executives represent women?

With women joining the executive branch so recently in both countries it is difficult to assess the impact on women's legislative representation and women's interests. In Liberia a woman president has so far not meant a dramatic increase in women's legislative representation, though nor was she already in power at the time of the last legislative elections. While women activists sought to have an electoral gender quota included in Liberia's 2004 electoral law, they were not successful. In the 2005 legislative election women won 17 percent of seats in the Senate and 12.5 percent of seats in the House of Representatives, below even the sub-Saharan African averages for women's legislative representation. It should be noted, however, that women were only 14 percent of candidates in those elections and therefore they were actually elected in proportion to their candidacies (Adams 2008: 481). In Rwanda, meanwhile, women have entered both cabinet and the legislature in high numbers. Cabinet members are not drawn from parliament in Rwanda, however, so the many women appointed to cabinet have been above and beyond those already in parliament. Rwanda's 2003 constitution requires 30 percent women in parliament "and *all other* decision-making bodies" and clearly this has been honored by President Kagame and other leaders (Burnet 2008: 369).

It appears that in both countries there has been a discernible impact of women's presence in the executive on women's interests. From the very beginning Ellen Johnson Sirleaf has made clear her commitment to Liberia's women. In her inaugural address, Johnson Sirleaf (2009: 271) recognized Liberian women's pivotal role in achieving peace in the country and in electing her; she pledged "to give Liberian women prominence in all affairs of our country." She has cited as purposeful her appointment of so many women to cabinet and other key government positions, for example, five of 15 county superintendents (Johnson Sirleaf 2009: 278). An early, though granted symbolic, act was to change the inscription on the front of the Supreme Court from "Let justice be done to all men" to "Let justice be done to all" (Ackerman 2009: 88). In addition, she nominated two women to the five-member body. In late 2008 Liberia introduced a specialized rape court to expedite rape cases; this followed changes to the law in dealing with gender-based violence, in particular domestic violence and rape, to increase penalties but also to shift blame from victims to offenders (Ackerman 2009: 88; Otieno 2008: 31). As one part of the reconstruction of the security sector, Johnson Sirleaf has sought to recruit women to the military and police; at least 20 percent of members of both the Armed Forces of Liberia and the Liberian National Police (LNP) are supposed to be women. By 2009 the LNP had met its target and Johnson Sirleaf had appointed a woman as police chief (Otieno 2008: 31; Ackerman 2009: 89). Other initial efforts by the Johnson Sirleaf administration include national programs that support school girls, market women and women farmers (Fuest 2008: 203; Bekoe and Parajon 2007). According to Otieno (2008: 32) President Johnson Sirfleaf is committed to gender mainstreaming throughout her government and to achieving gender equity in Liberian society.

In Rwanda, similar tangible gains for women can be identified. In 1995 a Minister of Gender and the Promotion of Women (MIGEPROFE) was established as the key government institution advocating for women's empowerment and gender-sensitive policy-making (Women for Women International 2004: 14) – before the Chamber of Deputies with nearly half or more women was elected. One of the first initiatives of the MIGEPROFE was the establishment of women's committees at the local level to encourage women's participation in politics. Also, women activists and women's organizations were involved in the drafting of the 2003 constitution. According to one of the participants, a member of parliament, women "got almost everything [they] asked for, including the 30 percent quota for women." In addition to ensuring the equal status of women, the constitution provides for the establishment of an independent Gender Monitoring Office (Women for Women International 2004: 16). In Rwanda, women members of parliament have organized themselves into a Forum for Women Parliamentarians and have pointedly worked together with women's organizations in order to achieve some of their goals. One of their most noteworthy accomplishments has been the introduction of Rwanda's Gender Based Violence Bill, the only bill to be introduced from the legislature rather than the executive. In part, according to Pearson and Powley (2008: 41), they were successful in moving the bill forward because of "powerful and supportive political will in the executive branch and the interest of international donors." In their study of the increased representation of women in Rwanda's parliament, Devlin and Elgie (2008: 251) state that "gender issues seem to have been established as part of the agenda prior to the increase in [women MPs'] numbers," from the beginning of parliamentary politics in Rwanda in 1994, echoing Pearson and Powley's assertion of the important influence of the executive branch on moving gender issues forward.[26] At the same time, many scholars such as Longman (2006: 149) have expressed concern that under an increasingly authoritarian government "the impressive representation of women in Rwanda's parliament and other government institutions will have only a limited impact on the lives of Rwandan women." Burnet (2008: 361) suggests that in the longer term, women's increased presence in government may help to undo current authoritarian trends – that "increased female representation in government could prepare the path for their meaningful participation in a genuine democracy because of a transformation in political subjectivity."

Conclusion

In most of sub-Saharan Africa women continue to be excluded from the pinnacle of executive power; in 50 years of political independence, only one woman has ever been elected president in Africa, in 2005. By contrast, women are slowly making inroads into cabinets; their representation at 20.2 percent in 2010 was slightly above the world average. While they continue to dominate in the socio-cultural ministries, they are increasingly holding portfolios such as foreign affairs, trade and industry, and the environment. There are good reasons for women's early under-representation in executives, and political liberalization in the last two decades has slowly but surely made more opportunities available to women. Indeed, conflicts and their aftermaths, in particular, have been seized by women activists and women's organizations for the political opportunities that they have offered. Liberia and Rwanda offer stunning evidence of the strides that women have made and can make in Africa when they come together across a myriad of dividing lines to heal wounds of the past and work together toward a common future.

This chapter provides support for a number of assertions made in recent studies of women in executives and a number of lessons learned. So, for example, Liberia and Rwanda are certainly two cases (and there are others in Africa such as South Africa and Uganda) in which political instability and the ensuing political transition led to women's ascension to executive office. A number of factors are at play here including the role of women and their organizations in ending conflicts and during critical transition periods when new constitutions and laws are drafted and promulgated. Also, women's own training and experiences during and after conflicts, as well as the influence and support of international organizations and movements, have provided ample cadres of available and qualified women for executive offices. In addition, Liberia and Rwanda – at the very bottom of all world social and economic indicators – demonstrate starkly that there is no necessary correlation between women's overall socioeconomic status in a country and some women's access to the highest political offices. They do show support for the assertion, however, that women rise to power as members of privileged groups. At the same time, as a rule and as these two cases show, women in Africa have not gained access to executive office through family ties as in some other areas of the world. Finally, in a part of the world where the needs of women are dire and where meeting the needs of women can have a significant impact on society as a whole, women executives do seem to be acting for women where they can. Historically in Africa, there is a tradition of women rulers and today, even where no such tradition existed, women are asserting themselves as traditional leaders at the local level and as executive leaders at the national level.

Notes

1 I would like to thank Sarah Bolen for assembling the two tables.
2 See Worldwide Guide to Women in Leadership (2009g).
3 In his article, Jibrin (2004) explores

> the dynamics of marginalising women from political power, and the ways in which "First Ladies" have sought to intervene through their special position as spouses of men in power. In many African countries, the First Lady phenomenon has opened doors for women that had previously been closed. At the same time, it has created a dynamic in which political space has been appropriated and used by the wives and friends of men in power for purposes of personal aggrandisement, rather than for furthering the interests of women.

4 See Inter-Parliamentary Union (2010c).
5 The eight countries are: Rwanda (56 percent), South Africa (45 percent), Mozambique (39 percent), Angola (38 percent), Uganda (31 percent), Burundi (31 percent), Tanzania (30 percent) and Namibia (27 percent). Every one of the countries also uses some kind of electoral gender quota, usually reserved or special seats or voluntary party quotas or both. See Bauer (2008).
6 In late 2010 Ellen Johnson Sirleaf dismissed all of her cabinet ministers in an effort to provide a "fresh start" going forward. The move was also seen as an effort to fight corruption. As of early 2011 a new cabinet was not yet listed on the Executive Mansion website.
7 Timothy Longman, personal email communication, 30 July 2009.
8 Liberian Constitution and Election Laws Forum (n.d.).
9 CIA (2010a) pages for Liberia and Rwanda; Inter-Parliamentary Union (2010a) for Liberia and Rwanda.
10 In order to describe the evolution of women in executive positions, some historical background is required. Liberia and Rwanda are both immensely complex societies with rich histories; only a brief sketch can be provided here.
11 Today 95 percent of Liberia's population belongs to one of several indigenous African ethnic groups, often referred to in Liberia as "country;" the remaining 5 percent are Americo-Liberian or "Congo" (Harris 2006: 384). In her memoir, Johnson Sirleaf (2009: 15) explains that once the slave trade was outlawed in the early 1800s but slaving continued, ships were intercepted and their human cargo, rather than being returned to their homelands in Benin, Nigeria, Congo, etc., would be liberated in Monrovia or Freetown. The Americo-Liberians dubbed these peoples Congo because of coming from the Congo Basin area; cut off from their own roots these peoples became assimilated into settler society and the term came to refer to both groups.
12 Information on women in cabinets in Liberia comes from Worldwide Guide to Women in Leadership (2009d), accessed July and August 2009; Dunn *et al.* (2001) and personal email communications with Elwood Dunn, August 2009.
13 Government of the Republic of Liberia Executive Mansion – President's Cabinet (n.d.).
14 I am grateful to Veronika Fuest for reminding me of this information on deputy and assistant ministers in Liberia.

15 Information on women in past cabinets in Rwanda comes from Worldwide Guide to Women in Leadership (2009e), accessed July and August 2009.

16 Official Website of the Government of Rwanda – Cabinet (n.d.).

17 Forty percent of South Africa's cabinet ministers are women with 45 percent women in the National Assembly. Republic of South Africa Government Communications (2009); Inter-Parliamentary Union (2010a) for South Africa.

18 Figures for these two paragraphs are drawn from CIA (2010a) pages on Liberia and Rwanda; UNDP (2009a) country data sheets for Liberia and Rwanda.

19 For women's legislative representation Tripp and Kang (2008) found that the single most important determinant of women's presence today is whether or not the country uses some type of electoral gender quota. This is certainly true in sub-Saharan Africa.

20 Liberia had the first female president of an African national university and relatively high female enrollments and female lecturers at the two Liberian universities. A Liberian woman was also the first female African president of the United Nations General Assembly. Fuest (2008), Harris (2006).

21 Bauer (2009: 207), citing Moran and Pitcher (2004), states that Liberia, at the outbreak of war, "had a large population of educated, professional women ... from which to draw potential leaders."

22 The property clause was dropped some time between the 1975 and 1985 elections in Liberia, during which time the voting age was also lowered from 21 to 18. See the following pages from Inter-Parliamentary Union (2010a): www.ipu.org/parline-e/reports/arc/LIBERIA_1975_E.PDF; www.ipu.org/parline-e/reports/arc/LIBERIA_1985_E.PDF; accessed August 2009.

23 See the following pages from Inter-Parliamentary Union (2010a): www.ipu.org/parline-e/reports/arc/RWANDA_1981_E.PDF; www.ipu.org/parline-e/reports/arc/RWANDA_1983_E_2.PDF; www.ipu.org/parline-e/reports/arc/2265_88.htm. Until that time the national legislature in Rwanda was a unicameral body; accessed August 2009.

24 This was not the first time that Ellen Johnson Sirleaf ran for president. In 1997 she ran against Charles Taylor (the first time a woman ran for president in Africa), polling less than 10 percent of the vote to Taylor's 75 percent. According to Adams (2008: 478–9), Taylor won that election largely because of fears that Taylor would return to war if he lost the election and because of his control over key resources including the only radio station capable of broadcasting outside Monrovia.

25 Adams (2006: 195) argues that it was African women's networks – "drawing on and building from norms embedded in regional and international documents" – that mobilized and fought to achieve these gender equity provisions within the AU.

26 Devlin and Elgie (2008: 251) further note that many Rwandan MPs perceive that "a gender agenda is now ... 'guaranteed' by the presence of more women."

7 Latin America

Tiffany D. Barnes and Mark P. Jones

Introduction

As late as the second half of the 1980s, there were, for all intents and purposes, no women in executive positions (president, vice president, cabinet minister) in Latin America. For instance, in 1987 there were no women presidents among the region's democracies, there was a single "second" vice president (in Costa Rica), and an average of only 2 percent women in cabinets, with the median and modal number of cabinet ministers in the region's countries zero (Htun 1997; Iturbe de Blanco 2003; PROLID 2007). By the 1990s, however, women had begun, slowly but steadily, to occupy a larger share of executive branch positions in the region, although the record was mixed, with advances more prominent in appointed cabinet posts than among directly elected presidents and vice presidents.

This chapter begins by evaluating progress in the presence of women in executive branch in 18 Latin American democracies from 1998 to 2008.[1] It then provides an in-depth focus on the evolution of women's presence in executive positions since World War II in two influential cases, Argentina and Chile, examining both the election of women presidents and vice presidents and the presence of women in cabinets. In line with the general regional trends, the presence of women in executive positions prior to the 1990s was minimal in these two countries (with the important exception of the presidency of Isabel Perón [1974–6] in Argentina), but has improved notably in the past decade, with both Argentina and Chile governed in December 2009 by a democratically elected female president whose respective cabinets contained noteworthy numbers of female ministers.

Regional overview

This section evaluates the evolution of women's presence in Latin American executive branches by comparing women's leadership in 1998 to that in 2008.[2] Data from the mid-point year of 2003 are also utilized in order to provide a better assessment of trends, as well as to serve as a reliability check on the data in those cases where the small number could potentially result in a high level of volatility with a value at one specific point in time possibly not representative of recent general trends in that category. The fundamental question driving this evaluation is to what extent women's presence in principal executive offices of the region's countries has improved during this time frame.

In 1998, none of the region's 18 countries had a female president (see Table 7.1).[3] By contrast, in 2008, the region had two female presidents, Cristina Fernández de Kirchner of Argentina and Michelle Bachelet of Chile. While an increase from zero to two presidents is not to be minimized, it is important to note that the percentage of women presidents in Latin America remained a paltry 11 percent in 2008.[4] Furthermore, this increase in the number/percentage of women presidents is not statistically significant, with the number of women presidents in 2008 statistically indistinct from that in 1998.[5]

For the purpose of this study, the top three presidential candidates (in terms of the number of votes won in the first or only round of the presidential election) are considered relevant, as long as they received at least 10 percent of the popular vote. Coincidentally, across the 18 countries there were a total of 47 relevant candidates in both 1998 and 2008 (in 2003 there were 48). In 1998, two women had been relevant presidential candidates in their country's most recent presidential election.[6] In Honduras, Alba Gúnera de Melgar was the candidate of the National Party, but lost the presidential contest to Carlos Flores of the Liberal Party. Gúnera de Melgar was the widow of former Honduran President Juan Alberto Melgar (1975–8). In Panama, Mireya Moscoso was the candidate of the Arnulfista Party (PA) dominated Democratic Alliance, but narrowly lost the election to Ernesto Pérez Balladares of the Democratic Revolutionary Party. Moscoso was the widow of PA founder, and three-time president (1940–1, 1949–51, 1968), Arnulfo Arias.

Between 1998 and 2008 the number of relevant/main women presidential candidates increased from two to five.[7] The most noteworthy case was Argentina, where in 2007 the winning presidential candidate and the first runner-up were women. In addition to the victorious Cristina Fernández de Kirchner (Front for Victory), Elisa Carrió (Civic Coalition) placed second in the election. In Paraguay, Blanca Ovelar of the National Republican Association finished second in the 2008 presidential election to Fernando Lugo of the Patriotic Alliance for Change. In Peru, Lourdes Flores of the National Unity coalition placed third in the first round of the 2006 election behind Ollanta Humala (Union for Peru) and Alan García (Peruvian Aprista Party). The final case of a relevant female presidential candidate in the 2008 era was that of Michelle Bachelet of Chile, who was the victor in the January 2006 runoff.

Overall, while the respective increase in the number of women presidents from zero to two and of relevant female presidential candidates from two to five does certainly represent movement in a positive direction, the fact that in 2008 women represented merely one out of ten presidents and relevant presidential candidates cannot be considered a positive state of affairs. When examining the period 1998 to 2008 it is difficult to conclude that there was significant advancement in the presence of women in the most powerful and influential (Stein and Tommasi 2008) political posts in Latin America.

Table 7.1 Presidents, presidential candidates and vice presidents in selected Latin American countries, 1998, 2003 and 2008

Office	1998 Nb (%)	2003 Nb (%)	2008 Nb (%)	2008 vs. 1998 difference	Significant difference[b]
President (18, 18, 18)	0 (0.0)	1 (6.0)	2 (11.0)	2 (11.0)	No
Main presidential candidates (47, 48, 47)[a]	2 (4.0)	2 (4.0)	5 (11.0)	3 (7.0)	No
All presidential candidates (197, 141, 159)	18 (9.0)	12 (9.0)	17 (11.0)	–1 (2.0)	No
Vice president (15, 15, 16)	1 (7.0)	2 (13.0)	2 (13.0)	1 (6.0)	No

Source: *The Europa World Book* (1998, 2003, 2008).

Notes
a Top three candidates (excluding any candidates with less than 10 percent of the vote).
b Significant at the 0.05 level for a two-tailed test.

In late 2009, 16 of the 18 Latin American countries possessed vice presidents.[8] Overall (see Table 7.1), there was a very minor increase of 6 percent (not statistically significant) in women vice presidents in Latin America between 1998 and 2008.[9] In 1998, there was one woman vice president, Rosalía Arteaga of Ecuador (elected in 1996). In 2008, there were two female vice presidents, Laura Chinchilla of Costa Rica and Ana Vilma Albanez de Escobar of El Salvador, who were elected in 2006 and 2004, respectively.[10]

Drawing on the lists of cabinet ministers contained in the 1998, 2003 and 2008 editions of *The Europa World Year Book*, Table 7.2 lists the percentage of cabinet ministers who were women in 1998, 2003 and 2008 for the 18 countries. Overall in the region, the percentage of women cabinet ministers grew from 8 percent of all cabinet ministers in 1998 to 25 percent in 2008, an increase that is highly significant.[11] In sum, we can state with extreme confidence that there was a statistically significant rise in the proportion of female cabinet ministers between 1998 and 2008. This improvement is best explained by two factors. The first factor is a combination of the progressive trend in voter preferences, generational replacement of sexist voters with less sexist voters, international commitments made by political leaders to gender equality, the adoption of formal or informal quota legislation for cabinet ministers, and the replacement of center-right presidents by left and center-left presidents (Buvinic and Roza 2004; Escobar-Lemmon and Taylor-Robinson 2005; Schwindt-Bayer 2007). The

Table 7.2 Percentage of female cabinet ministers in selected Latin American countries, 1998, 2003 and 2008

	1998	*2003*	*2008*	*2008 vs. 1998 difference*
Argentina	10.0	27.0	25.0	15.0
Bolivia	7.0	0.0	25.0	18.0
Brazil	5.0	13.0	8.0	3.0
Chile	15.0	18.0	41.0	26.0
Colombia	19.0	50.0	23.0	4.0
Costa Rica	6.0	40.0	35.0	29.0
Dominican Republic	7.0	17.0	14.0	7.0
Ecuador	7.0	24.0	35.0	28.0
El Salvador	8.0	8.0	23.0	15.0
Guatemala	0.0	23.0	8.0	8.0
Honduras	6.0	20.0	33.0	27.0
Mexico	13.0	11.0	17.0	4.0
Nicaragua	12.0	8.0	50.0	38.0
Panama	8.0	31.0	25.0	17.0
Paraguay	8.0	0.0	10.0	2.0
Peru	6.0	6.0	23.0	17.0
Uruguay	8.0	0.0	31.0	23.0
Venezuela	8.0	27.0	25.0	17.0
Region average	8.0	16.0	25.0	17.0

Source: *The Europa World Book* (1998, 2003, 2008).

second factor is the considerable autonomy enjoyed by the president in naming her or his cabinet in the Latin American presidential democracies (Payne *et al.* 2007).

There also existed a wide range in levels of female representation in cabinets in the region in 2008. One extreme was represented by Nicaragua (with 50 percent women in cabinet) and Chile (with 41 percent women in cabinet), where half or nearly half of the ministers were women – the result of explicit, albeit informal, policies by the countries' respective presidents (Daniel Ortega and Michelle Bachelet) to promote gender parity in their cabinets. The other extreme was represented by Guatemala and Brazil (both with 8 percent women in cabinet), where slightly less than one of every ten cabinet ministers was a woman.

In sum, we found strong and significant improvement between 1998 and 2008 in women's appointment to cabinet posts. At the same time, while positive growth was detected in the presence of women in uni-personal executive positions (president, vice president, relevant presidential candidates), these increases were statistically insignificant. Furthermore, in contrast to the case for cabinets where robust improvement in the status of women leaders was uncovered, it is difficult to view the minimal increases which took place in these uni-personal posts from 1998 to 2008 as signs of substantial progress in women's access to political leadership positions in Latin America.

Country cases: Argentina and Chile

Description of the political regimes

The 1945 to 2009 period in Argentina witnessed several democratic presidential elections (1946, 1973, 1983, 1989, 1995, 1999, 2003 and 2007), semi-democratic presidential elections (1951, 1958, 1963 and 1973) and military coups (1955, 1962, 1966 and 1976). Over these more than 60 years, the regimes that have governed Argentina have been fully democratic (1946–51, 1973–6, 1983–), semi-democratic (1951–5, 1958–66) and dictatorial (1955–8, 1966–73, 1976–83). Since 1983, however, Argentina has enjoyed uninterrupted democracy, and, as of 2009, it is safe to say that the current Argentine democratic regime is quite consolidated, and that the country faces no short- or medium-term risk of a democratic breakdown.

During the post-World War II era Argentina has been a federal republic with a presidential form of government. Since the return to democracy Argentine presidents have been empowered to name and remove the members of their cabinets without consulting Congress (or any other countervailing power), with the very partial exception of the position of Chief of Cabinet Ministers (since 1994) who can be removed by an absolute majority of the members of each chamber of the country's bicameral legislature. During the 1983–2009 period Argentina's executive ranged from eight to 14 cabinet ministers (including the Cabinet Chief of Ministers since the 1994 constitutional reform). Ministers in Argentina normally have ties to (or are members of) the president's political party or the party of allied parties that helped elect the president, or else they are independent technocrats chosen for their expertise in the area covered by their ministry. There is no requirement that ministers be members of Congress; in fact, holding a position in the executive branch is incompatible with occupying a seat in Congress (though it is possible for sitting deputies to take a leave of absence).

Since 1945, the president has at times been elected via an electoral college (1946, 1958, 1963, 1983, 1989) and at other times been elected directly (1951, 1973, 1973, 1995, 1999, 2003, 2007). At all times the national legislature has been bicameral (Chamber of Deputies and Senate); at present the Chamber is elected from multi-member districts using closed and blocked lists with seats allocated using proportional representation (PR) and the Senate is elected from closed and blocked lists with two seats going to the plurality list and one seat to the first runner-up (Jones 2008).

Similar to Argentina, Chile has experienced some (albeit less) democratic cycling since 1945. From World War II until 2009 Chile held eight democratic presidential elections (1952, 1958, 1964, 1970, 1989, 1993, 1999, 2005), interrupted by a military coup in 1973, which was then followed by almost 17 years of uninterrupted dictatorship until 1990. Since its return to democracy in 1989 (when democratic elections were held), Chile has been quite stable and, like Argentina, can at present safely be considered a consolidated democracy, with no risk of a short- or medium-term democratic breakdown.

Since World War II Chile has been a presidential republic. Chilean presidents are able to name and remove the members of their cabinet without consulting Congress (or any other countervailing power). Between 1990 and 2009, Chile's executive has had between 14 and 20 cabinet ministers. During the period covered by this chapter, the Concertation Alliance controlled the presidency. Under the four Concertation presidents, cabinet members were almost exclusively drawn from members of the constituent parties which made up the Concertation, although at times independent technocrats also occupied cabinet positions. There is no requirement that ministers be members of Congress; as in Argentina, holding a position in the executive branch is incompatible with occupying a seat in Congress. The bicameral legislature consists of the Chamber of Deputies and the Senate which, since 1989, have been elected using a binomial electoral system (Navia 2008). All electoral districts contain two members, who are elected using closed and unblocked lists, with seats allocated between the coalitions of parties using PR and within the coalitions using the plurality formula.

The evolution of women's presence in the executive

With one exception, women were conspicuously absent from the executive branch in Argentina during the post-World War II era until the late 1990s (Iturbe de Blanco 2003; PROLID 2007). In 1973, Isabel Perón (Juan Perón's third wife) was elected as vice president on a ticket with her husband. Following Perón's death, she assumed office on 1 July 1974, becoming the world's first female president. She then presided over an increasingly conflict-ridden and economically distressed Argentina, until being removed from office on 24 March 1976 by a military coup.

The most influential female politician in Argentine history never occupied a formal executive post. Eva "Evita" Perón (Perón's second wife), between the election of Perón as president in 1946 and her death in 1952, was responsible for profound advances in the promotion of women's political rights and in the design and implementation of public policies that benefited women (Fraser and Navarro 1996; Rock 1987).

It was not until May 1989 that Argentina had its first female cabinet minister. However, Susana Ruiz Cerruti (a career foreign service officer) was merely a placeholder, occupying the post of Minister of Foreign Relations for the final six weeks of President Raúl Alfonsín's term in office following the resignation of Alfonsín's long-time (1983–9) Minister of Foreign Relations, Dante Caputo. The first female cabinet member to occupy a ministry in full capacity was Susana Decibe, who was the Minister of Education from 1996 until the end of the second term of President Carlos Menem (1989–95, 1995–9) in 1999.

Figure 7.1 charts the evolution of the presence of women in Argentine cabinet positions as well as in the Argentine Chamber of Deputies (percentage elected in that year's partial renovation of the Chamber) using data from the Inter-Parliamentary Union (2009b), *The Europa World Year Book* (multiple years), and Escobar-Lemmon and Taylor-Robinson (2005). The values reflect the percentage of women cabinet members as of January of that year as well as the percentage of women deputies elected that year.

The presence of women in the Argentine cabinet paralleled that of women in the Chamber of Deputies from 1983 to 1991, with an extremely low percentage

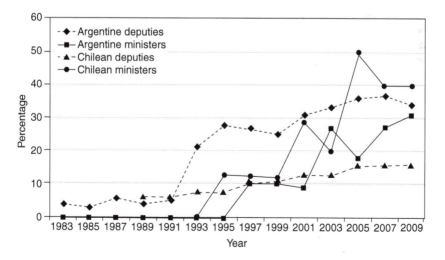

Figure 7.1 Percentage of women deputies elected and cabinet ministers in office in Argentina and Chile, 1983–2009.

(0 percent) of female cabinet ministers. In the late 1990s, the percentage of women cabinet ministers registered above zero for the first time (11 percent, one minister), before beginning an upward climb during the presidencies of Eduardo Duhalde (2002–3), Néstor Kirchner (2003–7) and Cristina Fernández de Kirchner (2007–).[12] With an approximately ten-year lag, the percentage of female cabinet ministers has moved in recent years to a level that comes close (albeit slightly below) that for women in the Chamber of Deputies, where an effective gender quota law had been in force for Chamber elections since 1993 (Jones 1996).

Cristina Fernández de Kirchner was selected (hand-picked) as the governing Front for Victory's (Peronist Party) 2007 presidential candidate by her spouse, then President Néstor Kirchner (2003–7). Fernández de Kirchner had previously obtained and occupied a series of important political positions (ranging from provincial deputy to national senator) with the assistance of Néstor Kirchner, and while in office (first as a provincial legislator and then as a national deputy and national senator) built a reputation as an accomplished and skillful politician (constructing, by 2007, a considerable level of autonomous political capital). Elected in October 2007 for a four-year term, Fernández de Kirchner, however, struggled during the first two years of her term in office, with her approval ratings plummeting from 60 percent in January 2008 to 20 percent in December 2009. Moreover, her role as chief executive has been often overshadowed by the prominent (if not pre-eminent) role in governance occupied by her husband Néstor Kirchner until his death in late 2010.

Women did not play a pronounced role in Chile's executive branch prior to the mid 1990s, though a few token females received ministerial posts prior to this period. Chile's first female minister was Adriana Olguín de Baltra, Minister of Justice (PROLID 2007). She was appointed at the very end of President Gabriel González Videla's (1946–52) term in 1952, only serving a short period of time. When President Carlos Ibáñez del Campo (1952–8) assumed power later that year, he appointed María Teresa del Canto as the Minister of Education (1952–3). In the following years women were occasionally appointed to serve as ministers. But women never played a prominent role in the executive branch. This same trend continued under the dictatorship of General Augusto Pinochet (1973–90). Women were scarcely involved in his regime, with few exceptions, one being Marie Therese Infante Barros, Minister of Labor and Social Affairs during the dictatorship's final year (1989–90).

After the transition to democracy in 1990, women were absent from the Chilean executive branch for several consecutive years.[13] In 1995 Adriana Del-Piano Puelma and Soledad Alvear were appointed to the Chilean cabinet as Minister of National Resources and Minister of Justice, respectively. They remained the only two women to have served in the Chilean cabinet during the post-1990 era until 2001, when President Ricardo Lagos assumed office and dramatically reversed this trend. During his campaign, Lagos faced significant pressure from social movements (Ríos Tobar 2008) and a few political insiders from within the governing Concertation coalition (Franceschet 2008) to increase women's representation in the executive branch. As a result, following his elect-oral victory, Lagos named five women (36 percent) to his first cabinet. These appointments paved the way for women (two in particular, Michelle Bachelet and Soledad Alvear) to increase their political presence and gain popularity within the electorate, thus positioning them for future political opportunities (Franceschet 2008; Ríos Tobar 2008; Segovia 2005).[14]

Figure 7.1 also charts the evolution of the presence of women in Chilean cabinet positions as well as in the Chilean Chamber of Deputies using data from the Inter-Parliamentary Union (2009b), *The Europa World Year Book* (multiple years) and Escobar-Lemmon and Taylor-Robinson (2005). The percentage of deputies reflects the total percentage of female deputies elected to the Chamber that year. The cabinet data reveal the percentage of women cabinet members as of January of that year.

As detailed in Figure 7.1, women have successfully increased their represen-tation in the Chilean executive branch over time. They were absent from the executive branch immediately after the transition to democracy in 1989. They made moderate progress under President Eduardo Frei (1994–2000), who appointed two women to his cabinet (approximately 12 percent). In 2000 Presid-ent Ricardo Lagos (2000–6) nominated five women to his cabinet, thus increas-ing the percentage of women in the executive branch to 36 percent in January 2001. Finally, when President Michelle Bachelet assumed office in 2006 she appointed an executive cabinet with gender parity (50 percent male and 50 percent female).

The trends in female representation in the Chilean Chamber of Deputies and Chilean executive branch are distinct from those in Argentina. Unlike Argentina, where women gained ground in the legislative branch before making inroads into the executive branch, Chile has not experienced significant legislative gains for women. Unlike Argentina, Chile does not have any national level institu-tional mechanisms to aid the progress of women in the legislature (i.e. gender quota legislation; Jones 2009). Rather, the relationship observed here can be pri-marily credited to elite political women entrepreneurs who explicitly sought to increase women's representation in the executive branch (Franceschet 2008), with Michelle Bachelet representing the pinnacle of these efforts. As a result, in the past decade, Chile has made great strides in increasing the presence of women in the executive branch, whereas the legislative branch continues to fall short in its level of female representation.

On 11 March 2006 Michelle Bachelet became Chile's first female president. Unlike all directly elected Latin American female presidents who preceded her, Bachelet did not have personal connections to a politically relevant man who helped (directly or indirectly) advance her political career. Bachelet first began to gain political visibility when she was appointed Minister of Health in 2001. After holding this portfolio for two years, she was appointed to a more prestig-ious post, Minister of Defense, the first woman in Chile to hold a cabinet position of this stature. Her service in the Lagos administration was crucial toward the development of her reputation as a skilled politician, allowing her to successfully climb the political ladder within the Concertation. Most import-antly, these political appointments provided Bachelet with the opportunity to increase her name recognition and popularity. By December 2004, 35 percent of the population reported they would like to see Bachelet as the next president (Segovia 2005). Her popularity continued to rise until she was clearly the strong-est candidate for the governing Concertation alliance and her opponent (Soledad Alvear) dropped out of the Concertation's primary election rather than suffer a certain loss to Bachelet. This is one of the most unique aspects of Bachelet's political success. Bachelet owes her success primarily to her own popularity and ability, not to other political elites (Ríos Tobar 2007).

Factors explaining women's access to the executive

The penultimate portion of this section is devoted to a systematic analysis of the factors that influence the appointment of women to cabinet ministries in Argentina and Chile. We analyze time-series sample populations for the Argentine and Chilean cabinets from 1991 to 2009. Given that the number of women cabinet ministers was consistently zero prior to 1991 in both countries and that Chile was a dictatorship between 1973 and 1990, we exclude these years from our analysis. Our dependent variable is the percentage of female ministers in each respective cabinet at time t (January of the year in question). Given the temporal nature of our data we first employ a Generalized Least Squares model (i.e. Prais-Winsten) and then an autoregressive integrated moving average model (ARIMA, AR1 process).

Our time-series analysis first considered a host of factors potentially related to variance in the presence of women in the Argentine and Chilean executive branches. Given the small number of cases (19 in each country), however, we could not analyze more than a handful of variables at once. Moreover, many potential variables of interest were either completely or practically invariant. In all, after the analysis of multiple preliminary models, we selected the variables and econometric procedures discussed in detail below.[15] Compared to large N cross-national analysis, the type of time-series analysis conducted here provides the advantage of allowing us to better identify causal relations (e.g. the percent-age of women deputies' impact on the percentage of women cabinet ministers), since it is difficult in the former analysis to adequately control for country-level fixed effects which are often invariant over short to medium periods of time (e.g. level of gender egalitarianism, political culture, religion, religiosity, the strength of the women's movement). The downside of this time-series approach, however, is that many variables of interest in the study of women's representa-tion are essentially invariant in the short to medium term, thereby inhibiting efforts to determine their impact, in contrast to the case in cross-sectional (or time-series cross-sectional) studies where there exists inter-country variation for these variables. Another difficulty with time-series analysis in the two cases examined here is the limited number of temporal observations (19).

First, we examine the impact of the presence of women in the national legis-lature via a variable which accounts for the percentage of women in the lower chamber. Second, we examine the effect of the level of gender development in the country using the United Nations Development Programme's (2009a) Gender-related Development Index (GDI). The GDI is an unweighted average of three gender indices which measure gender equality in the areas of life expectancy, education (both adult literacy rate [accounting for two-thirds of the education component of the index] and percentage of pupils in tertiary education [one-third]) and estimated earned income. As a measure of gender inequality, the GDI has many advantages in terms of validity and reliability over examining all of its constituent elements separately (Schüler 2006; United Nations Development Programme 1995).

Third, we include a variable which assesses the influence of the ideological position of the president for each cabinet appointed in our sample. Between 1990 and 2009, Argentina elected presidents with conservative (Menem [1989–9]), centrist (De la Rúa [2000–1], Duhalde [2002–3]) and progressive (Kirchner [2004–7], Fernández [2008–9]) ideological orientations. Thus our analysis for Argentina includes two separate dummy variables, one variable for centrist presidents (coded one) and another variable for progressive presidents (coded one). The conservative president serves as the baseline category. Chile, by contrast, only elected centrist (Alywin [1990–3], Frei [1994–2000]) and progressive (Lagos [2001–6], Bachelet [2007–9]) presidents during this time frame. Thus, in the Chile models we include a dummy variable for progressive presidents (coded one) and exclude the centrists as the baseline category.

Finally, we incorporate a binary variable to account for the president's sex. For each year, this variable is coded one if the president who appointed the cabinet was female, and zero otherwise. In both the Argentina and Chile sample one of the two presidents with a progressive ideology was also a female president. Thus, we estimate two separate models for each country and econometric approach (GLS, ARIMA). In all, there are four models that include the binary variable for female presidents and four models that include binary variables for presidential ideological orientation.

Table 7.3 provides an analysis of the impact of these socioeconomic and political variables on the percentage of cabinet members who were female. All eight of the models indicate that the percentage of women in the lower house has no effect on the percentage of females who are appointed to cabinet posts. Further, the estimated coefficients in six of the eight models are in the opposite direction of what we would expect if the percentage of women in the legislature were positively influencing cabinet composition. While we do not report the results here, other specifications of the model explored the lagged effect of women in the legislature. Given that the composition of the legislature changes every two years in Argentina and every four years in Chile, we considered the effect of two-, four-, six- and eight-year lags. This lagged analysis revealed no significant relationship between the percentage of women in the legislature and cabinet composition. Given the consistency of our findings, we can be reasonably confident in concluding that the percentage of women in the legislature is unrelated to the percentage of women in cabinet posts in Argentina and Chile.

Table 7.3 Determinants of the presence of women in the Argentine and Chilean cabinets, 1991–2009[a]

Independent variables	Argentina				Chile			
	(1)	(2)	(3)	(4)	(5)	(6)	(7)	(8)
Percentage of women in chamber	-0.338– (0.340)	-0.339– (1.438)	-0.323– (0.310)	-0.322– (1.118)	1.127– (1.590)	1.193– (1.833)	-0.507– (1.364)	-0.507– (2.301)
Gender Development Index (GDI)	2.680c (1.059)	2.685– (3.208)	3.059b (0.770)	3.057– (1.683)	0.582– (1.589)	0.580– (3.182)	2.792c (1.169)	2.793 (2.096)
Progressive president	4.800– (6.163)	4.748– (13.31)			16.916– (8.001)	16.352– (13.364)		
Centrist president	5.353– (5.723)	5.367– (11.79)						
Female president			13.130– (7.148)	13.130– (14.507)			23.080b (6.115)	23.060c (9.396)
Constant	-203.301c (79.781)	-203.703– (228.78)	-233.300b (56.449)	-233.242c (111.296)	-48.892– (117.258)	-49.181– (245.188)	-209.515c (83.484)	-209.725– (152.721)
Sigma		6.421b (1.052)		5.980b (0.940)		6.887b (1.225)		5.461b (1.338)
R-squared	0.755		0.779		0.639		0.848	
Observations	19	19	19	19	19	19	19	19
Model type	GLS	ARIMA-(AR1)	GLS	ARIMA-(AR1)	GLS	ARIMA-(AR1)	GLS	ARIMA-(AR1)

Notes

a Standard errors are in parentheses.

b p < 0.01.

c p < 0.05 (two-tailed test).

That is, increases in the percentage of legislators (concurrently or lagged) were unrelated to increases in the percentage of female cabinet ministers in these two countries between 1991 and 2009.

Three of the four GLS models and one of the ARIMA models report that GDI has a positive and significant impact on the percentage of women who occupy cabinet posts in Argentina and Chile. The results for GDI presented in the models for Argentina are robust for both of the GLS models (Models 1 and 3). However, neither of the ARIMA models provides similar significant results, though both do possess a GDI estimated coefficient that is in the hypothesized direction, with that in Model 4 significant at the 0.10 level.

In Chile, in Model 7 there exists a significant positive relationship between GDI and the percentage of women in the cabinet. This relationship does not hold for any of the other models, however. As a consequence, we cannot draw any firm conclusions about the relationship between GDI and the percentage of women in cabinet positions in Chile.

Models 1 and 2 for Argentina and Models 5 and 6 for Chile account for the ideological orientation of the president. The analysis for both countries demonstrates that there exists no significant relationship between presidential ideology and the percentage of cabinet ministers who are female.

Finally, Models 3, 4, 7 and 8 control for the presence of a female president. In Argentina, the existence of a female president appears unrelated to the proportion of female cabinet members. In Chile, however, the relationship between the sex of the president and the percentage of female cabinet ministers is much stronger. In the GLS and ARIMA specifications (Models 7 and 8), the relationship is statistically significant at the 0.01 level and 0.05 level, respectively. Overall, though, given the presence of only one female president in each country, it is not possible to draw any credible conclusions from these data regarding the general relationship between presidential gender and cabinet composition. For instance, with the present data we cannot conclusively know whether the impact of presidential sex in Chile is due to the fact that Michelle Bachelet was a woman or to the fact that Michelle Bachelet was Michelle Bachelet, although it would be reasonable to assume that Bachelet's sex had an impact on her decision to appoint a parity cabinet (initially, and maintain a near-parity cabinet over time).

In sum, this analysis, hampered by small sample size, uncovered only a tenuous relationship between several key socioeconomic and political variables and women's cabinet representation in Argentina and Chile over the past 20 years. Some of the findings differ somewhat from those of Escobar-Lemmon and Taylor-Robinson (2005) (e.g. the impact of the percentage of women legislators and the effect of presidential ideology). However, given the different models, populations and time periods examined by them and us, we have no reason to doubt the overall veracity of the substantive conclusions made by Escobar-Lemmon and Taylor-Robinson (2005) regarding the relationship between these variables and the presence of female cabinet ministers in Latin America.[16]

In the analysis presented here, none of the significant results are what one could call robust over space in time, although the findings for GDI in Argentina and for a female president in Chile do suggest that those variables may be relevant for understanding variance in the proportion of female cabinet ministers, although additional data and enhanced variance in the variables (e.g. additional female presidents) will be needed before any more definitive conclusions can be made.

Do women executives represent women?

The presidencies of Cristina Fernández de Kirchner and of Michelle Bachelet differ markedly in the extent to which the president represents women's interests. Upon assuming office in December 2007, President Fernández de Kirchner developed a governance style in which she was the visible face of the government, while a majority of the principal political and policy decisions were made by Néstor Kirchner (though most commonly in consultation with her). Other than a minor increase in the number of female cabinet ministers, there are few, if any, ways in which President Fernández de Kirchner has actively worked to improve the status of women in Argentina. Furthermore, by allowing her husband to govern from the shadows, President Fernández de Kirchner does not serve as a positive role model to future generations of Argentine female politicians in the same way that Chilean President Michelle Bachelet did.

From the moment she assumed office in 2006, Bachelet worked to actively promote gender equality in Chile. This was most visible in her cabinet appointments. Bachelet appointed Latin America's first gender parity cabinet composed of ten male ministers and ten female ministers. Furthermore, her gender parity initiative was not restricted to cabinet level appointments. Rather, Bachelet implemented the parity initiative in all her political appointments, including undersecretaries, regional governors and other high-ranking state officials (Ríos Tobar 2007). Finally, Bachelet's commitment to gender equality was not limited to her political appointments; rather it pervaded her political rhetoric and public policy priorities. In her first annual address to Congress she used the word "woman" 36 times and cited two prominent feminist figures (Ríos Tobar 2007). Bachelet's policy priorities included a pension overhaul to increase payouts to homemakers, free childcare for working parents with children under the age of four, and several advances in women's reproductive rights. For example, in 2006, Bachelet's Ministry of Health approved the new National Norms on Fertility Regulation, allowing for the distribution of emergency contraception to all females 14 years or older without parental consent. She also signed a law to make sexual education mandatory in all government regulated schools.

Finally, it may be argued that Bachelet also served as a more positive role model than her Argentine counterpart due to the fact that her presidency was viewed as successful by a large majority of the Chilean population, leaving office with an approval rating of approximately 85 percent in March 2010. This is a sharp contrast to Cristina Fernández de Kirchner's approval rating, which hovered in the 20 to 30 percent range for all but the first five months of her presidency. The sustained political popularity of Bachelet and her commitment to gender equality is an archetype for future generations of female political leaders.

Conclusion

In her mid 1990s diagnosis of the status of women's political leadership in Latin America, Htun (1997) found that women were woefully under-represented in the region's executive branches. Fast-forwarding to 2008, it is clear that women were still, on average, woefully under-represented in political leadership positions in the region. At the same time, between 1998 and 2008 there were several important advances in women's political leadership in Latin America (e.g. into cabinets and national legislatures). Nevertheless, in other critical areas progress was extremely limited (e.g. the presidency, vice presidency, relevant presidential candidacies).

Women dramatically increased their presence in the cabinets and national legislatures of Latin America during this period. The percentage of women ministers jumped from an anemic 8 percent in 1998 to 25 percent in 2008. To date, we lack a comprehensive explanation for this increase, although it is most likely the consequence of a combination of factors including the continuing trend of feminization of Latin American democracy (Buvinic and Roza 2004; Escobar-Lemmon and Taylor-Robinson 2005), the decision (and ability due to the lack of congressional approval of ministerial appointments) by presidents to appoint a cabinet that better reflects the diversity of their country's citizenry, and a replacement of primarily center-right governments (which were predominant in the region *c.*1998) by primarily center-left and left governments (which were predominant *c.*2008).

Similar to the case for cabinet ministers, the proportion of national legislators who were female increased in Latin America from 10 percent to 18 percent between 1998 and 2008. Here, the principal explanation for this growth is the adoption of well-designed gender quota legislation by a sub-set of countries in the region (Jones 2009).

In the area of directly elected executive posts, considerable challenges continue to thwart significant advances by women in Latin America. Between 1998 and 2008, the number of women presidents and relevant female presidential candidates did not increase significantly. Furthermore, as of 2008 only one in ten presidents and relevant presidential candidates were women. A similar story holds for the category of vice president, where the percentage of women did not change significantly over this time frame. Nonetheless, while there was not a significant increase in women's presence in any of these categories between 1998 and 2008, in all categories the percentage of women did increase during this period, albeit only modestly.

The two case studies in this chapter focused on Argentina and Chile. They underscored the limited presence of women in the executive branch in each country prior to the first decade of the twenty-first century, but also highlighted the recent election of women presidents in both countries (in 2007 in Argentina and 2005 in Chile). With regard to the representation of women's interests, the mandates of Cristina Fernández de Kirchner and Michelle Bachelet clearly differed. During her four years in office, President Bachelet actively worked to enhance the status of women in Chile and served as an outstanding role model. In contrast, President Fernández de Kirchner has done virtually nothing to enhance the status of women in Argentina during her two-and-a-half years as president, and the secondary role in governance that she played to her spouse (former President Néstor Kirchner), along with the severe operational deficiencies of her government, make her a less than stellar role model for the country's younger generations.

Notes

1 That is Argentina, Bolivia, Brazil, Chile, Colombia, Costa Rica, Dominican Republic, Ecuador, El Salvador, Guatemala, Honduras, Mexico, Nicaragua, Panama, Paraguay, Peru, Uruguay and Venezuela. Only since 1995/6 were all 18 of these countries functioning democracies.

2 1998 is chosen as the base year since it is ten years prior to the most recent year for which complete data using this study's methodology are available. A majority of the data and information for the comparisons were drawn from the 1998, 2003 and 2008 editions of *The Europa World Year Book*, which in turn reported the occupants of the various posts as of the first semester (on dates ranging from January to May) of that year. Where data from elections were utilized, the elections reported in *The Europa World Year Book* were employed (i.e. the elections were the ones held closest to 1998, 2003 and 2008 respectively, but not later than the first semester of that year). Where *The Europa World Year Book* data were incomplete, additional sources were consulted, but following the first semester of 1998/2003/2008 criteria for inclusion utilized by *The Europa World Year Book*.

3 Prior to 1998, only one woman had been directly elected president in Latin America (Schwindt-Bayer 2008). Violeta Barrios de Chamorro (the widow of Pedro Joaquín Chamorro, the assassinated editor of the newspaper *La Prensa*) was elected president of Nicaragua in 1990, and held office from 1990 to 1997. In addition to Barrios de Chamorro, three women had (prior to 1998) served as an interim president for periods ranging from two days (Rosalía Arteaga in Ecuador [1997]) to almost 21 months (Isabel Martínez de Perón [1974–6] in Argentina; the first female president in Latin American history). Bolivia's Lidia Gueiler (1979–80) served as interim president for eight months.

4 Between 1998 and 2008, one additional woman was directly elected as president in the region. In 1999, Mireya Moscoso (1999–2004) was elected president of Panama as the candidate of the Arnulfist Party.

5 Only those differences at a 0.05 level or above for a two-tail test are considered to be statistically significant. Depending on the executive position, the statistical analysis consisted either of a difference of means test or a binary logit regression.

6 For the 2003 mid-point, two women had been a relevant candidate in the most recent presidential election. Mireya Moscoso won in Panama, while in Peru Lourdes Flores finished a close third.

7 This modest increase from 4 percent to 11 percent of the relevant presidential candidates in the region cannot be considered statistically significant.

8 The office of vice president does not exist in Chile and Mexico, nor did it exist in Venezuela in 1998. At the time of the 2003 mid-point the office of vice president was vacant in Argentina. A handful of Latin American countries have multiple vice presidents, although only the first vice president is included in this analysis.

9 Prior to 1998, four women had served as vice president in Latin America. Of these four, only one was directly elected as the first in line for presidential succession (Isabel Perón, Argentina, 1973–4).

10 In 2003 there were also two female vice presidents, Astrid Fischel Volio of Costa Rica and Milagros Ortiz Bosch of the Dominican Republic.

11 For 2003, the percentage of women cabinet ministers in the region was 16 percent.

12 Fernando de la Rúa (1999–2001) assumed office on December 10, 1999, Eduardo Duhalde on January 1, 2002, Néstor Kirchner on May 25, 2003, and Cristina Fernández de Kirchner on December 10, 2007.

13 In 1991 President Patricio Aylwin created the National Women's Service and appointed Soledad Alvear as its director, although at this time this post was not considered to be a formal cabinet position (Escobar-Lemmon and Taylor-Robinson 2005).

14 In 2006 Michelle Bachelet and Soledad Alvear were the two leading internal presidential candidates for the governing Concertation (a coalition composed of four parties). Bachelet was supported by her own Socialist Party, the Party for Democracy, and the Social Democratic Radical Party. Alvear was backed by her own Chilean Christian Democratic Party.

15 Among the other variables which were examined but not included in the final models were popular attitudes toward women political leaders, a variable which, for instance, worsened slightly in Chile and increased only modestly in Argentina during this time period.

16 When discussing the relationship between presidential ideology in Latin America and the presence of women cabinet ministers, it is important to keep in mind, that unlike in Western Europe (e.g. Davis 1997), most Latin American political party systems tend to be highly personalist and/or clientelist in orientation, a notable contrast to the generally programmatic party systems found in Europe (Payne *et al.* 2007; Stein and Tommasi 2008). This distinction is especially stark when one considers that in these Latin American presidential systems, the unit of analysis is an individual president in contrast to an institutionalized and programmatic political party as is generally the case in Europe.

8 North America

Farida Jalalzai and Manon Tremblay[1]

Introduction

In North America, as in many other regions included in this volume, women have made great strides in attaining cabinet positions, in particular since the 1990s. Still, overall, women continue to comprise a minority of executive officials, serve at lower cabinet ranks, and disproportionately in positions that are considered stereotypically female. There is some evidence that women cabinet ministers substantively represent women's interests, though further research is required before this can be confirmed. At the highest levels of power, Canada has been led by a female prime minister briefly and only once (Kim Campbell) and, despite Hillary Clinton's historic candidacy, the United States (US) has a presidential glass ceiling still firmly intact. Overall, findings suggest that as far as Canada and the United States are concerned, socioeconomic factors do not work against women's promotion to executive positions, though gender stereotypes continue to interact with political institutions and processes to significantly hinder women's advancement.

This chapter provides a comprehensive overview of women's participation in the executive branches in the United States and Canada. More specifically, the three major executive posts examined in the United States are the president, federal cabinet secretaries and state governors, and in Canada the federal prime minister (PM) and the provincial premiers (hereafter "first ministers"), and the cabinet ministers at both the federal and province levels. A regional overview examines women's presence in North American[2] executive posts while subsequent sections focus on the United States and Canada. American and Canadian political systems, processes, and institutions are assessed, as well as important trends in the proportions of women in executive posts since World War II. The relationship between cultural, socioeconomic, and political factors and women's access to executive posts is of paramount importance and is described. Next, an analysis of the potential impact of women's presence in executive office on the representation of women's interests is provided. Finally, the conclusion suggests some lessons to be learned from the US–Canada comparison.

Regional overview

As in Australasia and Western Europe, North America is among the world regions offering the best quality of life and most solid democratic credentials. Greatly respected for the reliability of its observations on women's legislative representation, the Inter-Parliamentary Union shows that as of January 2010, women occupied 33.3 percent of ministerial positions in the United States with still lower proportions in Canada and Mexico – 29.7 percent and 10.5 percent, respectively.[3] Studies examining factors related to the feminization of cabinets identify a clear correspondence between the presence of women in parliament and in government: the former is a strong predictor of the latter (Davis 1997: 34–5, 88–9; Escobar-Lemmon and Taylor-Robinson 2005; Siaroff 2000; Studlar and Moncrief 1997). Yet, it seems that North America offers a counter-example to this expectation given that at the beginning of 2010, Mexico had the highest proportion of women legislators (27.6 percent) and the United States the lowest (16.8 percent) with Canada in the middle (22.1 percent). These numbers remind us that there is no cause and effect relationship between women's legislative and executive representation. In fact, a host of factors influence appointments to top-level executive roles.

Still, since the mid twentieth century, women are increasingly numerous in the Canadian, Mexican and US cabinets, even if progress may be considered too slow and the presence of women in cabinets is still largely unsatisfactory. In Canada, the average percentage of women federal and provincial cabinet ministers progressed from 1.1 percent during the 1950s to 3.3 percent during the 1960s, 4.1 percent during the 1970s, 10.1 percent during the 1980s, 23.4 percent during the 1990s, and 24.4 percent from 2000 to 2007. In the United States, prior to the late 1970s, women's cabinet representation was less than 1 percent; some presidential administrations were completely devoid of women, like Truman's in the 1940s and Kennedy's and Johnson's in the 1960s. Women's representation increased to 19 percent during Carter's administration in 1976, falling to 10 percent during the Reagan years in the 1980s, only slightly recovering under George H.W. Bush in the late 1980s/early 1990s. While Clinton advanced many women in cabinet posts, when considering the total number of appointments he made, they represent only 17 percent of cabinet officials from 1992 through 2000. However, George W. Bush filled only 12 percent of his posts with women. Most recently, 27 percent of Obama's cabinet is female.

In Mexico, it was not until the end of the 1950s (from 1958 to 1962) that a woman first entered the cabinet, and then only at a sub-secretary level;[4] by the mid 1970s only three women had been appointed to high-level executive positions (Camp 1979). In 1980, a woman was first elevated to the position of full minister though it was not until 1988 that the next women (two) were appointed *Secretarias*. In 1994, President Zedillo included three women in his cabinet.[5] His successor, President Fox, did not improve these numbers; the percentage of women cabinet ministers deteriorated during his term, dropping from approximately 16 percent in 2000 to 6 percent in 2006 (Schwindt-Bayer 2008: 9).

In fact, in 2006 Mexico had the lowest percentage of female cabinet ministers in the Americas, and only one of the 32 provinces had a woman governor (Schwindt-Bayer 2008: 11). In December 2009, under the Calderon administration, the situation somewhat improved with two out of 19 (10.5 percent) full ministers being women and one, Patricia Espinosa Cantellano, holding the traditionally male and prestigious *Secretaria de Relaciones Exteriores*.[6] One explanation for the enduring low proportion of female ministers in Mexico may be that women are too new on the political scene to have developed the networks to be part of the inner circle of (male) party elites that decides who will hold top executive positions (Escobar-Lemmon and Taylor-Robinson 2005; Zetterberg 2008). While Mexico would make an interesting case study of women's low representation in the executive, especially compared to recent gains in the legislature, we now focus on Canada and the United States.

Country cases: Canada and the United States

Description of the political regimes

To understand women's executive representation, essential characteristics of the US and Canadian government systems must be outlined. Canada and the United States are federalist states; the former with a parliamentary regime inherited from the United Kingdom and the latter a presidential system. Federal government, on the one hand, and state (in the United States) and provincial (in Canada) governments, on the other, have independent legislative and executive structures and officials, each playing a vital role. While Canada and the United States are federal states, the share of powers between their own levels of governments differs substantially. However, in both countries each level of government has full autonomy in appointing (or electing) its executive officials.

US presidential elections are linked to the national popular vote, though the state distribution of popular votes is pivotal to election. By contrast, in Canada the first ministers are not elected by an at-large popular vote; rather, they reach the top of the executive hierarchy because they are themselves a Member of Parliament (MP) or Member of the Legislative Assembly (MLA) and lead the party with the largest legislative representation.

The Canadian constitution does not explicitly mention the cabinet. In practice, the first ministers are the architects of their cabinets in terms of their structure and organization, the definition of departmental portfolios and their number as well as the person responsible for each of them. At the same time, the freedom of the first ministers in building their cabinets is not without limitations. Thus, the first ministers must craft their cabinets by taking into account a series of representational criteria (including sex). And, even more constraining, the first ministers must select their ministers from among members of their parliamentary caucus. Put another way, ministers in Canada are federal or provincial legislators, and they must retain their parliamentary role while exercising their executive mandate. By contrast, US cabinet members are barred from concurrently holding a congressional seat; current members of Congress must first resign their post before accepting a cabinet position. While the US constitution does not explicitly outline a presidential cabinet, article II generally allows the president to appoint public ministers. Departments are created or abolished by Congress, however. Nominees require Senate confirmation, which may be more difficult when the opposite party controls Congress, a further check on presidential power. Still, presidents may extend cabinet rank to other directors of executive institutions. So, from this point of view, it appears that US presidents are less limited in their ability to nominate their desired choices than their Canadian counterparts who must select their ministers from among the MPs or MLAs of their party.

Governors head the executive branch within the state. While powers of governors are highly dependent upon their particular state, most have the power to initiate a state budget and have the power to veto legislation. They also appoint heads of state agencies. However, often the most important executive officials are actually elected to their posts, not appointed, including attorneys general and secretaries of state. Though their powers greatly diverge around the country, governors are still often the most visible player in the entire state, and can use this to their advantage in the policy-making process. In sum, the US and Canadian political regimes differ on several dimensions. Yet, women remain strikingly under-represented in both Canadian and US cabinets.

Evolution of women's presence in the executive

The US presidency has never been filled by a woman nor has a woman ever received a major party nomination. Hillary Clinton, the woman who has come closer than any other to attaining a major party nomination, was married to former president Bill Clinton. Her failure to secure the nomination illustrates the difficulties associated with women breaking the presidential glass ceiling in the United States. Not only is the president the single most important actor in the US political system, her/his powerful international standing provides her/him with virtually unparalleled significance. Related expectations are for her/him to exude strength and independent leadership.

Kim Campbell was prime minister of Canada for a brief period – from June 25 to November 3, 1993.[7] She is the only woman who occupied this position at the federal level. Her time at the head of the federal government occurred in a very unfavorable conjuncture: her party, the Progressive Conservative, was considered to be in a freefall by public opinion polls only a few months before the general elections were to be called, and her predecessor, Brian Mulroney, had resigned as a consequence of a series of scandals and strong unpopularity attached to his leadership. The party led by Kim Campbell during the 1993 Canadian federal elections suffered one of the most bitter defeats by a political party ever since the founding of Canada in 1867. According to Bashevkin (2009: 9), this defeat contributed to electoral failures among other women leaders as well.

What about the feminization of cabinets? It is difficult to compare the proportion of women within each US presidential administration since cabinet members change throughout the course of a presidency. The first female cabinet secretary was Frances Perkins who was appointed Secretary of Labor in 1933 by Franklin D. Roosevelt. Still, post-World War II, women's progress in attaining cabinet office was relatively slow (see Table 8.1). In fact, the Truman administration had no women secretaries.[8] It was not until the Eisenhower administration in the 1950s that a woman held a cabinet post again (Oveta Culp Hobby: Health, Education, and Welfare).[9] Women were completely unrepresented in the Kennedy, Johnson, and first Nixon administrations in the 1960s. Since Nixon's second administration (1973), at least one woman has held cabinet or cabinet-level posts within each presidential administration. A major turning point in women's prospects began under the Carter presidency (1977–81) when three women were appointed to four cabinet posts. Both Reagan and George H.W. Bush promoted similar numbers to Carter. Not until the Clinton administration did major changes in the quantity and quality of appointees occur again. Above all, women finally broke through to some of the most powerful posts – Attorney General (Janet Reno) and Secretary of State (Madeleine Albright). Progress continued under George W. Bush who appointed the first female African-American Secretary of State (Condoleezza Rice). Barack Obama's cabinet choices appear to con-

Table 8.1 US female cabinet appointments, 1933–2010

President	Party	Years	Cabinet	Cabinet level	Total
Roosevelt	Democrat	12	1	0	1
Truman	Democrat	8	0	0	0
Eisenhower	Republican	8	1	0	1
Kennedy	Democrat	2	0	0	0
Johnson	Democrat	6	0	0	0
Nixon	Republican	6	0	1	1
Ford[a]	Republican	2	1	0	1
Carter[b]	Democrat	4	4	0	4
Reagan	Republican	8	3	1	4
G.H.W. Bush[c]	Republican	4	3	1	4
Clinton[d]	Democrat	8	5	9	14
G.W. Bush	Republican	8	6	2	8
Obama	Democrat	–	4	3	7
Total			28	17	45

Source: Center for American Women and Politics (2009b).

Notes
a Ford retained Nixon's cabinet level appointee Anne Armstrong (Counselor to the President).
b Carter appointed Patricia Harris to two different positions.
c G.H.W. Bush's Special Trade Representative (Carla Anderson Hills) was also Ford's Secretary of Housing and Urban Development. His Secretary of Labor (Elizabeth Hanford Dole) was also Reagan's Transportation Secretary.
d Clinton appointed Laura D'Andrea Tyson to two cabinet level posts-Chairs of National Economic Council and Chair of Council of Economic Advisors.

tinue gender and racial diversity in appointments. In his 2009 cabinet, four of 15 (26.7 percent) of his cabinet are women and, if cabinet ranked members are also included, seven of 21 (33.3 percent) are women. As of January 2010, 40 women have held cabinet or cabinet-level rank in a total of 45 positions. This is dispersed between 32 different cabinet and 12 different cabinet-level posts. Either way, considering that women's congressional representation is at an all time high at 17 percent, this is proof that women can fare better as presidential appointees than as elected office holders. Still, these represent only a handful of positions available.

Gubernatorial office is a major springboard to the US presidency and, more recently, the cabinet. As of January 2010 only 31 women had been governors and, of these, slightly over one-third were appointed or moved up the ranks to succeed male governors or were elected to their husband's posts.[10] Further, women rarely lead more populous and politically consequential states.[11] In mid 2009, six women were governors of their states, comprising only 12 percent of the overall total, less than women's percentage in Congress which was 17 percent.[12]

Women's involvement in Canadian governments, and notably as cabinet ministers (286 women were ministers in a provincial or federal cabinet from 1921 to December 2007), may be conceptualized according to three periods. The first one, which starts in 1921 and finishes in the mid 1980s, is characterized by a "symbolic" presence of women in cabinets, because their proportion does not exceed 12 percent. Two features mark this period. First, this moment witnessed the first women nominated to cabinets. In 1921 the first woman was appointed cabinet minister in British Columbia (Mary Ellen Smith, appointed minister without portfolio). A few months later a second woman became minister, this time in Alberta (Irene Parlby, also appointed minister without portfolio). Second, by the end of the first period all Canadian provincial and federal cabinets had welcomed at least one female cabinet minister, Nova Scotia being the last all-male cabinet to fall in 1985. At the federal level, it was not until 1957 that a woman was invited to take a seat at the cabinet table. The second period, which lasted from the mid 1980s to the mid 1990s, was characterized by a "supporting role" presence of women in cabinets, during which their proportion varied between 12 percent and 25 percent. All federal and provincial cabinets support this model, but two: Newfoundland and Labrador, and Saskatchewan. In the 1990s, in these last two provinces the proportion of female cabinet ministers jumped from less than 10 percent to more than 25 percent. In other words, whereas Newfoundland and Labrador and Saskatchewan were once laggards regarding women's participation in cabinets, abruptly they became leaders. Finally, the third period, from the mid 1990s until 2007, is characterized by a "significant" presence of women in cabinets – that is, at least 25 percent. Through the 1990s, all federal and provincial cabinets crossed this threshold except for three provinces: Alberta, Nova Scotia and Prince Edward Island, where the highest proportion of female cabinet ministers reached was 21, 17 and 22 percent, respectively. Indeed, in the 1990s some provinces had cabinets comprising at least 30 percent women: British Columbia (1991–2005, except in 1999), Manitoba (1999–2003, with a slight decline in 2002), Ontario (1990–5, and since 2006), Quebec (since 2003), and Saskatchewan (1995–9).

In sum, the participation of women in Canadian and US cabinets is a quite recent phenomenon. Indeed, women are still a minority in the executive, although their presence has increased steadily since World War II. We now turn to the factors that may explain why women still constitute a minority in the US and Canadian cabinets.

Factors explaining women's access to the executive

Studies have shown that a large array of factors influences women's access to legislative arenas, factors that may be reduced into three broad categories: cultural, socioeconomic, and political (Tremblay 2008b). One may assume that the same factors are at play when it comes to accessing the top of the executive political hierarchy. Cultural factors refer to the attitudes, values, beliefs, and opinions underpinning the social fabric of a country and its institutions, and inspiring the population's ways of being, talking, and doing. For instance, cultural factors include socialization and gender stereotypes. Research conducted in the US and Canadian contexts finds that women and men are considered competent in different policy arenas by the public and that this may impact their advancement to particular offices.

Huddy and Terkildsen (1993) distinguish between gender-trait and gender-belief stereotypes. Belief stereotypes link gender to perceptions of party and ideological leanings – so, in the United States men are associated with the Republican Party and conservatism and women with the Democratic Party and liberalism. The same is true in Canada where men are more readily associated with parties situated to the right on the political spectrum, and women with those on the left (Gidengil *et al.* 2003). Based on party stereotypes, Republicans are depicted as stronger on issues like national security while Democrats are considered better skilled at providing social services. As a result, men are deemed more proficient on defense and military issues and women superior on a host of compassion issues including welfare and education. That said, a recent study conducted in Canada shows the importance of partisan stereotypes in attributing feminine traits particularly when all political leaders are female. Comparing the Canadian Progressive Conservative PM Kim Campbell and the New Democratic Leader Audrey McLaughlin, Gidengil *et al.* (2009: 175) found that "the woman leading the left party [A. McLaughlin] was perceived to be more compassionate and trustworthy than the woman leading the right party [K. Campbell]."

Gender-trait stereotypes are based on male and female personality characteristics; toughness associated with masculinity and compassion with femininity, again leading to assumptions about men's superiority at handling military conflicts and women's supremacy at alleviating poverty (Huddy and Terkildsen 1993). Toughness favors men in executive positions while compassion is a liability for women (Fox and Oxley 2003; Huddy and Terkildsen 1993). These findings are bolstered by cross-national studies indicating that leaders are viewed as possessing masculine traits and that men are more likely to be seen as displaying these traits (Sczesny *et al.* 2004). Women are less hindered by perceptions of their collaborative and deliberative abilities than by perceptions of their (in) capacities to lead quickly, decisively, and independently (Duerst-Lahti 1997), also favoring their legislative as opposed to executive prospects. In contrast, executives are expected to lead quickly and decisively, traits more often associated with masculinity (Duerst-Lahti 1997; Jalalzai 2008). Executive power arrangements are also considered masculine because they are centralized and hierarchical (Duerst-Lahti 1997). Thus, women's prospects for breaking through to executive posts, particularly the more masculine ones, are considered less auspicious. Presidents and governors deal with both male and female issues for the presidency and governorship while masculine traits are valued for both. In contrast, the gendering of cabinet posts is specific to departments, though most posts still represent masculine domains. Processes related to attaining respective positions also affect women's prospects.

Considerable research evaluating the impact of gender-trait stereotypes on Canadian women politicians has approached the topic using a media lens. Such research has shown that the media use gender-trait stereotypes in depicting political women (among others, Bashevkin 2009: 160–5; Gingras 1995; MacIvor 1996: 209–12; Robinson *et al.* 1991; Robinson and Saint-Jean 1996). On the one hand, gender-trait stereotypes may emphasize political women's feminine-trait stereotypes, notably by defining them as private beings, an ideological mechanism that Sapiro (1984: 73) calls privatization: "Even where women are involved in public life, as in ... politics, their activities and concerns are expected to be imbued with the private significance of being a woman." One may suggest that political women in Canada are still privatized since, as Bashevkin (2009: 109) notes, the media scrutinize their private life more than men's, a subtle way of sending the message that even in politics women belong to the private realm (see also Trimble *et al.* 2010). On the other hand, gendered mediation may focus on masculine stereotypes, using them to gauge women's decisions and behaviors. Several studies conducted in Canada have shown that the media approach politics in general, and report on elections in particular, according to a game frame based on sports and war, valorizing conflict, performance, and violence. Yet, political women are put at a disadvantage by such a gendered mediation which is contrary to traditional women's role expectations. Analyzing leaders' debates in the 1993, 1997, and 2000 federal elections, Everitt and Gidengil (2003; see also Gidengil and Everitt 2000, 2003) concluded that the gendered nature of reporting electoral campaigns (that is, through a media frame based on masculine-trait stereotypes) poses a serious barrier to women seeking the highest executive position in Canadian politics – that of prime minister (see also Gidengil and Everitt 1999, 2000; Sampert and Trimble 2003). The good news is that the influence of stereotyped mediation on the electorate is unclear, and certainly not definitive, with voters stereotyping political leaders on other labels, notably their party (Gidengil *et al.* 2009). In short, women politicians are sitting between two chairs

– those of gender-role expectations they cannot satisfy: on the one hand, their presence in politics challenges the traditional feminine stereotypes; on the other, women's performance has every chance of being evaluated as disappointing since the media analyzes politics through male stereotypes.

The supply of women who can compete for executive positions must be taken into account since they represent a potential pipeline from which presidents and first ministers may choose. A common factor thought to be important to women's political success is their educational attainment and their workforce participation, particularly in high-rank professions. These are the socioeconomic factors which determine the social and economic conditions qualifying women to be recruited into an executive role: women's access to university education, the proportion of women in the labor market, the female/male revenue ratio, and per capita gross national product (GNP) are examples of such socioeconomic parameters. As concerns legislative politics, one hypothesis explains the small number of women in politics by their under-representation in the pool from which parties recruit their potential candidates (Darcy *et al.* 1994: 104–5). Consequently, an improvement in women's socioeconomic conditions should contribute to an increase in the proportion of women in politics.

Early US studies found a connection between women's educational and employment levels and the proportion of women legislators (Darcy *et al.* 1994: 107–16; Rule 1987). Women in the United States enjoy near parity with men in education, income, and health.[13] Despite these promising measures, however, women are still seldom represented among the highest professional ranks. Degrees earned and employment patterns are concentrated in fewer and less prestigious fields compared to men and a large gap in women's earnings remains (McBride-Stetson 2004). More recent research fails to find a connection between women's education and employment and political representation (Matland 1998; Moore and Shackman 1996). Still, cabinet secretaries are highly educated and politically experienced; female secretaries are no exception. Men are slightly more apt to have an advanced degree while women are more likely to have attended private higher education institutions (Dolan 2001). Women more often come from families with professional backgrounds (Martin 2003). A majority of men and women hail from a local, state, or federal level position and women are slightly younger than men upon appointment, and generally have fewer children (Borrelli 2002: 110–31). Of the 40 women cabinet appointees 14 were lawyers and 12 were academics.[14] Women are also more often recruited from inside Washington, DC, suggesting a closer connection to the national political scene (Martin 2003) although they are also more often treated as outsiders in their confirmation hearings (Borrelli 1997). Women are also more prone to gain experience in the same executive department they ultimately head (Borrelli 2002). Twenty-six women held another federal executive office before serving in the cabinet.[15] Some also served previously in elective office: three were governors of their state,[16] while four (including Hillary Clinton[17]) were in Congress.

Women north of the United States also enjoy quite favorable social and economic conditions, allowing them to imagine a career in politics. In 2001,[18]

14.9 percent of Canadian women compared to 16 percent of men had a university degree (i.e. a bachelor's/first professional degree, master's or doctorate; Statistics Canada 2005: 99). During the academic year 2001–2, women represented 56.7 percent of the full-time university enrollment and they constituted a majority in all fields of study but engineering/applied sciences and mathematics/ physical sciences (Statistics Canada 2005: 100). In 2004, 57.8 percent of women were employed in the paid workforce, representing 46.8 percent of total employment (Statistics Canada 2005: 119). More interestingly, 72.5 percent of women with children under 16 were engaged in paid labor, this proportion being 39.1 percent in 1976 (Statistics Canada 2005: 121). Not surprisingly, more than two out of three (68.8 percent) part-time employees were women (Statistics Canada 2005: 124). In 2003, women's income as a percentage of men's was 62.1 percent (Statistics Canada 2005: 148). Despite the fact that women's social status still lags behind that of men (particularly as concerns employment and income/earnings), significant numbers of women enjoy social and economic levels rendering them eligible for a political career.

In Canada as elsewhere, women politicians constitute an elite compared to women in general: they have a higher schooling level and a more exceptional professional profile than women who are not politicians (see Black 2000; Black and Erickson 2000; Kohn 1984; Oakes 1994: 163, 166–7; Tremblay 2010: 100–5; Tremblay and Trimble 2004; Young and Cross 2003). Since women legislators constitute an elite compared to the Canadian female population, and since the executive stands higher than the legislative within the Westminster hierarchy of power, one may suspect that women cabinet ministers have a more elitist profile than political women who have not been invited to serve in the executive. This argument should be qualified: generally speaking, women cabinet ministers in Canada from 1921 to December 2007 did not have a profile distinguishing them significantly from their legislative sisters who had never been part of the executive. Generally, women ministers and those who have never been members of cabinets are similar though they exhibit some few differences. For the highest diplomas earned, federal and Quebec female cabinet ministers are more educated than women legislators who have never been ministers.[19] Regarding their principal employment before their first election in politics, women ministers were no more likely to occupy top professions (notably as senior managers, professionals, lawyers, notaries, and physicians) than women who were never ministers, Prince Edward Island being an exception. More intriguingly, women cabinet ministers in Alberta were significantly less likely to occupy a top profession before their first experience in provincial politics than women who were never cabinet ministers. A preliminary explanation may reside in party adherence to the appointment of women cabinet ministers almost all of whom are considered conservative – a party more populist and more working-class than others. Future research should explore this interpretation.

Political factors are related to demand for women in politics; in other words, the demands of party elites for women legislators and cabinet members. These demands are intrinsically linked to the political regime and how its traits shape the parties' processes for selecting their legislative and executive personnel. As mentioned previously, an important difference between Canadian and US political regimes is that Canadian first ministers must recruit and select their cabinet ministers from among the members of their parliamentary caucus, a constraint that US presidents do not face; in fact, there are few specific qualifications women must meet to be part of the US cabinet. Despite this difference in the regime, however, the first ministers as well as US presidents are the principal selector-agents (but not the only one) of those who will be part of their cabinets.

Are women more likely to be appointed by liberal administrations than conservative, as comparative research suggests (among others, Escobar-Lemmon and Taylor-Robinson 2005)? In the US two-party system, this reflects possible differences in Democrat and Republican administrations. One important distinction, however, is the number of years each party has held the executive. Since World War II, Republicans have held the presidency for 36 years and Democrats for 30 years. Both parties have appointed identical numbers of female cabinet members – 14 each. Since Republicans have held the presidency longer, this suggests Democratic administrations have been more inclusive of women. Still, the Republican Party has actually appointed a slightly higher proportion of women to male posts (64 versus 57 percent) and the Democratic Party a higher percentage of women to female posts (29 versus 21 percent). However, differences are negligible given the low number of women appointees. The Democratic Party has taken the lead in promoting women to cabinet-level posts. Sixty percent of Republican cabinet-level female appointees and 83 percent of Democrats are to male positions; 20 percent of Republican appointees and 17 percent of Democratic appointees are to female posts while the remaining 20 percent of Republican appointees are to gender-neutral posts. Still, again, the overall number of female cabinet-rank Republican appointees is much smaller than Democratic appointees.

Overall, however, it seems that the growing number and variety of posts women are appointed to is representative of changes within both parties. Presidents on both sides of the aisle have actively recruited women. Still, the pioneering efforts of President Carter and President Clinton were integral to the development of more positive trends. For example, though Clinton was adamant that he was against being a "bean counter" (someone who was just concerned with appointing the right numbers of women to his cabinet), his commitment to appointing the first female attorney general was evident in his nomination of two other female nominees (who were not confirmed) prior to Janet Reno. Still, George W. Bush appointed a greater number of women to his traditional cabinet than Clinton, though Clinton promoted four times the number of women to cabinet-level rank. While the Obama administration is still in its infancy, President Obama has already promoted several women to cabinet or cabinet-level rank. While still far from parity, it is unlikely that women would be relegated to only a few appointments within female departments in future administrations, Democrat or Republican.

In Canada, do left-wing cabinets contain higher proportions of women than their right-wing counterparts? Analyzing the determinants of appointment to federal cabinets from 1935 to 2008, Kerby (2009) observes that conservative cabinets were slightly more feminized than liberal ones: 14 versus 12 percent. From the 1920s to 2007, those cabinets categorized as right-wing cabinets were those formed by federal and provincial conservative and progressive conservative parties, the Saskatchewan Party, the Social Credit parties and the United Farmers parties. Since "left-wing" parties are quite marginal in Canada compared with their European counterparts, center-left parties (that is, the Cooperative Commonwealth Federation and the New Democratic parties) and parties of the center (the Liberal, Quebec Parti québécois and Manitoba Liberal-Progressive parties) were categorized together for the purpose of this analysis. This "right-wing cabinets" versus "center and the center-left cabinets" comparison shows that these latter have higher levels of feminization than cabinets set up by conservatives and progressive conservative parties: 12.9 versus 8.5 percent.

Two observations can be drawn from these numbers. First, the gaps separating the levels of feminization of right-wing cabinets on the one hand, and center and center-left cabinets on the other are sometimes quite weak: less than 5 percent in New Brunswick, Newfoundland and Labrador, and Nova Scotia, and less than 6 percent in British Columbia and at the federal level. Second, the opinion that right-wing parties would manifest a firm and systematic hostility to women's involvement in cabinet affairs must be qualified. Of course, the levels of feminization of right-wing cabinets are lower than those of center and center-left ones. However, the contrary is sometimes true. For instance, from 1996 to 2007, right-wing cabinets were more feminized than center and center-left ones in Prince Edward Island (20.7 versus 18.2 percent), New Brunswick (23.9 versus 9.1 percent) and Saskatchewan (27.8 versus 23.6 percent). Of course, these cases are exceptions and not the rule, but they prevent any possibility of establishing a causal relationship between right-wing cabinets and weak proportions of women ministers – even if such a relationship is true most of the time. In fact, these unusual observations oblige us to envisage that the election of a strong contingent of women in the legislature, and especially in the parliamentary caucus of the government party, puts pressure on first ministers that even right-wing ones cannot ignore without potential electoral costs. Future research should explore this hypothesis.

Comparative research finds that masculinized posts such as defense are not only more prestigious but disproportionately held by men; women are overly concentrated in feminine ministries such as family and women's issues (Blondel 1988; Escobar-Lemmon and Taylor-Robinson 2005; Paxton and Hughes 2007: 97). These patterns also surface in North America. In the United States, among the 28 cabinet posts occupied by women, 61 percent headed male departments, 25 percent led female, while 14 percent have no clear gender bias[20] (see Table 8.2). While the only explicitly female departments in the United States are education and health and human services, women's appointment to these posts

Table 8.2 US female cabinet positions, 1933–2010

Position	Women	Democrat	Republican	Gender
Labor	7	3	4	Male
Health/Human Services	4	3	1	Female
State	3	2	1	Male
Education	2	1	1	Female
Housing/Urban Development	2	1	1	Neutral
Commerce	2	1	1	Male
Transportation	2	0	2	Male
Attorney General	1	1	0	Neutral
Agriculture	1	0	1	Male
Homeland Security[a]	1	1	0	Male
Interior	1	0	1	Neutral
Energy	1	1	0	Male
Health, Education and Welfare[b]	1	0	1	Female
Defence	0	0	0	Male
Treasury	0	0	0	Male
Veteran's Affairs	0	0	0	Male
Total	28	14	14	

Source: Center for American Women and Politics (2009b).

Notes
a Created under G.W. Bush administration.
b No longer exists – separated into other departments.

is very high, thus confirming comparative trends. However, more recent administrations show a more varied pattern of female appointments. For example, a different woman has served as Secretary of State (a key player in foreign policy) in each of the last three presidential administrations. Janet Napolitano's appointment as Secretary of Homeland Security also represents an important development for women, somewhat compensating for their inability to become Defense Secretary. This relatively new position leads the effort to protect the country from both foreign threats and various domestic dangers, directly challenging stereotypes of women's inability to lead during crises. US presidents are provided with further opportunities to promote women to executive leadership through classifying their posts as "cabinet-level" rank. Bill Clinton elevated nine women this way, the vast majority serving in economic positions, generally considered masculine, including the Chair of the Council of Economic Advisors, Chair of the National Economic Council and Director of Management and Budget. Three women have been promoted to the cabinet as Administrator of the Environmental Protection Agency. Finally, two women have also served as Ambassador to the United Nations. Seventeen cabinet-level positions have been occupied by 15 different women (see Table 8.3). Thirteen (76 percent) are to male positions, three (18 percent) to female, and one (6 percent) does not have a clear gender distinction (Counselor to the President).

Table 8.3 US female cabinet level positions, 1933–2010

Position	Women	Democrat	Republican	Gender
UN	3	2	1	Male
Environment	3	2	1	Female
Economic Advisers	3	3	0	Male
Trade Representative	3	1	2	Male
Personnel Management	1	1	0	Male
Small Business	1	1	0	Male
Economic Council	1	1	0	Male
Councilor to President	1	0	1	Neutral
Office of Budget	1	1	0	Male
Total	17	12	5	

Source: Center for American Women and Politics (2009b).

Studies conducted in Canada have also found that ministerial departments are distributed according to a gender divide: women inherit portfolios reminiscent of their maternal and domestic roles in the private sphere (Bashevkin 1993: 88; MacIvor 1996: 283–5; Moncrief and Studlar 1996; Studlar and Moncrief 1999; Trimble and Tremblay 2005). In fact, a clear majority of women cabinet ministers in Canada have been responsible for social portfolios, some fulfilling an economic mission (such as education, environment, employment and human resources, immigration, municipal and regional affairs, tourism and leisure) and others a cultural one (citizenship, culture, identity, and multiculturalism, family and children, health and social services, women's status). However, a few of them have also headed the male-defined *régalien* (that is, the functions intrinsic to state sovereignty and formerly held by the king notably defense, justice and international affairs/relations) and economic/finance departments (particularly at the federal level). From 1921 to 2007, 286 women were members of federal and provincial cabinets and were responsible for a total of 1,011 portfolios. More precisely, 591 were senior responsibilities and 420 junior, and 734 out of these 1,011 portfolios (or 72.6 percent) had a socioeconomic or a socio-cultural mission. The importance of social portfolios may be explained (at least in part) by the fact that many more women have been cabinet ministers in provinces than at the federal level (845 versus 166) and that the Canadian constitution confers on the provinces a primary role in cultural and social affairs. In fact, from 1921 to 2007, 75.5 percent (638/845) of the socioeconomic and socio-cultural portfolios in provincial cabinets were held by a woman compared to 57.8 percent (96/166) in the federal government. However, this latter assigned to women 34.9 percent (58/166) of *régalien* and economic/finance portfolios, two fields where the federal government enjoys a leading role according to the constitution, with this proportion falling to less than 20 percent (159/845, or 18.8 percent) in the provinces.

As suggested earlier, not all cabinet positions are created equal. The US executive literature recognizes a hierarchy in prestige signified by the "inner" and

"outer" cabinet dichotomy. The inner cabinet comprises the four original departments – defense, state, treasury, and justice (Borrelli 2005). Not only are these
policy areas perennially higher profile, but these secretaries are generally thought
to have open access to the president (Borrelli 2005). In contrast, the outer cabinet
posts were created more recently and feature departments with fewer connections to the president. Instead, they tend to be closer to the particular interest
groups they represent. Only four women to date have broken through to the inner
cabinet (Condoleezza Rice, Janet Reno, Madeleine Albright, and Hillary
Rodham Clinton). According to Borrelli (2005), even Reno's appointment as
attorney general did not challenge the tendency to appoint women who are
policy generalists and unlike most attorneys general, she did not have a close
relationship with the president. Again, women have never served as Secretary of
Defense or Treasury. Thus, not only are some cabinet appointments more powerful and prestigious than others, but this has gendered implications.

Canada's cabinets are also hierarchical spaces structured according to the
inner/outer split (White 2005: 43–6). The law of the discrepancy proportion
(Putnam 1976: 33) suggests that the higher a political position, the fewer women
will be found, a hypothesis supported by a wealth of literature (Bashevkin 1993:
65–92; MacIvor 1996: 283–5; Studlar and Moncrief 1999; Vickers and Brodie
1981). Yet, this hypothesis is not fully confirmed with regard to women cabinet
ministers in Canada from 1921 to 2007. In fact, almost 60 percent (591 of 1,011,
or 58.5 percent) of the portfolios women held at the cabinet level during this
period were at the full minister level against 41.5 percent (420 of 1,011) that
were of a junior caliber. This gap in favor of full minister holds true for both
federal and provincial cabinets. Indeed, the proportion of women full ministers
has been about the same in the provincial and Ottawa cabinets: 58.7 percent in
the former and 57.2 percent in the latter. In short, it is not entirely true that
women are located at the bottom of the Canadian executive hierarchy, although
it is the lot of about 40 percent of women cabinet ministers. At the same time,
women have taken up only a minority of the *régalien* ministerial portfolios at
both the federal and provincial levels: 14.5 percent (24/166) and 6.4 percent
(54/845), respectively. From this point of view, if *régalien* departments are not
completely beyond women's reach, their control over these most powerful, influential and desirable cabinet positions is limited, which in a way gives credence
to Putnam's law of discrepancy proportion.

To summarize, a host of factors influences women's access to Canadian and
US executive positions. In particular, gender stereotypes exert a strong influence
on the ministerial portfolios women inherit. Since gender expectations structure
women's participation in cabinet, one may expect that women cabinet ministers
substantively represent women, a question to which we now turn.

Do women executives represent women?

Important questions remain regarding the substantive representation of women:
do women in the cabinet lead differently than their male counterparts, and

notably do they represent women from a substantive perspective? There is still little attention devoted to women's substantive representation in executives in either Canada or the United States.

The available findings indicate that women appointees in the US executive are more feminist and liberal than men appointees and, according to surveys, they are also more supportive of abortion rights, childcare, and equal rights regardless of party (Dolan 2001).[21] However, given that women have generally been relegated to weaker cabinet positions, their ability to substantively represent women's interests has been curtailed (Borrelli 2002). Still, in analyzing some of the more powerful women cabinet members to date, some do represent women's interests, particularly among secretaries of state. Shortly after becoming Secretary of State, Madeleine Albright ordered diplomats to make the pursuit of women's rights a central component of foreign policy (Lippman 2004). Hillary Clinton has heightened this priority as well. She created a special Ambassador for Global Women's Issues and in her diplomatic travels continually references the importance of women's rights. For example, she spoke out against the rape of women in eastern Congo (Landler 2009). While Condoleezza Rice is also noted to have spoken in favor of women's rights internationally, particularly in the Middle East, many viewed this with more skepticism given that George W. Bush's administration curtailed women's reproductive and economic rights (Stevens 2005).

With regard to Canada, evidence that women cabinet ministers substantively represent women is far more intuitive than obvious. In fact, if some research indicates that female legislators represent women from a substantive point of view (Tremblay 1998, 2003; Tremblay and Mullen 2007; Trimble 1993, 1997), this observation is not as clear where women cabinet ministers are concerned. Of course, several women who have been cabinet ministers in Canada since 1921 may without a doubt be described as feminists,[22] including Nancy Allan (appointed Manitoba Labour and Immigration Minister in 2003), Marion Boyd, Jenny Carter, and Frances Lankin (who served in the Ontario Rae government from 1990 to 1995), and Lise Payette (who was responsible for several ministerial portfolios in the first Quebec Parti québécois government from 1976 to 1981). Now, whether they were able to put their gender/feminist consciousness into consequential action is another question that cannot receive a clear assessment from the current state of knowledge – even if ministers are also legislators and several studies indicate that women parliamentarians substantively represent their female fellow citizens. In fact, many factors may prevent women ministers from substantively representing women. Some are intrinsic to the parliamentary regime: the secrecy of cabinet discussions in conjunction with the rules of ministerial solidarity and party discipline, and the policy priorities of the first minister and her/his government team. Other factors are external to the parliamentary rules of the game: the (sometimes) painful contacts between women cabinet ministers and the women's movement, the ideological orientations (and feminist beliefs) of female ministers as well as their own electoral and political ambitions.

In short, more research must be conducted before concluding that women ministers act for women's interests – or put another way, that the access of women to the Canadian and the US executives is a fruitful and significant strategy for women's substantive representation.

Conclusion

Even though the cabinet is the heart of executive power, the US and Canadian executives differ on several dimensions. A significant difference resides in the pathway for accessing cabinet, notably the pool of candidates at the disposal of the chief executive (i.e. the US president and the Canadian prime minister) for choosing, selecting, and appointing her/his nominees to the cabinet. In fact, generally speaking the latter must draw her/his ministers from the legislative delegation of her/his party while US presidents are bound by no such limitation. Thus one may conclude that the feminization of the executive is a more attainable objective in the United States than in Canada, since the president may appoint whom s/he wants while the Canadian prime minister must limit her/his choices to the women members of her/his legislative caucus.

Yet, the second part of this chapter has shown that this rationale does not hold: despite a larger room for maneuver offered to the president for constituting her/his cabinet, US cabinets are not significantly more feminized than their Canadian counterparts. In both countries women are still a minority in cabinets and their progress in reaching executive positions has been relatively slow – even though the pace of their move has accelerated a bit since the 1990s. An economic-inspired supply-demand approach has been suggested to account for the weak presence of women in cabinet circles. With regard to the supply side, at first glance socioeconomic factors appear quite secondary to cultural ones (i.e. gender stereotypes). The ideology of the government party is one of the demand-side political factors which helps us to understand why there are so few women in Canadian and US cabinets. In addition, the traditional vertical and horizontal divide is still in force for making sense of women's involvement in cabinets: generally speaking, women are located at the lower echelons of the cabinet hierarchy and are responsible for female-related portfolios. Most recently, however, this model has been evolving. Finally, the question of whether women cabinet ministers substantively represent women remains unresolved. The complexity of the problem (for instance, the intertwining of variables which compose the societal fabric) and the working rules of cabinet (the secrecy rule, for example) postpone into the distant future credible responses to what for the moment appears to be an enigma.

To conclude, what lessons may be learned from this US–Canada comparison? First, there is no link between wealth, democracy, and women's presence in cabinets. Indeed, considerable research has shown that the proportion of women in parliaments is related to neither the level of economic development nor the level of democracy (Paxton and Hughes 2007: 309–12; Paxton and Kunovich 2003; Reynolds 1999). At first glance, it seems that such a pattern also holds true for women's participation in the pinnacle of executive power: Canada and the United States are among the richest countries in the world, and yet the levels of feminization of their cabinets are about the same as those in Liberia and Rwanda – which are very poor countries – as Chapter 6 shows. Second, there is a need to refresh and refine analyses of women's participation in politics. In fact, women's status and material living conditions have greatly evolved since the 1990s, and it is not clear that yesterday's body of knowledge is still suitable for understanding today's patterns of women's involvement in politics. For instance, women members of executives are no longer systemically confined to female-defined and less powerful portfolios. Third, there is a huge hole to fill in knowledge regarding the representational role of women members of political executives: do they speak and act for women's interests? Nothing is so uncertain, and future research must address this important question.

Notes

1 Manon Tremblay would like to thank Sarah Andrew for collecting data on women in Canadian cabinets.
2 North America may be defined in several ways, as restricted to Canada and the United States only, or as including also Mexico, Central America, and the Caribbean islands. The adoption of the North American Free Trade Agreement in the mid 1990s imposed a largely accepted vision of North America as composed of Canada, Mexico, and the United States. This chapter adopts this understanding of North America.
3 Inter-Parliamentary Union (2010d).
4 See Worldwide Guide to Women in Leadership (2009f).
5 Thanks to Dr. Magda Hinojosa (Arizona State University) for providing data on women ministers in Mexico.
6 CIA (2009b).
7 Two women have served as provincial premiers: Rita Johnston in British Columbia (July to October 1991) and Catherine Callbeck in Prince Edward Island (January 1993 to October 1996).
8 While Truman came to power upon the death of F.D. Roosevelt, he did not retain Perkins.
9 Center for American Women and Politics (2009b).
10 Center for American Women and Politics (2009a).
11 Exceptions are Jennifer Granholm of Michigan, Beverly Perdue of North Carolina, and former governors of Texas Miriam Ferguson and Ann Richards.
12 Center for American Women and Politics (2009a). The record number of women governors is nine, or 18 percent, reached in 2005 and 2008 (Center for American Women and Politics 2010).
13 UNDP (2009e). This is based on the Gender-related Development Index. With a GDI scoring of 0.942, the United States is ranked nineteenth in the world.
14 Center for American Women and Politics (2009b).
15 Center for American Women and Politics (2009b).
16 Christie Todd Whitman, Janet Napolitano, and Kathleen Sebelius were governors; Lynn Martin, Margaret Heckler, and Hilda Solis are the other three from Congress.
17 Hillary Clinton also served as First Lady – arguably an important unofficial executive post.
18 All the numbers presented in this paragraph are based on the 2001 Canada census and the pages in the parentheses refer to Statistics Canada (2005).
19 However, this gap is statistically significant at $P \leq 0.10$.

20 Our coding is in line with the vast literature on gender stereotypes, including that dealing with male/female legislative issues and comparative assessments of gendered domains in cabinet office, though taking into account specific gender dynamics within the United States (Madeleine Albright–Bill Clinton, Condoleezza Rice–George W. Bush, and Hillary Rodham Clinton–Barack Obama).
21 Some of these findings are drawn from state executive studies as well (see Carroll 1987; Havens and Healy 1991).
22 Thanks to Sylvia Bashevkin (University of Toronto), Shannon Sampert (University of Winnipeg), and Linda Trimble (University of Alberta) for their advice on this point. As concerns Ontario, see Byrne (2009).

9 Western Europe

Fiona Buckley and Yvonne Galligan

Introduction

In a 2009 photograph of political leaders in Europe the German chancellor, Angela Merkel, stands out.[1] She is wearing a colorful pink jacket that contrasts strongly with the dark suits worn by the other leaders of European states. And she is the only woman sitting on the platform. The image is striking in a region of the world where women's representation in politics has been an issue for three decades. So, how is it then that Angela Merkel is a rare[2] instance of a woman as executive leader in Europe? This chapter discusses women's political leadership in Germany, the United Kingdom (UK) and Spain since World War II in an effort to identify the conditions under which women achieve high office in these countries. It analyzes women's participation in the political executive as senior ministers and as heads of government. The chapter begins with an overview of women's recruitment to cabinet office in Western Europe and introduces a gendered categorization of executive portfolios. This is followed by country case studies beginning with an overview of the political systems in the UK, Germany and Spain and an examination of the formal and informal rules of access to executive office in these countries. The next section analyzes the evolution of women in UK, Germany and Spain executive positions since World War II. A discussion of the socio-cultural, economic and political variables influencing women's access to executive positions then follows. The chapter concludes by estimating the impact of executive women in these countries on women's legislative representation and on women's interests.

Regional overview

Prior to the 1980s few women occupied ministerial positions in Western Europe. This reflected women's significant under-representation in parliament at the time. It also reflects the more general pattern of European executives being drawn from the legislature which, as Davis (1997: 8, 30) observed, provides the "pool of eligibles" from which a cabinet is formed. Thus, women's absence from executive office is inextricably linked with the prevailing cultural expectations of gender roles, and the consequent individual, societal, and political obstacles that prevented women from entering politics in the 1950s and early 1960s. Their absence from parliament at that time meant that women were essentially disqualified from membership of the political elite (Davis 1997: 30; Aberbach *et al.* 1981). Over the following decades, the cultural liberalization of gender roles, increasing educational and employment opportunities, legal reforms in the status of women and the politicization of gender equality contributed to a growth in women's parliamentary presence so that by the 1990s women's opportunities for entry to executive office had increased. In 1994, women comprised 16 percent of those holding full cabinet posts in the 15 member states of the European Union (European Commission DG EMPL 2009: 43). By January 2009, this figure had risen to 26 percent amongst the 27 European Union (EU) member states – a significant increase in a relatively short period of time.

Research on European cabinets indicates that the portfolios allocated to women often reflected the educational and occupational categories into which women have traditionally been directed (Davis 1997: 16). In the 24-year period between 1968 and 1992, about one-half of the 438 female executive appointments were made in health, social welfare, education, family, culture and consumer affairs (Davis 1997: 16). The European Council[3] adopted the BEIS typology in 1999 as a method of analyzing the distribution of women ministers' portfolios in EU member states. This classifies government functions into four areas: basic (B), economy (E), infrastructure (I) and socio-cultural (S). The application of the typology demonstrates that women tend to be appointed to socio-cultural portfolios at a greater rate (43 percent) than they are appointed to basic (18 percent), economic (16 percent) or infrastructural (23 percent) portfolios[4] (Table 9.1).

While there is no formal hierarchy of cabinet portfolios, it is universally considered that finance and foreign affairs are the most prestigious of all government functions. These responsibilities fall into the two categories (economic and basic) where female ministers are least represented. Since the early 1990s, though, as women's parliamentary representation has grown, there is evidence of more women being appointed to ministries of finance, defense and foreign affairs (Borrelli 2002: 23–4). In 2009, women occupied 17 percent of these positions across the EU member states.[5] This still lags behind women's holding of infrastructural (23 percent) and socio-cultural portfolios (43 percent), but marks a breakthrough into ministries that have traditionally been seen as comprising the inner cabinet of government. In the next section we describe the political systems of our three cases, the UK, Germany and Spain, as background to a more detailed consideration of the cabinet recruitment norms prevailing in each country.

Table 9.1 Distribution in percentage of senior ministries in EU member states by BEIS typology in 2009

	Basic		Economic		Infrastructure		Socio-cultural	
	Women	*Men*	*Women*	*Men*	*Women*	*Men*	*Women*	*Men*
Austria	40.0	60.0	0.0	100.0	0.0	100.0	60.0	40.0
Belgium	14.0	86.0	33.0	67.0	0.0	100.0	100.0	0.0
Bulgaria	38.0	62.0	0.0	100.0	33.0	67.0	25.0	75.0
Cyprus	0.0	100.0	0.0	100.0	0.0	100.0	33.0	67.0
Czech Republic	25.0	75.0	0.0	100.0	0.0	75.0	0.0	100.0
Denmark	0.0	100.0	60.0	40.0	25.0	75.0	50.0	50.0
Estonia	0.0	100.0	0.0	100.0	0.0	100.0	75.0	25.0
Finland	50.0	50.0	25.0	75.0	75.0	25.0	83.0	17.0
France	20.0	80.0	29.0	71.0	43.0	57.0	56.0	44.0
Germany	33.0	67.0	25.0	75.0	0.0	100.0	75.0	25.0
Greece	14.0	86.0	0.0	100.0	0.0	100.0	25.0	75.0
Hungary	13.0	87.0	0.0	100.0	0.0	100.0	33.0	67.0
Ireland	0.0	100.0	33.0	67.0	0.0	100.0	50.0	50.0
Italy	0.0	100.0	0.0	100.0	50.0	50.0	60.0	40.0
Latvia	14.0	86.0	0.0	100.0	0.0	100.0	50.0	50.0
Lithuania	0.0	100.0	33.0	67.0	0.0	100.0	25.0	75.0
Luxembourg	13.0	87.0	0.0	100.0	0.0	100.0	50.0	50.0
Malta	25.0	75.0	0.0	100.0	0.0	100.0	50.0	50.0
Norway	50.0	50.0	75.0	25.0	33.0	67.0	33.0	67.0
Poland	0.0	100.0	20.0	80.0	0.0	100.0	67.0	33.0
Portugal	0.0	100.0	0.0	100.0	0.0	100.0	40.0	60.0
Romania	0.0	100.0	0.0	100.0	0.0	100.0	0.0	100.0
Slovakia	0.0	100.0	0.0	100.0	0.0	100.0	25.0	75.0
Slovenia	0.0	100.0	0.0	100.0	0.0	100.0	60.0	40.0
Spain	43.0	57.0	0.0	100.0	100.0	0.0	57.0	43.0
Sweden	50.0	50.0	25.0	75.0	50.0	50.0	50.0	50.0
The Netherlands	17.0	83.0	40.0	60.0	67.0	33.0	0.0	100.0
United Kingdom	46.0	54.0	17.0	83.0	100.0	0.0	0.0	100.0
All	19.0	81.0	17.0	83.0	25.0	75.0	47.0	53.0
Percentage of all female ministers	18.0		16.0		23.0		43.0	

Sources: European Commission Directorate-General for Employment, Social Affairs and Equal Opportunities (DG EMPL) (2009, 2010).

Country cases: Germany, Spain and the United Kingdom

Description of the political regimes

The political arrangements of the UK, Germany and Spain are described as parliamentary democracies, as the government is dependent on retaining majority support in parliament for its continuing survival. The party or combination of parties commanding a majority in parliament forms the government. The head of government, the prime minister, is leader of the largest party in the legislature and has the task of selecting a cabinet that is then formally appointed by the head of state. Although our three cases appear similar, on closer observation they differ in important respects in terms of their constitutional, political and electoral arrangements.

Until 2010, the use of the single-member plurality electoral system (first-past-the-post) was viewed as having contributed to the continuing dominance of the two-party system in the UK. However, a hung parliament after the May 2010 general election brought the first coalition government since World War II to office. A Liberal Democrat condition for sharing power with the Conservatives was that of electoral reform. It remains to be seen if the Alternative Vote will replace the plurality vote, and if so, the traditional two-party system will become a three-party one, with the Liberal Democrats playing a small but pivotal role. Parliament consists of two houses – the popularly elected House of Commons (lower house) and the appointed House of Lords (upper house). Although there is a provision whereby the head of government can look to the House of Lords for cabinet appointees, cabinet ministers are almost always drawn from the lower house and within this house, drawn exclusively from among the members of the largest political party. The head of government, the prime minister (PM), is the leader of the largest party in the House of Commons.

Appointment to the British cabinet is a classic example of the generalist system of cabinet recruitment, where government ministers are drawn from the party or parties that hold the majority in parliament. Davis (1997: 40–1) identifies a number of prerequisites for appointment to the British cabinet that are features of all executives drawn from a parliamentary base: membership of parliament, significant parliamentary tenure and "prowess" in parliamentary debate. She calculated that 95 percent of ministers in UK governments from 1968 to 1992 were members of parliament and each possessed on average 12.2 years of parliamentary service. She emphasized the importance of "competence in parliamentary debate ... to win the notice of British prime ministers" and noted that "ministerial aspirants are advised to seek out opportunities to speak not only in Commons ... but also outside the house, with the press and in constituency meetings" (Davis 1997: 40–1). Theakston (1987) notes that in generalist systems such as that of the UK, a minister's competence and experience in one area is thought to readily transfer to a number of other functional areas. The practice serves to reinforce the value of the generalist background (Davis 1997: 42).

The political development of post-World War II Germany is well documented. The German political system was constructed as a federal arrangement in West Germany (Federal Republic of Germany, FDR) while the Soviet-controlled East Germany (German Democratic Republic, GDR) followed a communist regime. In November 1989 under severe pressure from a groundswell of public opinion, the communist party of East Germany relinquished its monopoly of power and opened its borders with the West. Demands for unity grew, and on October 3, 1990, East Germany joined the Federal Republic. After reunification, the *Grundgesetz*[6] or Basic Law became the constitution of all Germany. It defines Germany as "a democratic, federal and social state, operating under the rule of law, whose authority derives from the people" (Bendix 2007: 6–7). The federal institutions bear all of the hallmarks of parliamentary democracy, with the *Bundestag* (lower house) producing the chancellor (prime minister) who is the parliamentary leader of the largest party. Bundestag members are elected every four years according to a predetermined timetable. Germany uses the mixed members' proportional (MMP) system (also known as the Additional Member System) to fill its Bundestag seats. One half of the seats are filled using the first-past-the-post system in single-member constituencies. The remaining seats are filled using party lists in multi-member districts. The *Bundesrat* (upper house) consists of appointed representatives of the 16 *länder* or state governments. Bendix (2007: 7) describes the Bundesrat as "a body specifically responsible for ensuring the national government does not violate the legitimate interests of the states laid out in the Grundgesetz."

Unlike the British system where the prime minister is the "first among equals," the German chancellor is "the leader of a government whose composition he determines and whose policies he defines" (Goetz 2003: 32). In her study of recruitment patterns of government ministers across Europe from 1968 to 1992, Davis (1997: 44) found that 74 percent of ministers in (West) German governments were members of parliament and each possessed on average 7.7 years of parliamentary service. The results would suggest that parliamentary service and length of tenure are still important criteria for cabinet membership in Germany. However, these are not the only criteria. In an important distinction from British practice, federal ministers need not be members of parliament. Gerhard Schröder made extensive use of this provision when appointing his first cabinet in 1998 with five of the 15 ministers coming from outside the parliamentary arena (Goetz 2003: 26). In another contrast to the UK experience of cabinet formation, German executives are often coalition arrangements. In these circumstances, the chancellor's powers of cabinet appointment are restricted due to the need to include members of the coalition party or parties at the cabinet table. It is not unusual for the chancellor to have little or no input into the choice of cabinet representatives by the coalition partners. In addition, the chancellor's options are determined by features that the British PM also needs to take into account – regional, religious, political and, more recently, gender balance (Goetz 2003: 27).

Spain is often described as having a co-constitutional political system as it is neither a federal nor unitary state but has a number of autonomous regions within the Spanish nation-state. The death of General Francisco Franco in late 1975 brought an end to a 36-year authoritarian dictatorship which had emerged during the 1936–9 Spanish civil war. Since the restoration of democracy, all 11 governments have been one-party executives. The centrist Union of the Democratic Centre (UCD) were in power for three terms from 1977 to 1982; the Spanish Socialist Workers' Party (PSOE) enjoyed four terms of office between 1982 and 1996. The right-leaning Popular Party (PP) came to power in 1996, and remained in office for two terms until April 2004, when the PSOE, under the leadership of José Luis Rodríguez Zapatero, returned to power. Zapatero led his party to victory again in the April 2008 parliamentary elections.

Similar to the prime minister in the United Kingdom and the chancellor in Germany, the president of the government (*presidente del gobierno*) occupies a central position within the political system in Spain. Responsibility for the formation of a cabinet (*Consejo de Ministros*) rests with the president and, similar to the British model, ministers are drawn from one of the two chambers of the national parliament – the Congress of Deputies (*Congreso de los Diputados*) or the Senate (*Senado*). When appointing a cabinet, the president considers what combination of promotions to executive office will offer the optimum conditions for retaining parliamentary support and securing re-election (Real-Dato 2009: 7). Policy preferences of party members, placation of adversaries, the promotion of ambitious politicians, rewarding loyalty and seniority, ensuring regional representation, and assessing the impact of decisions on public support are factors a president is required to bear in mind when shaping an executive. In 2004 and 2008, Zapatero allowed one of his electoral pledges, that of gender parity, to guide his cabinet appointments (Real-Dato 2009: 16). In mid 2010 there were an equal number of men and women in the Spanish cabinet.

As can be seen from the previous discussion, the executives of these three parliamentary democracies are generalist in character. The formal requirement of parliamentary membership is a predominant, but not an exclusive, condition. A wide range of informal conditions related to party, individual ambition, seniority, the representation of geography, gender and, when required, coalition partner, play more strongly than formal rules of access to the executive.

Evolution of women's presence in the executive

In parliamentary democracies, the number of women in cabinets generally reflects the number of women elected to the lower houses of parliament. Figures 9.1, 9.2 and 9.3 illustrate this point in relation to our three cases.

Spain has made significant efforts to introduce positive action to reduce inequality in the numbers of men and women participating in electoral politics. On the re-establishment of democracy in Spain in 1977, women held only 6 percent of seats in the Congress of Deputies. By 1993, women's representation had risen to a modest 16 percent. In March 2007, the left-leaning PSOE government introduced a gender equality law (*Ley de Garantía de la Igualdad entre Hombres y Mujeres*) which introduced the principle of "balanced presence" into the

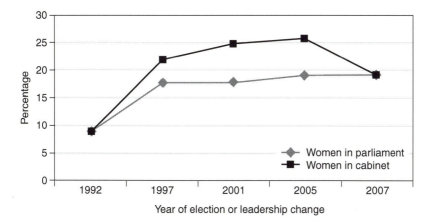

Figure 9.1 Women in parliament and cabinet in Britain, 1992–2007 (source: authors' own, created using data from Inter-Parliamentary Union (2010a), Centre for Advancement of Women in Politics (2010)).

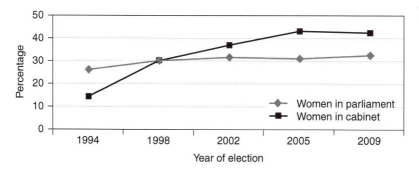

Figure 9.2 Women in parliament and cabinet in Germany, 1994 onwards (source: authors' own, created using data from Inter-Parliamentary Union (2010a)).

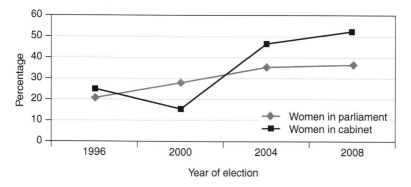

Figure 9.3 Women in parliament and cabinet in Spain, 1996 onwards (source: authors' own, created using data from Inter-Parliamentary Union (2010a)).

electoral laws. This required party lists to have a minimum of 40 percent and a maximum of 60 percent of either gender in all elections. The proportion of women in parliament as a result has increased from 14 percent in 1989 to 36 percent in 2010. The law also imposes gender parity in all selection committees in state administration, public organizations and on the boards of directors of large private corporations. The current Spanish prime minister is strongly committed to gender parity and, as noted earlier, there are an equal number of men and women serving in his cabinet. Women's representation in the Spanish cabinet government has increased gradually since the late 1990s. Up to that time only five women served in cabinet government. Since the late 1990s, a total of 22 cabinet appointments have been assigned to women. The rise in the number of women in cabinet is the combination of an increasing number of women in parliament and the introduction of positive action measures such as the gender equality law.

In Germany, political parties began to introduce formal mechanisms to increase the levels of female representation in the late 1980s. The Green Party was the first to introduce a gender quota of 50 percent for party candidates in 1983. This prompted a lively debate in the Social Democratic Party (SPD) which followed with a 40 percent gender quota in 1988. The conservative Christian Democratic Union (CDU) set a target, or soft quota, in 1996 under which one-third of all party candidacies and officer positions would be held by women. These measures have contributed to increasing women's representation in the Bundestag from 8.5 percent in 1980 to 33 percent in 2010. The commitment of leftist parties in particular to the principle of parity has helped shape the gender profile of cabinet government. The so-called red-green[7] governments under the chancellorship of Gerhard Schröder saw women appointed to a number of ministries. McKay (2003: 8) asserts that "after 16 years in opposition, the election of the red-green coalition ... gave the SPD an opportunity to put its principles regarding gender equality into practice." Schröder appointed women to five of 15 ministerial portfolios in 1998, with this figure rising to seven in 2001. He continued his commitment to gender equality in 2002 when six of the 14 government ministries were headed by women. Throughout the time of Schröder's governments, an average of 42 percent of all cabinet appointees were women. This represents a significant improvement on the cabinets of Helmut Kohl,[8] where only an average of 12.6 percent of cabinet portfolios were assigned to women. The formation of the grand coalition[9] in 2005, under the chancellorship of Angela Merkel, marked a milestone moment for Germany. It was the first time that the country had a female chancellor. Merkel's government saw five women hold ministerial office with this figure rising by one to six in October 2008. The election of the CDU/CSU[10] and the Free Democratic Party (FDP) coalition government in September 2009 saw five women appointed to cabinet.

Attempts to improve women's political representation in the UK have been less successful, despite a vigorous debate on the issue during the 1990s. In 1993, the Labour Party adopted a policy of all-women candidate shortlists in one-half of the party's winnable seats in the 1997 general election. A controversial measure for increasing women's low political representation, it was deemed illegal in 1997. Nonetheless, the 38 women already selected under this process continued to stand and 35 went on to win a seat in the 1997 general election. In 2002, all-women shortlists were legalized when the Blair government passed the Sex Discrimination (Election Candidates) Act 2002 to enable political parties to take positive action to reduce inequality in the numbers of men and women. Of our three cases, though, the UK continues to have the lowest proportion of female representatives, constituting 22 percent of the House of Commons in 2010. This is also evident in cabinet appointments where women rarely hold more than 25 percent of cabinet portfolios.

As noted previously, access to the highest rungs of executive leadership is often a consequence of parliamentary experience, service and performance. With this achieved, the next stage on the route to cabinet membership is appointment to a junior ministry that brings ministerial responsibility but does not include a seat at the cabinet table. A cursory examination of the parliamentary careers of women cabinet ministers in the UK, Germany and Spain indicates that all have held at least one junior ministry at some point in their careers. Indeed, more women are appointed to junior ministries than senior ministries. In the UK, of the 107 women who have held a ministerial position since 1945, only 25 have achieved full cabinet membership. Thus, 77 percent of all women ministers in Britain have never been promoted from junior to senior ministerial rank. The comparable figure for Germany is 62 percent since 1949 (or 47 out of a total of 76 women ministers). However, in Spain, a majority of women junior ministers since 1979 (52 percent, that is 32 out of 62) have gone on to serve as cabinet ministers.

As can been seen from the earlier discussion, the position of prime minister is a particularly powerful one in parliamentary democracies. Margaret Thatcher served as British prime minister from 1979 to 1990 and Angela Merkel has occupied the office of German chancellor since 2005. No woman has yet to serve as president of the government in Spain, but two women have served in the powerful position of vice president of the government, María Teresa Fernández de la Vega Sanz (2004) and Elena Salgado Méndez (2009). In her study of European executives, Davis (1997) found a positive correlation between the proportion of women in government and the sex of the prime minister. Similar findings have occurred at other levels of government. In their study of local government in the UK, Bochel and Bochel (2008: 431) found that "there was a statistically significant relationship between the sex of the council leader and the proportion of the cabinet who are women ... with women leaders being more likely to have more women in their cabinet." Angela Merkel has been a supporter of female cabinet appointees. During her first term as chancellor, a total of seven women served in her cabinet,[11] while in her second government formed in September 2009, women were appointed to five of the 15 ministerial portfolios. However there are no steadfast rules about this. For much of her 12-year period as premier, Margaret Thatcher was the only woman serving in cabinet.

As we have seen, the majority of female appointees to cabinet have served in socio-cultural roles indicating a gendered division of labor in cabinet portfolios.

Only in Spain has there been some effort to allocate women non-traditional executive responsibilities. In 2002 Ana Palacio Vallelersundi was appointed to the position of external (foreign) affairs. This was followed by the appointment of Carme Chacón i Piqueras as minister for defense in 2008. In 2009, Elena Salgado Méndez was appointed as minister for finance and vice president of the government. Interestingly, a woman head of government does not necessarily break the gendered pattern of women's participation in cabinet government. Of the five[12] women Angela Merkel appointed to her cabinet in September 2009, four were appointed to socio-cultural portfolios.

Factors explaining women's access to the executive

The above evidence suggests that while women are making their way into senior cabinet positions, their responsibilities replicate a gendered division of labor arising from stereotypical sex role expectations unless, as in the case of Spain, conscious efforts are made to counter this trend. This pattern is difficult to fathom, as the socioeconomic indicators of these countries place them among the most economically and socially advanced nations of the world. In terms of gross national product, the UK is the eighteenth wealthiest country in the world, followed by Germany (twenty-second) and Spain (thirty-seventh).[13] The 2009 Human Development Index (HDI) ranked Spain fifteenth among the "very highly developed" category of countries, with the UK and Germany in twentieth and twenty-first places, respectively.[14] All are highly urbanized states, ostensibly offering more opportunities for women's self-realization than rural-dominated societies: 90 percent of the UK population lives in towns and cities, while 77 percent of Spanish people and 75 percent of German residents do likewise.[15] Furthermore, when one interrogates the development indices to account for gender inequalities in achievement and attainment, the results remain positive, with Germany ninth in the world in the gender empowerment measure (GEM), Spain ranked eleventh and the UK in fifteenth place out of 109 countries. As one can see, these economic and social trends are too general to enable us pick apart the variables that are likely to contribute to the dominance of women in socio-cultural ministerial offices. Instead for possible explanations we turn to social statistics. We will examine the religious composition of these states, attitudes to gender equality, women's educational achievement, fertility and employment patterns.

The three countries share a pattern of increasing secularization and a declining interest in religious life since the 1960s. Spain is a strongly Catholic country, with 76 percent of the Spanish population professing attachment to that religion. Although after World War II German Protestants outnumbered Catholics, by 1987 the religions were equally represented, at 42 and 43 percent of the population, respectively (Glatzer *et al.* 1992: 291, 295). In 2010, German Protestants and Catholics each comprised 30 percent of the population, and in the UK 72 percent of the population professed attachment to Christian churches. In all three countries, Islam is a statistically identifiable, but small, religion, with adherents accounting for 4 percent or less of the population. The growing secularization of these societies is indicated by the proportions indicating atheism or non-religious attachment. Over one-third of the German population, one-quarter of those living in the UK and over one-fifth of Spanish residents today are of no religion. The decreased attachment to formal church-going from the mid 1960s onwards and the current significant minority in each country that declare as non-religious suggests a "liberalization" of underlying social norms and values that find expression in increased support for gender equality. A 2008 survey on discrimination in the European Union found that in Spain, over one-half of the population (54 percent) considered that gender discrimination was still widespread, while 38 percent of British respondents were also of this view. Attitudes in Germany were the most supportive of gender equality, with just under one-quarter (23 percent) of the population feeling that gender discrimination was widespread (European Commission 2008: 74). This can be traced back, to some degree, to the loosening of religious ties experienced in Germany and the liberalization of social policy impacting on women's lives. As Glatzer *et al.* (1992: 104) remark: "the paradigmatic model of the housewife in marriage ... remained untouched until the marriage and divorce law underwent reform in 1977."

Education, too, played a part in expanding women's social horizons. In each country, the expansion of tertiary level education from the 1960s onwards provided greater opportunities for young women that had been denied to their mothers. Indeed, Folgueras and Martin (2008: 1520) comment on this point in relation to Spain "where less than 5 per cent of Spanish women born in the late 1930s had access to university education, nearly one-third of women born in the early 1970s have attended college." Similarly, Glatzer *et al.* (1992: 105) observe that women's take-up of expanding educational opportunities during the 1960s in Germany led to a reduction in gender-based discrimination in this area, while Dyhouse (2006: 97–117) documents a similar growth in women's higher education in the UK from the late 1960s. By 2007, women noticeably outnumbered men as college graduates across the three countries.

One consequence of women's higher education levels and wider support for gender equality in society is the increased presence of women in the workforce. In 1970, at the point of educational and social change, almost half of all working-age women were in the labor force in Germany and the UK, attesting to the more conducive conditions for women's opportunities existing in those countries. In Spain, by contrast, less than one-third of women between 15 and 64 years were in the labor force. Over the course of the following decades, women's labor force participation grew in all three countries, but most dramatically in Spain during the years 2000–8. By 2008, two-thirds of all women of working age were connected to the labor force in Germany and the UK, while over half were in Spain.

It is a long-proven fact that women's employment opportunities are structured by children and childcare considerations. One contributory factor to women's entry to the labor force in each country is the decline in women's fertility rates since the 1970s. In 1970, the average female fertility rate was two children or more in the two cases, and almost three in Spain. By 2007 this had declined to under two. The most dramatic decline is evident in the case of Spain, where fertility rates halved between 1970 and 2007, from 2.9 to 1.4 children per woman.[16]

There appears to be a causal connection, then, between higher educational attainment, increased labor force participation and declining fertility levels in these three countries over two generations, with the most significant changes occurring in Catholic, conservative Spain. It is not surprising, therefore, to find that the strongest resistance to gender equality occurs in Spain, as women's increased opportunities for self-realization come into conflict with the more traditional gender role expectations underlying these trends.

The socio-cultural, economic and political factors above created the important resource of "social capital" for women with political ambitions. Shifts toward acceptance of equality between women and men accompanied by lower fertility rates brought about a liberalization of women's roles from the 1970s onwards. In turn, women's aspirations to self-fulfillment expanded beyond, as well as in, the home. Through high educational achievement and increased workforce participation, female ambition became socially accepted. Women with political ambitions acquired networks, public skills and civic knowledge as a result of these expanding socioeconomic opportunities. Given these developments over a generation, the absence of women from cabinet government came under increasing question in the UK, Spain and Germany in the late 1990s. Thus, when Tony Blair and Gerhard Schröder consciously appointed women in numbers to their respective cabinets in 1997 and 1998, they were responding to a pent-up demand grounded in societal expectations of modern government. In 2004, the new prime minister of Spain, Zapatero, recognized that a modern cabinet required the inclusion of women ministers. He went further than Blair and Schröder, appointing a gender equal executive. That these three men were elected to head a government based on modernizing agendas also contributed to the breaking of this particular glass ceiling. But it would not have been possible for them to bring women into cabinet had the background factors discussed above not influenced women's capacities to serve in executive office.

Do women executives represent women?

Feminist scholars have long considered the impact of women's representation in political life. Phillips (1998: 224–40) identified four arguments to support women's political representation. First, women politicians act as role models for aspiring women candidates; second, women should be equally represented for justice reasons as they compose 50 percent of most populations; third, women's interests are inadequately addressed in a politics dominated by men; and finally, women's political representation revitalizes democracy. Others have demonstrated that having female candidates and representatives boosts women's political interest, knowledge and efficacy (Burns *et al.* 2001: 355). Catalano (2009: 50) argues that women should be equally represented for symbolic reasons as "the historical absence of women in political institutions may be associated with perceptions of women's second-class citizenship and the notion that politics is a 'male domain'." These arguments were developed to support and advocate women's presence in legislatures. As we have seen, there is often continuity between the legislature and the executive, thus the essence of these debates can reasonably be utilized to address the impact of executive women on women's legislative representation and on women's interests.

To begin, the presence of women in executive office is normatively desirable as political institutions should reflect the social composition of society. Second, women's presence in executive leadership may act to sever the strong association between masculinity and political leadership. As more women are appointed to cabinet, women's political leadership becomes increasingly seen as normal and achievable. Third, the appointment of women to cabinet in one country may have a contagion or diffusion effect on women's participation in public life in other nations. Much positive international political commentary greeted Spanish prime minister Zapatero's appointment of a gender balanced cabinet in April 2008. The Spanish cabinet and those of the Scandinavian regions were held as beacons of female representation in Europe. The promotion and progress of women in these countries has obliged many nations to evaluate their policies with regard to the advancement of women in politics. Buckley and Galligan (2010) suggest that European countries can be grouped into two distinct categories when it comes to the promotion of women in public office – the recognizers and facilitators. Recognition of the importance of women's role in political decision-making is oftentimes accompanied by the development of promotional strategies such as funding academic research into the role of women in politics. These measures fall short of adopting concrete mechanisms to increase the number of women in political life. In contrast, countries such as those in the Scandinavian region, the Netherlands, Belgium, Spain, Austria, Germany, Portugal, France and Slovenia have introduced institutional changes such as quotas and laws promoting affirmative action that have facilitated an increased number of women in public life.

Fourth, and arguably the most important impact of women in executive leadership, is their influence on policy outcomes. In parliamentary democracies such as the UK, Germany and Spain, policy typically originates in cabinet. For the passage of female-friendly social policy, Atchison and Down (2009) argue that the presence of women in cabinet is of greater importance than the presence of women in legislatures. Given, as we have seen, that women predominate in holding socio-cultural ministries, it would appear that women in executive office are well placed to directly influence policy associated with a wide range of women's interests. In their study of a number of Organisation for Economic Cooperation and Development (OECD) countries including the UK, Germany and Spain, Atchison and Down (2009) found that the representation of women in social welfare ministries in particular was key to explaining the extent of female-friendly social policies.[17] Many argue that the appointment of women to these portfolios is a means of excluding women from the highest political offices of finance, defense and home affairs. This may be the case, but Atchison and Down

(2009: 6) note, "ministers enjoy a significant measure of negative agenda control – that is they are well placed to block policies they do not support." Holding a portfolio may give ministers a veto over any policy (O'Malley 2006: 320).

Mushaben (2005) assessed the presence of women in the Schröder-led cabinet of the SPD and Greens in Germany between 1998 and 2002. Five women were brought into this cabinet, four of whom held socio-cultural portfolios. She found that during this five-year period, women's issues became a routine part of the policy agenda.

> The prevailing political discourse has been modified at a number of levels, beginning literally, with the addition of *innen* (the feminine noun form ending) to all job ads, political speeches, etc.... There is ample evidence now that collective displays of *girl power* are beginning to reshape policy even in non-traditional, heavily male-normed domains, e.g., agriculture and national security policy.
>
> (Mushaben 2005: 157)

Thus, the German experience would suggest that the type of ministerial portfolio held should not be underestimated in terms of the influence it can impart.

As we can see, there are a number of actual and potential impacts of executive women on women's legislative representation and interests. However, not all advancements in women's political and interest representation can be attributed solely to the increasing number of women serving in executive office. Structural and contextual features of the political system also play a role. The existence of proportional based electoral systems, positive discrimination measures and gender equity laws, as well as the presence of a dedicated and resilient women's movement, all combine to improve the representation of women in politics. It must also be recognized that some women holding executive office have done little to advocate for women's interests. As noted earlier, for much of Thatcher's 12-year premiership she was the only woman serving in cabinet. Thatcher can be seen as representing archetypal "masculinised women [who] work as much as possible to blend in with their male counterparts and avoid challenging the gendered norms of an institution" (Rincker 2009: 47). One contextual explanation for this masculinized behavior on the part of executive women is that the more adversarial the political system, the more masculinist its expectations. Sykes (2008: 3) argues that in the combative environment of the British adversarial system, Thatcher practiced "conviction-style leadership" to convey "requisite masculinist attributes" in an effort to appear "tough, firm and determined" and therefore worthy of leading a country.

Conclusion

The gendered nature of political executives continues to present challenges for female politicians. The masculinist norms and expectations of this high level political world remain. However, from this analysis of women's presence in executive office in the UK, Germany and Spain, we can conclude that change is afoot. The number of women holding ministerial office is growing, and there are slow changes in the types of portfolios held by women. This, combined with the increasing number of women being elected to national parliaments, suggests that the situation is encouraging for women's entry to cabinet in Europe. These developments point to exciting possibilities with regard to women, politics and gender in the years to come.

Notes

1 'Angela Merkel Hosts a Meeting of Key European Leaders'. Online. Available at: www.flickr.com/photos/londonsummit/3301762324/ (accessed June 2010).
2 Angela Merkel is one of only a handful of women who have held the position of prime minister in Europe. Others include Margaret Thatcher, British prime minister from May 1979 to November 1990; Édith Cresson, French prime minister from May 1991 to April 1992; Gro Harlem Brundtland, Norwegian prime minister from February to October 1981 and again from May 1986 to October 1989 and from November 1990 to October 1996; Anneli Jäätteenmäki, Finnish prime minister from April to June 2003; Jóhanna Sigurðardóttir, Icelandic prime minister from February 2009 to present; and Jadranka Kosor, Croatian prime minister from July 2009 to present. Iveta Radicova became the first female prime minister of Slovakia in June 2010.
3 The European Council is a regular meeting of ministers in a particular policy area from all EU member states, e.g. all ministers for finance will meet as a European Council to make decisions on EU finance policy.
4 For further information, see the European Commission DG EMPL (2009, 2010).
5 See European Commission DG EMPL (2009).
6 In 1949, the West German *Grundgesetz* "was explicitly formulated as a substitute for a constitution until such time as the country reunified" (Bendix 2007: 6). After reunification, this became the constitution of the reunified Germany.
7 A coalition government consisting of the SPD and Green parties. It served in government from 1998 to 2002, and again from 2002 to 2005.
8 Helmut Kohl was chancellor of Germany from 1982 to 1998. A member of the CDU party since his teenage years, he became chairperson of that party in 1973.
9 A coalition goverment consisting of CDU/CSU and SPD parties. It served in government from 2005 to 2009.
10 Christian Socialist Union.
11 In the 2005–9 Merkel government, women holding ministerial office were: Heidenmarie Wieczorek-Zewl (Economic Co-operation and Development Aid); Ilse Ainger (Consumer Protection, Food and Agriculture); Brigitte Zypries (Justice); Ulla Schmidt (Health); Ursula von der Leyen (Family, Seniors and Youth); Dr. Annette Schavan (Education and Research); Ursula von der Leyen (Family, Senior Citizens, Women and Youth). The 2009 onwards Merkel government contains the following female members of cabinet: Sabine Leutheusser-Schnarrenberger (Justice); Ursula von der Leyen (Labour and Social Affairs); Ilse Ainger (Consumer Protection, Food and Agriculture); Kristina Schröder (Family, Senior Citizens, Women and Youth); Dr. Annette Schavan (Research and Education).
12 Kristina Schröder, Federal Minister for Family Affairs, Senior Citizens, Women and Youth; Annette Schavan, Federal Minister of Education and Research; Ilse Aigner, Federal Minister of Food, Agriculture and Consumer Protection; Ursula von der Leyen, Federal Minister of Labour and Social Affairs; Sabine Leutheusser-Schnarrenberger, Federal Minister of Justice.
13 Rankings in 2008, from World Development Indicators (n.d.).

14 See UNDP (2009a). The 2009 HDI represents statistical values from 2007. The HDI presents an index composed of measurements of three dimensions – life expectancy, education and having a decent standard of living.
15 UNICEF (n.d.).
16 UNICEF (2010).
17 Atchison and Down (2009) did find, however, that high leave entitlements in Spain during the 1980s may well have derived from policy diffusion rather than significant pressure from women cabinet ministers to do so as, on becoming a democracy, the Spanish government instituted policies similar to those in other European countries.

10   The Nordic countries

Christina Bergqvist

Introduction

The region that is today called Norden consists of five independent countries: Denmark (including the Faroe Islands and Greenland), Finland (including Åland), Iceland, Norway and Sweden. From a comparative perspective, the Nordic countries are politically, socially and culturally rather similar. They all have high standards of living and generous public welfare systems. In a study by Inglehart and Norris (2003), the Nordic countries are the prime examples of post-materialist societies: egalitarian values, including gender equality, and high levels of individuation and secularization. All countries are parliamentary democracies and utilize a proportional representation electoral system. Despite their very modern image, three of the five Nordic countries are monarchies. The queen of Denmark, the king of Norway and the king of Sweden are formally the heads of the state.[1] Finland and Iceland have presidents and are often classified as semi-presidential systems. With the exception of Finland and to some extent Iceland, the heads of state in the Nordic countries have no real political power, their duties being merely representative. In Finland the president is directly elected by the people and holds real power in terms of foreign policy, European Union policy, major military decisions and the appointment of top civil servants. In Iceland the president is elected by direct popular vote for a term of four years, with no term limit.

The Nordic countries are well-known for their high level of gender equality in general and the significant representation of women in politics in particular. In 1980, Vigdís Finnbogadóttir became the first woman in the world elected president in a democratic election. Women's share in today's executives hovers between 40 and 60 percent and is generally slightly higher than the proportion of women in the Nordic parliaments. This chapter will provide an overview of the development of women's participation in executives in the Nordic countries and propose possible explanations for women's significant representation in Nordic governments today. The chapter will focus on Norway and Sweden as two representative cases of Nordic women's inclusion in executives.

Regional overview

Women's access to the Nordic executives has been highly connected to their integration into politics in general and especially to women's representation in the parliament. A majority of ministers have a background as parliamentarians or have had prominent positions in political parties or in regional or local political institutions (SOU 2007: 42; Holli 2008a). After the introduction of universal suffrage, between 1906 and 1920, women started to enter the Nordic parliaments. Normally very few women were elected in the first universal suffrage elections. In Finland, however, women and men attained the right to vote and stand for election at the same time, already in 1906, and as many as 10 percent of the parliamentarians in the first universal suffrage election were women (see Table 10.1). The other countries took between 50 and 60 years to reach this same outcome (see Table 10.2).

There is a gap between the time when women first entered parliament and the time when the first woman was appointed minister in a cabinet. In Denmark and Finland this happened in the 1920s, thus 10–20 years after the first women had entered the parliament. Again Finland was remarkable because the first female minister, Miina Sillanpää, in contrast to the relatively short incumbency of Denmark's first female minister, Nina Bang, stayed in office for as long as 20 years. In Norway and Sweden the first female ministers were not appointed until after World War II and in Iceland not until 1970 (Raaum 1999).

Women's representation in parliament increased after World War II and there was a real upswing in the 1960s and 1970s, except in Iceland where the increase

Table 10.1 Historical data on women's access to parliament and the executive in the Nordic countries

	Denmark	Finland	Iceland	Norway	Sweden
Parliament					
Introduction of universal suffrage	1915	1906	1920	1913	1919
First election to parliament with women candidates	1918	1907	1922	1921	1921
Share of women elected in the first election to parliament with women candidates (%)	3.0	10.0	2.0	1.0	2.0
Executives					
First woman minister in a cabinet	1924	1926	1970	1945	1947
First woman prime minister	Never	2003	2009	1981	Never
First woman president	–	2000	1980	–	–

Source: Denmark's Governments since 1848; Finnish Cabinets and Ministers since 1917; Norwegian Government Ministries and Offices since 1814; Raaum (1999: 32); Stjórnarrád Íslands; Sweden (2007).

Table 10.2 The proportion of women in parliament and in government (cabinet ministers) in the Nordic countries, 1950–2009

	1950	1960	1970	1980	1990	2000	2005	2009
Denmark								
Parliament	8	9	11	20	31	37	37	38
Government	7	6	8	17	16	45	26	42
Finland								
Parliament	9	15	17	26	32	37	38	42
Government	6	8	11	13	26	45	44	60
Iceland								
Parliament	3	3	2	5	21	35	30	43
Government	0	0	7	0	10	33	25	42
Norway								
Parliament	5	7	9	24	36	36	38	36
Government	7	7	13	25	44	42	47	47
Sweden								
Parliament	10	13	15	25	38	43	45	47
Government	3	7	11	25	30	55	50	45

Sources: Denmark's Governments since 1848; Finnish Cabinets and Ministers since 1917; Norwegian
Government Ministries and Offices since 1814; Raaum (1999: 32); Stjórnarrád Íslands; Sweden (2007).

came in the 1980s. In most cases substantial changes also took place in the cabinets. As will be further expanded on below, the role of the social democratic
parties and the mobilization of women's movements are usually seen as important factors for women's political integration in Norden. The social democratic
parties have traditionally had a strong role in the Nordic countries and have led
many governments throughout the period (Raaum 1999). Strong left and social
democratic influences in politics often facilitate women's access to political
office. However, as we will see, there is no clear pattern that social democratic
governments have taken the lead in appointing women ministers. Rather, there
seems to be a certain point at which there is no turning back. In most cases each
new government since World War II has, regardless of its political affiliation,
included more women than the former. In 2009 there were at least 42 percent
women in each of the Nordic executives (see Table 10.2).

By and by women's share in government has become about the same as in
parliament and from the 1990s until today a new pattern has emerged whereby
the proportion of women is higher in the executive than in the parliament. Thus,
in the last 20 to 25 years there has been a striking increase in women in executives. A very important occurrence was the appointment in 1981 of the first Norwegian female prime minister, Gro Harlem Brundtland, who led a social
democratic government for about a year. In 1986 she was back again and formed
a new government with eight women out of 18 ministers. In the former center-
right government there had been only four women. Since Bruntland's "women's
government" the executives not only in Norway, but also in Sweden and Finland

have followed suit. In Sweden the first government with 50 percent women was formed in 1994 and in Finland the government of 2009 had 60 percent women. Women's share in governments in Denmark and Iceland has been a bit more unstable, for example in Denmark the center-right government of 2005 only had 26 percent women while the center-right government of 2009 appointed 42 percent women (Table 10.2).

Despite the increase in the number of women ministers there have been only two female prime ministers apart from Brundtland. In Finland Anneli Jäätteen-mäki sat for only a couple of months in 2003 before she had to resign due to a scandal (Holli 2008a). Iceland got its first woman prime minister in 2009, Jóhanna Sigurðardóttir, a social democrat who is said to be the first openly homosexual head of government in the world. In Finland and Iceland the two women who have been presidents have been very popular.[2] Vigdís Finnbogadóttir was the president of Iceland between 1980 and 1996. Tarja Halonen was elected the first female president in Finland in 2000 and she was re-elected in 2006 for another six-year term. Before being elected president she was a social democratic member of parliament and between 1995 and 2000 she held the position of minister of foreign affairs (Holli 2008a).

Country cases: Norway and Sweden

Description of the political regimes

Norway and Sweden are chosen as two representative cases of the Nordic region. They are established parliamentary democracies where the government (the executive) has to be actively accepted or passively tolerated by a majority in the parliament (so-called negative parliamentarianism). In Norway the king plays a more prominent, but ceremonial, role than in Sweden when a new government is formed. It is the king of Norway who approves a government's application to resign and appoints the new government. The king asks, in most cases, the leader of the winning party to form a new government. In practice the political parties in the *Storting* (the Norwegian parliament) have the actual power over the formation of the government. In Sweden the speaker of the *Riksdag* (the Swedish parliament) holds consultations with party leaders and then proposes a candidate for the post of prime minister and the *Riksdag* votes on the proposal. If more than half the total number of members of the *Riksdag* votes against the proposal, it is rejected. If the *Riksdag* approves the speaker's proposal, the prime minister chooses which and how many members (ministers) are to be included in the government. Both countries employ a closed list proportional representation electoral system. These factors contribute to a political system in which coalition governments of several parties or minority governments are the norm.

During the period before World War II the social democratic parties in both countries became an important political force and since the introduction of universal suffrage they occasionally headed the government or were part of a coalition government. After World War II they strengthened their positions and established themselves as the dominant political party in each country. Norway was led by social democratic prime ministers between 1935 and 1963 and Sweden between 1932 and 1976, with the exception of a couple of months. During World War II the social democrats ruled in coalition with other parties; occasionally they managed to form a majority government, but the norm in both countries has been minority governments with the support of left-wing parties in the parliament. Left parties (including social democrats) in power are usually considered to be a positive factor for the inclusion of women into political positions but, as we will see, this has not always been the case here.

There are also some differences between the two country cases that make them interesting to compare and will shed light on the somewhat different routes they have taken. Although religious influence is comparatively weak in the Nordic countries, religious/cultural differences exist between Norway and Sweden. In fact, the influence of the Christian People's Party (*Kristelig Folkeparti*) in Norway has been cited as a factor which may account for the prevalence of more traditional gender views in Norway compared to Sweden (Leira 1992). In Norway, unlike in the other countries, the Christian People's Party was established early (in 1933) and has held a relatively strong electoral position (Karvonen 1994). From then on, peaking in 1973, the party has played a rather prominent role in Norwegian politics. In Sweden, the Christian Democratic Party was established in 1964, and it has only experienced some electoral success as late as in the 1990s. Overall, the party has played a minor role in Swedish politics (Sörensen and Bergqvist 2002).

Historically, there have also been some differences in the ideologies of the women's movements in the two countries; the Norwegian strategy has been based on an ideology of gender difference whereas the Swedish approach has been based on an ideology of gender neutrality or gender equality. The rhetoric of difference utilized by the women's movement in Norway has facilitated the use of quotas to enhance the proportion of women in political institutions and in the boards of public administration as well as in boards of private companies (corporate boards). There is a provision in the Norwegian Gender Equality Act, since 1988, that requires authorities to ensure a representation of at least 40 percent of both sexes on non-elected public boards, councils and committees – including the cabinet, but not the parliament (Raaum 1999: 36). In 2006 Norway also introduced a quota of 40 percent women in corporate boards. Voluntary party quotas have also been used more by political parties in Norway than in Sweden. In Sweden there has been a stronger emphasis on gender equality (sameness) and a reluctance to use measures such as quotas. Today in Sweden there are some parties that have adopted quotas, but rather than using quotas more widely parties are involved in a competition to appear equal; pressure from women's groups outside and inside the parties has been a rather successful strategy (Borchorst *et al.* 1999).

Evolution of women's presence in the executive

Today the proportion of women in executive positions is more or less in parity with the proportion of men, in both Norway and Sweden. This is a rather recent phenomenon and it has taken a long time to achieve.[3] There are some interesting differences between Norway and Sweden, such as that Norway leads Sweden when it comes to including women in executive positions. But Sweden has always had a higher percentage of women in parliament. Here we will take a closer look at the development of women's representation in the executives of the two countries. Even when women get access to the highest positions of power we often find a pattern of vertical and horizontal gender segregation that takes place inside an institution, in this case the executive. The vertical segregation makes it harder for women to attain the most powerful and prestigious positions as for example the post of prime minister and the horizontal segregation can be seen in a division of positions into certain "female" and "male" areas.

To pass the threshold to executive power has been harder than to pass the threshold to national legislatures. In neither country did any woman enter the executive until after World War II. In 1945 Kirsten Hansteen became minister without portfolio in the Ministry of Social Affairs. Sweden had to wait two more years. When the first Swedish government after World War II was installed in 1946 it consisted only of men, but a year later Karin Kock became the first Swedish female minister without portfolio. She was also the first woman economics professor in Sweden. Between 1948 and 1949 she was the Minister of Public Housekeeping. An analysis of all women who since 1945/6 have held an executive position when the executive was installed[4] reveals that Norway has had 91 women ministers (an average of 26 percent) and Sweden 78 (an average of 27 percent).

In both countries the period after World War II and well into the early 1970s is characterized by a pattern of one or two "symbolic" women ministers in junior positions without portfolio or with a portfolio in the Ministry of Social Affairs.[5] Many of the first women in executive positions were met with resistance; for example, Karin Kock said that it would have been easier for her if she had been a man (Niskanen 2007). It was not until 1965 in Norway and 1969 in Sweden that a newly formed government included more than one woman. It is interesting to note that in the case of Norway the "one-woman rule" was broken by a centre-right government, not a social democratic one. In 1973 the Norwegian Social Democrats were back in power and nominated four women out of 16 ministers, thus 25 percent.

In Sweden the social democratic government of 1969 to 1976 initially included two women without portfolio. In 1973 the government was re-elected and Prime Minister Olof Palme reshuffled the cabinet and included three female ministers without portfolio. It was not until 1976, however, when for the first time in 44 years a non-social democratic government was installed, that there was a substantial break with the pattern of "symbolic" women in junior positions. Five out of 20 ministers were women, an increase from 11 to 25 percent. Sweden got its first female Minister of Foreign Affairs when Karin Söder from the Centre Party Sweden was named to the post.

The commonly held belief that left governments are more prone to nominate women is not confirmed in these cases. The pattern is more complex; although the Norwegian case gives some support for the thesis, the Swedish case contradicts it. In Norway it was a woman, social democratic Prime Minister Gro Harlem Brundtland, who really made a difference during her second government in 1986. Not only did she again become the prime minister of Norway, she also increased the number of women cabinet ministers from four (22 percent) to eight (42 percent) thereby establishing a new norm for what is seen as acceptable in Norway as well as the other Nordic countries.

In Sweden we saw another pattern with center-right, rather than social democratic, executives taking the lead in nominating women. Paradoxically, a possible reason for the Swedish reluctance to appoint women to the executive could be the strong and powerful position the Swedish social democrats held through their long reign of executive power. Probably their long tenure made them less open to the influences of the new women's movement claims for representation that were very strong at the time. Historical research indicates that leading men in the party had formed strong networks and defended their positions against women newcomers (Karlsson 1996). The Swedish center-right parties who, more or less, had been outside the government for more than 40 years had not been in a position to build a strong network of powerful men. This situation opened a window of opportunity for politically active women in the center-right parties and their women's sections. Between 1976 and 1982 Sweden was governed by four different center-right executives who set the norm of including around 24 percent women. When the social democrats were back in power in 1982 they followed suit and then each new cabinet, despite the political orientation, has increased the number of women cabinet ministers. The success of the Norwegian gender equal executive was also important as there is a certain competition between the Nordic neighbors. The Swedish reputation as a leading star for gender equality had been hurt. The reputation was perhaps restored in 1994, when social democratic Prime Minister Ingvar Carlsson presented a cabinet with 50 percent women and 50 percent men and declared that gender equality would be a top priority during the coming years, and that gender mainstreaming was a key strategy of his government. In his governmental declaration he stated:

> For the first time in the history of Swedish democracy the newly appointed government consists of an equal number of women and men. Through this decision I have deliberately wanted to create a model for gender equality efforts in all areas of society. The deputy Prime Minister will have the overarching responsibility to scrutinize in advance the government's policy and ensure that it contributes to gender equality in working life and the community.
>
> (Sweden DS 2001: 64, my translation)

Despite the fact that the executives have reached a balance between women and men, vertical segregation has continued, even more so in Sweden than in Norway. The position of prime minister has never been held by a woman in Sweden and women have rarely been given the positions considered most prestigious. This pattern has weakened over time, however, as more women enter cabinet.

The literature on women in politics has found that women ministers as well as women parliamentarians often are more prominent in areas like social affairs, education and culture than in finance, defense and foreign affairs (Reynolds 1999; Bergqvist 1998; Wängnerud 2000). This means that women may be stereotyped into some areas because they are seen as more suitable. Often these positions do not have the highest status, so there is of course a relationship between vertical and horizontal segregation. But, a prestigious position is not always the same as a powerful position and a less prestigious position can actually be very important and give the executive minister a lot of power. In both countries we initially see a very strong gender pattern whereby a few women cabinet ministers are found in the ministry of social affairs. The pattern has prevailed over time and since 1945 very few men have actually been responsible for issues related to social affairs, culture, education and gender equality. More recently, with the expansion of more women into executive positions women ministers are common in most other areas as well. As mentioned, we have to keep in mind that it is not self-evident that "soft areas" are always powerless and therefore that women cabinet ministers have had little influence on important political decisions. Being responsible, for example, for social affairs and healthcare is of great importance and might give a female minister a better opportunity to act in women's interests than if she is responsible for defense (Bergqvist 1998; Atchison and Down 2009). In fact, in advanced welfare states like Norway and Sweden women have been in charge of ministries with very large budgets and for issues that are seen as very important by the citizens in those countries.

Factors explaining women's access to the executive

There are a number of structural, institutional, cultural and political factors that are usually seen as important to the development of women's representation. Early on, Norway and Sweden attained most of those characteristics such as a proportional representation electoral system, influential left parties and egalitarian political cultures. After World War II first Sweden and later Norway also developed into societies with high socioeconomic and educational levels and a substantial increase in women's participation in the labor market (Raaum 2005; Inglehart and Norris 2003). Thus, in both Norway and Sweden we find all the factors that are usually considered favorable to women's political representation in elected office. As the most important route to an executive position typically passes through political parties and parliament it is reasonable to assume that the same factors that have led to women's greater inclusion in parliament have contributed to the high level of women in executives in Norway and Sweden. Below

I will discuss how these factors have been important for women's access to executive positions. However, as the variation in women's representation in advanced western democracies shows, these factors do not automatically lead to high numbers of women in political institutions. I will also discuss the importance of taking women's agency and own strategies into consideration.

First, high socioeconomic standards when it comes to education, women's participation in the labor market and access to social welfare have probably contributed to women's inclusion in politics (Norris 1997a; Raaum 2005). Of special importance is the type of welfare state that is found in the Nordic countries. This type of welfare state (often referred to as the social democratic welfare state regime) is redistributive not only between classes, but also between women and men. The issues of, for example, parental leave and childcare have been politicized and are not seen only as private concerns. There is a whole package of public policies making it possible for women and men to reconcile work and family (Sainsbury 1999). The politicization of issues traditionally seen as women's responsibility in the private sphere have mobilized women and brought women and their concerns into politics. Their engagement and expertise have given them access to channels leading to executive positions especially, as we have seen, in the policy areas of social affairs, family, gender equality and culture. Second, culture is often mentioned as an important factor. In these cases an egalitarian culture and positive attitudes toward women's participation in public life have of course facilitated women's access to executive power (Inglehart and Norris 2003).

Third, researchers have found some institutional factors like early suffrage and a proportional representation electoral system to be favorable for women's integration into politics (Norris 1985). In both countries women obtained the right to vote and stand for elections early on in the twentieth century and both countries use a proportional representation electoral system. In a PR system the use of party lists allows parties to "compose" lists that are attractive to different groups of voters. A mix of candidates representing diversity of class, gender, age and ethnicity signals that the party is open for everyone. This has been an important factor in the egalitarian culture of the Nordic countries. Today gender is the dimension that more or less all parties have to take into consideration. As mentioned earlier some parties, especially the social democratic and left-wing parties, have quota regulations to ensure a balance between women and men. Norway has been a pioneer in using voluntary party quotas (Skjeie 2001; Raaum 2005).

Fourth, a factor that is not usually discussed in relation to women's access to political office is the existence of public gender equality machineries. The possibility to promote gender equality, both in numbers and in substance, has been facilitated by the development of public gender equality machineries. During the late 1970s and 1980s the two countries, like the other Nordic countries, made gender equality into a distinct policy area with its own agencies and legislation, and by the mid 1980s the core institutions were in place. The overarching responsibility for gender equality has been in the hands of a *Minister for Gender*

Equality, who is a full-fledged member of the government. The existence of a minister signals that this area is of importance, although the minister in charge of gender equality has always had additional areas of responsibility. From an international perspective, the establishment of this ministerial post at an early date has given gender equality policies a high political profile. The structure of the gender equality machinery at the national level has remained quite stable since the early 1980s (Bergqvist *et al.* 2007; Borchorst 1999).

Although the structural factors, the institutions and the culture of Norway and Sweden have been of importance and have contributed to women's increased access to executive positions they do not automatically lead to a higher number of women. In addition, the importance of political strategies and actors has also been pointed out in the literature on women's representation in the Nordic countries. These studies show that the pressure and campaigning from women's movements outside the political system and a public debate where gender equality and women's representation is scrutinized in combination with consistent work by women within the political parties and political institutions have been vital for their success. Occasionally there have been decreases in women's representation which have led to strong reactions from women's groups. The gains in political representation cannot be taken for granted, but have to be defended and fought for (Sainsbury 2004, 2005).

One example of women's agency comes from Sweden in 1991 when there was a decrease in women's representation in parliament from 38 to 33 percent. This led to a mobilization of women that had not been seen for a long time. The women's movement saw the decrease as a backlash against gender equality and as related to the neo-liberal political wind that was blowing over Sweden. The decrease in women's representation in parliament occurred when the social democratic government lost parliamentary support and a center-right coalition government took over.[6] The political establishment was shaken by the strong reactions from women with diverse backgrounds, some of them already well-known gender researchers and journalists, from all over the country. These politically independent women from the universities, the media and other parts of society formed a network, called the Support Stockings, to promote women's representation and press the parties to nominate more women in the next election. If the parties did not respond to this, the network threatened to form a women's party. Their well-known rallying cry was "half the power, full pay" (Sainsbury 2005: 207). The network received a lot of media attention and public polls gave them support from many women and men. In the end they did not form a party, but they were successful in reaching their goal of more women in parliament. This mobilization of women outside the party-political arena helped women active in political parties and women representing their parties in elected assemblies to put pressure on their nominating committees to include more women on their party lists.

In the 1994 election campaigns more or less all parties recommended that their party districts nominate women and men in equal numbers. A popular strategy was called "every other seat for a woman," which meant that every other position on the party list should be a woman. In three out of six parties represented in parliament, the Left Party, the Social Democratic Party and the Green Party, the recommendations also led to changes in party statutes (Christensen 1999). Since then all elections have resulted in an increase in women's descriptive representation in parliament and about half of the ministers have been women. Before the election in 2006 a feminist party was formed by some of the women earlier involved in the Support Stockings and several young radical feminists. Under the leadership of the former Left Party leader, Gudrun Schyman, they decided to stand for parliament, but did not manage to get enough votes. The election resulted in a center-right coalition government. In contrast to 1991, when the majority for a center-right coalition resulted in a decline in women's representation, women's share in parliament increased from 45 to 47 percent. However, the new government consisted of fewer women than the former social democratic one, nine women (41 percent) and 13 men.

To conclude, an equal distribution of women and men cannot be taken for granted, but has to be actively defended. Women have shown that they are ready to defend women's political representation.

Do women executives represent women?

In parliamentary democracies like Norway and Sweden policies normally originate within the cabinet, and governments have considerable control over the policy-making process. This is also noted by Atchison and Down (2009), who found that the proportion of cabinet portfolios held by women is positively associated with female-friendly social policies. From a comparative perspective, Norway and Sweden have a long history of a substantial number of women in executive positions and there are many examples of their engagement in women's interests and in improving the situation of all women. The Norwegian "women's government" under Prime Minister Gro Harlem Brundtland is the most obvious example of how executive women have had an impact on women's representation. As far as I know, she was the first woman prime minister in a democratic country who had a clear agenda for improving gender equality. In general, several researchers have shown the importance of women's movements and women's involvement in policy-making as cabinet ministers, parliamentarians and femocrats (feminist bureaucrats) in the formulation and implementation of policies in the interests of women in the Nordic countries (Borchorst 2003; Hobson 2003; Bergman 2004; Holli 2008b). In this section I will relate the roles of executive women to the demands from women's movements in the two countries. Women's movements have taken an integrationist approach in both countries, meaning that they have been positive and supportive of women entering politics. From the late 1960s and 1970s women increasingly became political insiders with possibilities to form political alliances to promote their interests. Here I will first give some examples of issues where women in parliaments and in executives have worked together to promote interests articulated by each country's women's movement. These issues are related to women's right to employment and the possibility to reconcile work and family, representation and bodily rights.

Reconciliation of work and family

Women's movement articulation of demands and some of their strategies have differed in the two countries. For example, due to a historically stronger emphasis on women as mothers, the demand for full-time public childcare and women's possibilities to participate in the labor market was less strongly articulated in Norway than in Sweden during the 1960s and 1970s, the time when women were attaining more prominent positions in the executive. The male breadwinner ideals and the rhetoric of women and men's separate spheres have been stronger in Norway, including among social democrats and women's groups. In Sweden a dual earner/dual career model where women and men have the same roles has been favored by both liberal and left women and many men as well. In addition, Christian values and the Christian Democratic Party have played a more prominent role in Norway than in Sweden. Norwegian researcher Leira (1992) claims that women's agency played a minor role in the policy process around childcare in Norway. That was not the case in Sweden where liberal and left/social democratic women who represented the "vision of gender equality" were well represented in public committees, in parliament and in the executive. The rhetoric of difference, or the ideology of separate natures of men and women, was abandoned within the women's movement in Sweden. In fact, the sex role and gender equality debates in the 1960s and 1970s involving the vision of gender equality in all spheres of life did away with the rhetoric of difference. The Swedish cabinet of 1970 contained two very strong campaigners for equal rights and conditions for women and men, Alva Myrdal and Camilla Odhnoff, who were responsible for family policy (Bergqvist 1999). In Sweden women in executive positions in alliance with women in other influential positions contributed to the introduction already in the 1970s of some – for the time – very radical policies such as paid parental leave for mothers and fathers, the expansion of public childcare and individual taxation.

Over time we can observe a convergence between the two countries in the views of women's participation in the labor market and the demand for the availability of full-time publicly funded childcare. An important factor in this regard was the Norwegian Labour governments in the 1980s and 1990s under the leadership of Gro Harlem Brundtland. During her time gender equality was strengthened in Norway. An example of an innovative measure is the father's quota introduced in 1993. Norway then became the first Nordic country to introduce a paid month exclusively reserved for the father, as a measure to encourage more men to use their right to paid parental leave and make it easier for women to return to the labor market. In Sweden this was introduced a year later.

Women's sexual integrity

Issues related to women's bodily rights and sexual integrity belong to the core issues of women's movement demands that have been taken up by women in parliament and government. After the Swedish election in 1994 when women's representation increased and the social democratic government took over and promised to make gender equality one of its first priorities, a public inquiry into women's inviolability (*Kvinnofrid*) was initiated (Bergqvist *et al.* 2007). The inquiry led to new legislation and reforms, which to a certain extent were in accordance with the feminist perspective on male violence and rape as related to men's power over women. The new legislation included, for example, a new kind of offence called "gross violation of a woman's integrity," a wider defini- tion of rape and the prohibition to purchase sexual services. The last measure was introduced in 1999 and is perhaps the most unusual and controversial as it only criminalizes the person (almost always men) who buys sex. Earlier research has shown that the so-called "prostitution law" was the result of intensive lobby activities from the women's movement, joint efforts by women's federations from all the political parties, except the conservatives, and joint actions by women in the parliament (Svanström 2004).

Women in corporate boards

Despite the successful increase of women in top political positions, women's share in other leadership positions has been very low in the Nordic countries. Since the 1990s the focus has turned from political representation to women's share in other top positions, for example at universities, in private corporations and especially on corporate boards. In the early 2000s the proportion of women on corporate boards was around 5 percent both in Norway and Sweden. In 2009 it was around 40 percent in Norway and 20 percent in Sweden (SVD 2009). This is the result of Norway taking the "fast track" with a quota law introduced in 2006 that requires the boards to nominate at least 40 percent women, while Sweden continues to follow on the "incremental track" (Dahlerup and Freiden- vall 2005). Interestingly, the first initiative toward a quota for Norwegian corpor- ate boards was taken during a center-right government in 1999 by Minister of Gender Equality, Valgerd Svarstad Haugland. She came from the Christian People's Party and suggested a minimum of at least 25 percent women. With social democrats back in power a year later they suggested a minimum of 40 percent. In 2001, a center-right coalition proposed the 40 percent quota to the parliament. In December 2003 all political parties in parliament, except the Progress Party, voted in favor of the law. This political consensus stands in sharp contrast to Sweden where the center-right parties are sturdily against quotas and where the social democrats have also been cautious not to challenge private corporations.

Conclusion

In comparative perspective, women's access to the executives of the Nordic countries stands out as extraordinarily high. In 2009 an average of 47 percent of the cabinet ministers were women, which was well above the average in parliament of 41 percent. When we see these figures and consider all the competent and successful women who have served in the executives of their countries it is sometimes easy to forget that the pioneers had to break through a very hard glass ceiling. The development has been incremental over a long period of time and has by no means only been an automatic response to favorable socioeconomic, institutional and cultural factors, but has been fought for by women actors from organizations, political parties, etc. The support from women and men inside the political system has also been important. Despite the overall positive picture there are still remnants of a gendered pattern whereby men dominate portfolios related to finance and defense, and since World War II women have been almost exclusively in charge of ministries related to social affairs, family policy and gender equality. The Norwegian and Swedish case studies support the finding that a high level of women executive ministers is positively associated with woman-friendly policies.

Notes

1 In 1980 Sweden adopted equal primogeniture, meaning that the eldest child of the monarch, regardless of gender, takes precedence in the line of succession. Sweden had previously (since 1810) used agnatic primogeniture, meaning that only males could inherit the throne. The oldest child of the current monarch, King Carl XVI Gustaf, is Crown Princess Victoria, Duchess of Västergötland. In Norway equal primogeniture was introduced in 1990 and in Denmark in 2009. The current Danish queen was installed because there were no male successors.
2 In mid 2010 Mari Kiviniemi became prime minister of Finland, so that both prime minister and president of Finland were women; also Iceland's prime minister, Jóhanna Sigurðardóttir, married her female partner in church the first day that a new law made the marriage possible.
3 *Norwegian Government Ministries and Offices Since 1945* (2010); Sweden (2007).
4 Thus I have not counted women ministers entering the government after a while when, for example, a man has resigned.
5 This is not to say that these women were without power. They were all very strong and competent women, but did not get the recognition they would have deserved.
6 It has not been much noted that the new government increased the proportion of women from 33 to 38 percent.

11 Conclusion

Manon Tremblay and Gretchen Bauer

The objective of *Women in Executive Power: A global overview* has been to examine women's participation within the executive branch of government, as chief executives (i.e. presidents and prime ministers [PMs]) or cabinet ministers. In order to accomplish this, *Women in Executive Power* uses an original approach, namely, comparing experiences across time and across nine geopolitical regions. Each chapter uses the same analytical framework comprised of five aspects. It begins by presenting a regional overview, since World War II, of female participation in government (as executive leaders, cabinet ministers or both). Then, restricting itself to a select number of case studies, it looks at four elements for each country: nature of the political regimes; evolution of female presence within cabinets; socio-cultural, economic and political factors that explain female participation in governments; and finally, the impact that female executives have had on the substantive representation of women. This concluding chapter of the book follows the same five-point structure; we extract a number of observations from each of the sections in order to compile an overall set of lessons learned.

Regional overviews

The book relies on a comparative approach that encompasses nine geopolitical spaces: the Arab states, Central and Eastern Europe, Latin America, the Nordic countries, North America, Oceania, South and Southeast Asia, sub-Saharan Africa and Western Europe. Generally, the objective of this section in each chapter was to provide a portrait of female participation in politics at the executive level for each world region.

A first observation that can be drawn from the nine regional overviews is that in light of their demographic weight, women are under-represented as both chief executives and cabinet ministers. According to the Inter-Parliamentary Union (2010d), on January 1, 2010, 15 countries had a woman chief executive. More specifically, four women were heads of state: Dalia Grybauskaite (Lithuania), Tarja Halonen (Finland), Mary McAleese (Ireland), Pratibha Patil (India); six acted as head of government: Luísa Días Diogo (Mozambique), Jadranka Kosor (Croatia), Angela Merkel (Germany), Jóhanna Sigurðardóttir (Iceland), Ioulia

Timochenko (Ukraine), Sheikh Hasina Wajed (Bangladesh); and five were both head of state and head of government: Michelle Bachelet (Chile), Ellen Johnson Sirleaf (Liberia), Cristina Fernández de Kirchner (Argentina), Doris Leuthard (Switzerland) and Gloria Macapagal-Arroyo (Philippines).[1] As concerns cabinet membership, the Inter-Parliamentary Union's numbers indicate that in January 2010 16.9 percent of the 4,100 ministers in 188 countries were women. While four countries had cabinets in which more than half of ministers were women (Finland [63.2 percent], Cape Verde [53.3 percent], Spain [52.9 percent] and Norway [52.6 percent]), this is in stark contrast to the 16 countries that had only male cabinet ministers. Indeed, the level of cabinet feminization varies significantly from one part of the world to another; the regions presented in this book demonstrate the complete range: 7.6 percent in the Arab states overall versus 49.7 percent in the five Nordic countries. Table 11.1 illustrates these variations.

The overall *regional* average proportion of women in ministerial positions varied from 7.6 percent for the Arab states to 22.7 percent for Europe as a whole – with regions defined, as indicated in Table 11.1, by the Inter-Parliamentary Union. Generally speaking, the regions can be split into two categories: those regions where female participation in cabinet falls below 15 percent (Arab and Asian countries and Oceania) and those regions where female participation in cabinet exceeds that level. Vânia Carvalho Pinto and Andrea Fleschenberg insist that the patriarchal culture that exists in Arab and Asian countries acts as an obstacle for female access to executive power. Moreover, female participation is low throughout the Arab states and Asia, with no significant *sub-regional* differences, whereas in Oceania there is a distinct difference between Australasia (26 percent of women in ministerial positions, and several holding important posts as shown by Jennifer Curtin and Marian Sawer) and the Pacific Islands (where only 8.6 percent of women are cabinet ministers).

A second observation flows from these findings: if the levels of female participation in cabinets vary amongst the regions, they also vary within the same region. Oceania is a good example, as is Europe and, to a lesser extent, the Americas and sub-Saharan Africa. The European case is particularly interesting with 11.2 percent female ministers in the Central and Eastern European countries contrasted with near parity in the Nordic countries, all of which underscores the challenges to unification that the rich European diversity represents.

A third observation reveals that the level of feminization of cabinets also varies within the same sub-region. Aside from Australasia, the Fertile Crescent and the Nordic countries where there is little difference between the maximum and minimum proportions of female cabinet members, the general rule is that there is an important difference between the highest and the lowest proportion of female cabinet members within sub-regions (for instance, in the Central American and Caribbean Islands, South America, all of the sub-regions of sub-Saharan Africa and Western Europe). These fluctuations within the region and particularly within the sub-region raise questions about the utility of using the notion of a "contagion effect" for explaining female participation in cabinets (Matland 2006; Matland and Studlar 1996). Indeed, there is no proof that the nomination

Table 11:1 Women in parliaments and holding ministerial positions, by region and sub-region, January 1, 2010

Region (Nb of countries) Sub-region	Percentage of women in lower/single House of Parliament	Ministerial positions		
		Average (%)	Minimum	Maximum
Worldwide	17.4	16.9	0.0	63.2
Americas (34)	18.2	20.0	0.0	45.5
Central and Caribbean Islands (20)	16.0	16.9	0.0	38.5
North (3)	22.2	24.5	10.5	33.3
South (11)	21.0	24.5	7.4	45.5
Arab states (19)	10.3	7.6	0.0	23.1
Arab Gulf States (7)	4.7	7.0	0.0	16.7
Fertile Crescent (5)	13.1	7.4	6.3	10.3
North Africa (7)	13.8	8.2	0.0	23.1
Asia (31)	17.4	8.4	0.0	21.4
South (8)	16.6	7.6	0.0	16.0
Southeast (10)	20.8	9.8	0.0	21.4
Other (central, east and north) (13)	15.0	7.8	2.9	16.7
Europe (46)	23.1	22.7	0.0	63.2
Central and Eastern (22)	17.6	11.2	0.0	27.8
Nordic countries (5)	41.4	49.7	42.1	63.2
Western (19)	24.6	29.1	9.1	52.9
Oceania (14)	6.5	11.1	0.0	28.6
Australasia (2)	30.5	26.0	23.3	28.6
Pacific Islands (12)	2.1	8.6	0.0	25.0
Sub-Saharan Africa (44)	17.1	20.2	0.0	53.3
East (10)	24.8	22.1	7.4	33.3
Southern (12)	21.8	21.8	0.0	34.3
Central (6)	9.4	15.3	3.7	38.5
West (16)	12.5	20.7	8.0	53.3

Source: calculated from Inter-Parliamentary Union (2010d).

of women to government in one country has a knock-on effect in neighboring countries. At the same time, the idea should not be completely rejected given the proximity of Australia and New Zealand and among the Nordic countries and their respective similar levels of cabinet feminization. In fact, Christina Bergqvist uses the notion of a contagion effect to help explain the dynamic between Norway and Sweden.

From this we can draw a *first* lesson: the notion of contagion effect, to explain female participation in cabinet, must be used cautiously. While at times it may appear that this explanation for female participation in cabinet applies (as the Australasian and Nordic countries illustrate), more often it fails to live up to its heuristic potential. As this conclusion demonstrates, socio-political phenomena cannot be explained by "magic formulae."

Country cases

Generally, the objective of this section was to provide two or three case studies from each of nine regions in order to offer a more in-depth analysis of women's participation in executives around the world. The country cases were evaluated along four lines: nature of the political regimes; evolution of female participation in governments since World War II; evaluation of the factors explaining women's participation (or not) in executives; and finally, consideration of whether women executives represent women. Twenty countries were included among the nine regional chapters: Morocco and the United Arab Emirates (the Arab states), Burma and Pakistan (South and Southeast Asia), Australia and New Zealand (Oceania), Croatia, Lithuania and the Czech Republic (Central and Eastern Europe), Liberia and Rwanda (sub-Saharan Africa), Argentina and Chile (Latin America), Canada and the United States of America (North America), Germany, Spain and the United Kingdom (Western Europe) and Norway and Sweden (Nordic countries). Here it must be stressed that the observations from these 20 cases may not be strictly construed as trends since the "sample" was not randomly selected; however, nor should the observations be lightly dismissed.

Description of the political regimes

Table 11.2 presents a number of institutional political traits of the countries that were studied. The aim was to identify some of the characteristics of the political regimes in order to place the countries into comparative perspective with one another.

The table presents a wide array of institutional political characteristics, including regime type, the nature of the state and the national parliament, the voting system used for electing the members of the lower or single house, and the selection process for cabinet (generalist versus specialist). This diversity enables us to compare different political configurations and to have a better understanding of the impact of these institutional traits on cabinet feminization.

Evolution of women's presence in the executive

Since World War II, about 70 women have been chief executives (i.e. presidents or prime ministers), three out of four of them since 1990 (Tremblay 2008c). As for cabinets, despite a general growth in cabinet feminization since the middle of the twentieth century, we observe, first, that this progression has not been linear and that the trajectory has at times stagnated, or even regressed. Most of the countries in this volume offer examples of this. The nature of this evolution threatens any assumption that, over time, women and men will equally share executive duties. At the same time, Christina Bergqvist proposes an interesting observation: in the Nordic countries at least, current cabinets set standards with regard to female representation that future cabinets cannot afford to ignore. Without completely excluding regressions in levels of female participation, these standards can at least considerably limit them. This point warrants further research, especially as it refers to the idea of a contagion effect, which in this case takes effect over time.

The second observation is that a more substantial female access to cabinet has been a recent phenomenon. While certain governments welcomed women's presence in cabinet early on (in the 1920s in Canada and 1930s in the United States, in the 1940s in Norway, Sweden and Yugoslavia, and in the 1950s in Burma and Chile), others did not include women until the 1990s or even the first decade of 2000 (for example Argentina, Morocco and the United Arab Emirates). Many of the first-time nominations of women were as ministers without portfolios. Jennifer Curtin and Marian Sawer write that one of the first women to be named minister without portfolio, Australia's Dame Enid Lyons, quipped that she was in cabinet "to pour the tea." The 1980s appeared to be a turning point for female participation in cabinets as their numbers grew markedly, a trend that coincided with the mobilization of national and international women's movements (spurred on by the United Nations Decade for Women and decennial conferences on women), as well as notable increases in women's access to parliaments. The 1990s also marked a considerable diversification of the portfolios held by women ministers.

A third observation concerns how women are appointed to cabinets, in particular the ministerial status of women and the portfolios with which they are charged. A well documented literature suggests that women can be found at the bottom of the executive hierarchy (i.e. as junior ministers instead of senior ministers) and responsible for traditionally female fields (i.e. education, health and social affairs). Even though many of the case studies in this collection substantiate these claims, other cases suggest a need to qualify them. Most of the chapters give examples of more and more women being named to traditionally male ministries (such as defense and national security, finance and foreign affairs) placing them at the top of the executive hierarchy. Thus, Farida Jalalzai and Manon Tremblay, writing about Canada and the United States, suggest the need to reconsider Putnam's law of increasing disproportion (1976: 33), which states that where power is women are not. As their presence in cabinet has increased

Table 11.2 Selected traits of the political regimes

Countries	Percentage of women in ministerial positions, January 1, 2010	Government regime type	Nature of the state and the national parliament	Voting system, lower or single house	Cabinet's selection process (generalist vs. specialist)
Argentina	20.0	Republic	Federal Bicameral	PR (Lists)	Specialist
Australia	23.3	Constitutional monarchy/ parliamentary (Westminster) democracy	Federal Bicameral	Plurality/Majority (AV)	Generalist
Burma/Myanmar	0.0	Military junta	Unitary No parliament	Plurality/Majority (FPTP)	Specialist
Canada	29.7	Constitutional monarchy/ parliamentary (Westminster) democracy	Federal Bicameral	Plurality/Majority (FPTP)	Generalist
Chile	45.5	Republic	Unitary Bicameral	PR (Lists)	Specialist
Croatia	15.8	Presidential/parliamentary democracy	Unitary Unicameral	PR (Lists)	Generalist
Czech Republic	17.6	Parliamentary democracy	Unitary Bicameral	PR (Lists)	Generalist
Germany	33.3	Republic/parliamentary democracy	Federal Bicameral	Mixed (proportional)	Specialist
Liberia	30.4	Republic	Unitary Bicameral	Plurality/Majority (FPTP)	Specialist
Lithuania	14.3	Parliamentary democracy	Unitary Unicameral	Mixed (parallel)	Generalist
Morocco	11.1	Constitutional monarchy	Unitary Bicameral	PR (Lists)	Both
New Zealand	28.6	Constitutional monarchy/ parliamentary (Westminster) democracy	Unitary Unicameral	Mixed (proportional)	Generalist
Norway	52.6	Constitutional monarchy/ parliamentary democracy	Unitary Unicameral	PR (Lists)	Specialist

Pakistan	7.5	Parliamentary (de facto presidential) democracy	Federal Bicameral	Mixed (parallel)	Generalist
Rwanda	33.3	Republic/presidential	Unitary Bicameral	PR (Lists)	Specialist
Spain	52.9	Parliamentary Monarchy/ parliamentary democracy	Unitary* Bicameral	PR (Lists)	Generalist
Sweden	45.0	Constitutional monarchy/ parliamentary democracy	Unitary Unicameral	PR (Lists)	Specialist
United Arab Emirates	16.7	Monarchy	Federal Unicameral	Indirect elections via an electoral college	Specialist
United Kingdom	22.6	Constitutional Monarchy/ parliamentary (Westminster) democracy	Unitary Bicameral	Plurality/Majority (FPTP)	Generalist
United States of America	33.3	Republic	Federal Bicameral	Plurality/Majority (FPTP)	Specialist

Sources: CIA (2010a); Inter-Parliamentary Union (2010a, 2010d); International IDEA (2010).

Note
* Spain is also described as a "regional state" because of its asymmetrical devolution through 17 decentralized autonomous communities.

and they have gained more seniority, women are holding a wider array of ministerial responsibilities. Furthermore, the chapters on Australasia and the Nordic countries demonstrate that the political importance of portfolios varies over time and according to the conjuncture, and that social portfolios can at times be more prestigious and powerful than others, potentially offering more opportunities for representing women. We suggest that future studies should investigate women's experiences heading traditionally female portfolios with those of women leading traditionally male portfolios, focusing especially on perceptions of their political competency and their political paths and future political ambitions.

The last observation, however, may come as a disappointment: there are no guarantees that a female chief executive, either as head of state or of government, translates into an increase in female members of cabinet – or, for that matter, into an increase in female members of parliament (in Chile and Liberia women executives accomplished the former but not the latter). Not only does this observation raise doubts about Davis' (1997) reported correlation between the level of feminization of cabinets and female heads of government, it also questions, once again, the notion of a contagion effect. A number of examples in the chapters contradict Davis' thesis (Andrea Fleschenberg recalls Indonesian president Megawati Sukarnoputri, Fiona Buckley and Yvonne Galligan remind us of British Prime Minister Margaret Thatcher, and for Argentina, Tiffany D. Barnes and Mark P. Jones note the low level of cabinet feminization under President Cristina Fernández de Kirchner), while others (Michelle Bachelet in Chile and Ellen Johnson Sirleaf in Liberia) strongly support it. Moreover, some chapters relate cases of male executives being very concerned to include more women at the ministerial level. In 2008 José Luis Rodríguez Zapatero, the Spanish Prime Minister, formed a cabinet containing equal numbers of women and men, following the example of Swedish Prime Minister Ingvar Carlsson in 1994; and, as noted by Tiffany Barnes and Mark P. Jones, Nicaraguan President Daniel Ortega made sure there was a substantial female presence in his cabinet. Fiona Buckley and Yvonne Galligan summarize as follows: "a woman head of government does not necessarily break the gendered pattern of women's participation in cabinet government." This observation revives the controversial assertion that passive representation does not necessarily engender active representation – or that sex representation does not translate into gender representation (Keiser *et al.* 2002). All told, it is probably too early and there are probably still too few female heads of state or government to be able to draw any credible conclusions about their impact on the feminization of cabinets. Nonetheless, a female chief executive still constitutes a role model for both girls and women, regardless of whether her political style and decisions are congruent with feminist ideals.

From this we can draw a *second* lesson: the analysis of female participation in governments must rethink its perspectives given the recent noteworthy gains made by women in the executive arena. While the general female participation in governments remains largely unsatisfactory, the proportion of women in executives has risen considerably in the first decade of the new millennium, and whilst this evolution has risen and fallen, it is generally a positive trend. If the pattern of vertical and horizontal gender segregation persists, it no longer fully accurately describes female participation in cabinets – given that women now frequently hold senior positions in the ministerial hierarchy and that they oversee traditionally male portfolios. Moreover, the importance of social portfolios can no longer be discounted not only because they form an important part of state budgets in an era when states are seeking to cut back on their social expenditures, but also because social rights are a masterpiece of twenty-first century citizenship (by commanding inclusion in or exclusion from the global community). This renewed perspective means that a new approach must be adopted when considering the consequences of women's inclusion in cabinets – notwithstanding that we still cannot assume that female chief executives' cabinets will necessarily be more feminized than those of their male counterparts.

Factors explaining women's access to the executive

Determining whether female participation in executives is related to any sociocultural, economic or political factors has generated some important research material. With regard to cultural factors, a first observation drawn from the chapters is that gender roles seriously limit female participation in governments. Vânia Carvalho Pinto explains that in the Arab world, traditional gender roles not only confine women to spousal and mothering roles but also generate stereotypes about women's ability to participate in politics. This may also explain why female ministers generally have diplomas: "accusations of lack of knowledge are difficult to level in these cases, and because women with high academic qualifications may feel more secure in entering a predominantly male and hostile environment." Contrary to this, Christina Bergqvist notes the positive impact that egalitarian gender roles have had on female participation at the highest levels of state power in the Nordic countries, in general, and Norway and Sweden, in particular.

A second observation can be made with regard to the essentially negative role that religion has played in the participation of women in executives. Though religion may at times seem to be a means by which to fight oppression, it nonetheless promotes gender roles that exclude women from political governance: Andrea Fleschenberg notes that in Burma "cultural Buddhism-based beliefs ... generate the thinking that women do not have the capacity to speak in public and, instead, occupy the prime role of family caretaker." The chapters on Western Europe and the Nordic countries suggest, in turn, that secularization has had a positive impact on female participation in those governments. Simply put, religion does not have a gender-neutral impact on women's participation in governments.

That said, traditional gender roles and religion are not insurmountable obstacles to women becoming ministers, as attested by several African, Latin American, Asian and Central and Eastern European countries where women can be found in the higher echelons of executive power. Typically, these women represent the national elite which may have consequences for other women when it comes to representing "women's interests." In their separate chapters on sub-Saharan Africa and South and Southeast Asia, Gretchen Bauer and Andrea Fleschenberg both observe that not infrequently women's elite status "trumps" their gender status, gaining them access to executive positions. Moreover, Andrea Fleschenberg confirms what many have observed for Asian women executives, namely, that coming from families with elite backgrounds often means that these women gain their political access and careers not on their own merit but thanks to family ties.

In her Presidential Address to the Canadian Political Science Association in Ottawa, May 2009, Miriam Smith (2009) wondered about culture's capacity to explain both social and political phenomena. As she notes, culture,

> should not be interpreted as a stand-alone explanatory factor that produces particular political outcomes. Nor ... should we consider "culture" as a confined and delimited arena in which we can consider questions of difference, diversity, identity and recognition. Rather, discussions of culture must be anchored in a consideration of the structural, historical, material and institutional context. Institutions, law and political economy only make sense in a cultural context; therefore, we should be cautious about separating culture from other aspects of social reality and carrying on conversations about cultural difference that are abstracted from these other dimensions.
>
> (Smith 2009: 835)

A *third* lesson, therefore, is that while culture is both useful and necessary to explain female participation in government, it does not provide a fully satisfying reading. Smith (2009) also notes that culture exists, of course, but not apart from a larger societal framework which gives culture its meanings. In other words, certainly any explanation of women's participation in government must take into account cultural factors, which in turn cannot be invoked in isolation or out of context – but must be inserted into a more complex explanatory model.

Economic factors round out the *fourth* lesson of this conclusion: no link can be found between the level of economic development and the level of cabinet feminization or women's presence at the pinnacle of executive power. Liberia and Rwanda are two of the world's poorest countries, yet recently women play an important role in executive politics there. By contrast, Australia, Canada, Germany, the United States and the United Kingdom are among the richest countries in the world and still have poor levels of female participation in government. That the level of economic development apparently has no impact on the feminization of executive ranks recalls its small influence on the proportion of women in parliaments (Reynolds 1999; Siaroff 2000; Tremblay 2008d). Economic development, however, is a complex concept, particularly in conjuncture with the welfare state. Thus, Christina Bergqvist believes that strong levels of female participation in Norway and Sweden are in some part linked to the type of welfare state (that is, social democratic welfare state regime) that these countries enjoy.

Political factors may have the most convincing impact on levels of cabinet feminization. Two types of factors can be identified: institutional, that is, traits that are intrinsic to the type of regimes, systems and political institutions, or contextual, that is, factors that are linked to events and extra-institutional actors in civil society at the national or international level. A second look at Table 11.2 allows us to draw links between certain institutional characteristics and women's access to ministerial positions. Some studies have argued that parliamentary regimes should be more open to women as executive power is shared among a number of actors (which requires them to collaborate, deliberate and negotiate) whereas in presidential regimes power tends to be more concentrated in the strong leadership of the chief executive (Jalalzai 2008; Jalalzai and Krook 2010). This seems to be confirmed by the case studies presented in this book. When comparing cases in which, *theoretically*, power should be shared among a number of actors with those cases where power should be concentrated in one actor, feminization levels are, respectively, 30.5 percent and 24.7 percent.[2] One must always use caution when dealing with theory as it is often far from practice, however. Sykes (2009) maintains that parliamentary regimes are becoming more and more presidential in nature, a trend that limits comparisons based on political regimes. In Canada, for example, power should theoretically be shared amongst the various actors, but in reality power is concentrated in the hands of the prime minister (Savoie 1999).

The number of legislative chambers does not seem to have any real impact on the number of female ministers: unicameral parliaments have 28.8 percent and bicameral parliaments have 27.7 percent. This does not mean that the presence of a second chamber is without consequence to women accessing cabinets; it all depends on national particularities. Bicameralism promotes female access to cabinets in Australia because the Senate represents a pool of eligible women to fulfill ministerial roles, whereas the Canada Senate and the British House of Lords do not play that same role. What about unitary states and federations – do the former have less feminized governments than the latter? The idea behind this question is that unitary states offer fewer opportunities to women to be a part of government as there are fewer ministerial positions than in federations. Not only do the studies in this book fail to support this thesis, they actually demonstrate the opposite: in unitary states, female levels of representation in cabinets are at 28.4 percent compared to 23.4 percent in federations. But in order to get a more accurate picture, it would be necessary to take into account all levels of ministerial representation, both national and sub-national, a task that future studies might undertake.

The proportion of women in parliaments and the proportion of female cabinet ministers do not seem to evolve at the same pace. In some countries they do – Rwanda, Canada, Norway and Sweden – but in other countries they do not. In both Chile and Liberia there were fewer women in parliament but many in cabinet, as well as women presidents (from 2006 to 2010). As for the former Soviet republics, Maxime Forest finds a discrepancy between women's presence in the legislative and executive branches in the pre-transition period: whilst a quota system was in place to ensure a certain level of female legislative representation, there was no such mechanism for executives. The same has been true in Pakistan. But Jennifer Curtin and Marian Sawer believe that legislative quotas could have a knock-on effect for executives if they were appropriately designed, even though a government's ideological leanings would still have an impact on cabinet feminization.

Indeed, political parties are also major institutional actors: they play an important part in women accessing parliaments and it would seem that that role is just as important for accessing executives. The chapters on North America and Western Europe show that left-leaning parties seem more inclined to nominate women to cabinets than right-leaning parties. There are, however, some exceptions that must be noted. In the mid 1970s, a Swedish center-right government allowed "a substantial break with the pattern of 'symbolic' women in junior positions:" these center-right parties operated from the margins for a number of years allowing women to climb the ranks and create important networks for themselves which worked in their favor when the coalition came to power in 1976. By contrast, the first cabinet after the dissolution of Czechoslovakia was made up of only men. Maxime Forest also finds that for Central and Eastern Europe,

> *all* female prime ministers and heads of state elected or designated since 1989 have been recruited from the center-right, and 41 out of 52 (79 percent) of the women who held major ministries (finance, economy, defense, interior or foreign affairs) during the past two decades, were designated by (center-) right parties.

The Australia case study underlines the fact that political parties are not uniform entities; instead they are spaces in which conflicting interests do battle, which can either promote or inhibit women's access to cabinet.

Electoral systems have also garnered a lot of attention with regard to their effects on female participation in political life. Whilst the role they play with regard to female representation in parliaments is well documented, the same cannot be said for female participation in cabinets. Whitford *et al.* (2007) authored one of the rare studies that consider the influence of the electoral system on the descriptive representation of women in ministerial positions. Examining 72 countries in the mid 1990s, they concluded that open-list proportional representation (PR) voting systems were associated with more women cabinet ministers than closed-list PR and single-member plurality voting systems. Their explanation for this interesting result is "that the parties in coalition in these [open-list PR] systems perceive and respond to what voters prefer … and not just what voters have done in actually delivering women to the legislature" (2007: 570). The case studies in our book seem to verify this finding. The level of cabinet feminization for countries using a proportional representation system is 32.6 percent[3] whereas the level is 27.9 percent using a plurality/majority voting system (excluding Burma/Myanmar as there are no elections) and 20.9 percent for mixed voting systems. It is an intriguing result that countries using a plurality/majority voting system have higher levels of cabinet feminization than countries using a mixed-member voting system because it contradicts the pattern identified for parliaments. In fact, legislatures produced from a proportional voting system are more feminized than those formed by a mixed voting system, which in turn have higher levels of female legislators than those using a plurality/majority voting system (Norris 1997b, 2004: 187).

It is relatively easy to understand the impact that the electoral system can have on the proportion of female cabinet ministers in political regimes where there is no separation of executive and legislative powers and cabinet members are *mostly* selected from the eligible pool of parliament, as is the case in Westminster-style parliamentary regimes. According to this ("generalist") model of recruitment, the prime minister selects her/his cabinet following general elections from her/his parliamentary caucus, and as such only the female legislators sitting on the government side can be selected to become cabinet ministers. Since several studies have identified strong correlations between the proportion of female cabinet ministers and the proportion of female members of parliament (Davis 1997: 88; Reynolds 1999; Siaroff 2000), particularly the number of female members of parliament from the governing party caucus (Studlar and Moncrief 1997, 1999), one may deduce that a situation combining voting systems yielding generous proportions of female legislators with a generalist model for selecting cabinet ministers should have a positive impact on the proportion of women cabinet ministers. However, the impact of the electoral system on cabinet feminization is not as clear in regimes where cabinet members are not selected from the eligible pool of parliament and instead are *mainly* brought in from the outside for their expertise in a certain field (the "specialist" model). This suggests, then, that the proportion of women in parliament, which is influenced by the electoral system (and political parties; Tremblay 2008d), acts as a yardstick in regimes where ministers are *mostly* selected from outside of parliament, that the chief executive would find difficult to ignore when it comes to naming her/his cabinet. This idea should be further explored in a future study.

To add to this puzzle, Davis (1997: 38–55) found in her study on female participation in cabinets in 15 parliamentary democracies from 1968 to 1992, that women were less likely to be selected as cabinet ministers in regimes that employed the generalist model, a fact also noted by Siaroff (2000). The same conclusion may also be drawn from the case studies in this book. When dividing the countries between those that use a *mostly* generalist model and those that employ a *mostly* specialist model, the levels of cabinet feminization are 23.6 percent for the generalist and 32.1 percent for the specialist.[4] Further studies are therefore required to ascertain the impact that both the electoral system and the method for selecting cabinet ministers have on the proportion of female cabinet ministers.

The *fifth* lesson finds that there are no institutional political traits that fundamentally favor or hinder female participation in executives. Nonetheless, of such institutional traits, type of recruitment system (generalist versus specialist) and political parties appear to have the most obvious impact on female participation in cabinet. Generally speaking, women are more present in left-leaning cabinets than in right-leaning ones. We must therefore turn our attention to those paradoxical cases where left-oriented cabinets have few women and right-oriented cabinets have more women in order to understand the underlying dynamics of this reasoning.

The case studies identify a few extra-institutional political characteristics that have had a positive impact on the number of female executives including: regime changes, adherence to regional or international norms and mobilized women's movements. Prolonged conflicts – and their resolutions in the form of political transitions – can profoundly change the political opportunity structure for women's participation and leadership. The genocide in Rwanda and the civil conflict in Liberia – and their aftermaths – altered the gender balance in those countries, allowing women to gain access to new legislative and executive roles – in some cases, such as Ellen Johnson Sirleaf's successful presidential bid, without having to face male (or any) incumbents. In several post-conflict situations the education, training or skills that women may have gained in the course of the conflict have prepared them well for participation in politics at many levels.

The case of New Zealand further supports the idea that a change in regime or a break with the past can create conditions that allow easier access for women to government. In the mid 1990s, New Zealand switched to a mixed-member proportional voting system which resulted in more female members of the House of Representatives and more who would be eligible for ministerial positions. However, transitions do not necessarily result in more women participating more at the executive level, as demonstrated by the situation in Chile *before* the presidencies of Ricardo Lagos and Michelle Bachelet.

Nominating women to ministerial positions can also be part of a larger project by the state. Vânia Carvalho Pinto believes that the Arab world is sending a message of modernity to the international community by nominating female ministers; Maxime Forest considers that by nominating women to ministerial positions, some Central and Eastern European countries are showing the European Union (EU) that they share the same norms and values (such as equality and transparency); Fiona Buckley and Yvonne Galligan interpret the Spanish Prime Minister Zapatero's gender-balanced cabinet as a component of a modernizing agenda.

Whatever gains women have made with regard to accessing government, however, would not have been possible without women's movements that steadfastly promoted women's political representation. The chapters in this book have shown that women's activism adopts a variety of forms and adapts itself to the conditions in which it operates. In Liberia, Gretchen Bauer records Ellen Johnson Sirleaf's own belief that it was the women of Liberia who helped her to win the presidential elections in 2006 (after having helped to secure the peace in the previous few years) – a view shared by outside observers as well. As for the Arab world, Vânia Carvalho Pinto suggests that the Moroccan women's movement has been lobbying government to expand women's rights, and in so doing has been compensating for the lack of female representation in the House of Representatives. She also argues that in a strongly gender-segregated society such as the United Arab Emirates, "women can have access to female members of the ruling families through kin connections, or through women's associations and Ladies Clubs" – arguably a kind of women's movement activism. Certainly in Australasia, the Nordic countries, Western Europe and North America, the successes that women have experienced in politics are as a direct result of the work of women's movements in putting pressure on the political class, especially on the left.

National women's movements do not operate in a vacuum but are instead a part of larger movements at both the regional and international levels. Since the mid 1980s, a number of supra-national organizations (such as the European Union, the Southern African Development Community and the United Nations) have worked in tandem with a global women's movement to promote the equal participation of women and men in the decision-making process. These transnational networks (True and Mintrom 2001), which are alliances between international organizations and women's movements, have been important in promoting gender mainstreaming mechanisms such as electoral gender quotas (Krook 2006, 2009) and gender equality machineries. The chapters in this book demonstrate that these gender equality machineries have significantly contributed to advancing women's rights. Norway and Sweden are two excellent examples of women's movements mobilizing themselves from within the women's sections of political parties in order to promote women's enhanced representation in politics. Croatia and Lithuania are further examples of countries in which women's sections of political parties have played an important role in cabinet feminization. In Australia, meanwhile, feminists have relied upon the feminist "ginger group," EMILY's List, to advocate for women's greater participation in politics.

A *sixth* lesson may be drawn from these observations: women's access to executives is a result of the coming together of a number of contextual factors. Thus, female participation in cabinets cannot be explained with an institutional approach that does not take into account context or national and international civil society actors that also play an important role in shaping governance and political opportunity structures. The case studies in this book have demonstrated the importance of women's movements in increasing female participation in executive branches of government. These studies have also shown the diverse circumstances in which these movements have been mobilized. This has occurred not only through women's movements but also with the help of external protagonists in many different fields. As Christina Bergqvist writes:

In general, several researchers have shown the importance of women's movements and women's involvement in policy-making as cabinet ministers, parliamentarians and femocrats (feminist bureaucrats) in the formulation and implementation of policies in the interests of women in the Nordic countries.

Similarly, around the world an unlikely constellation of factors, such as political transitions, regime changes, the propagation of international norms and values around gender equality and national machineries for women are having an increasing impact on women's access to legislative and executive office. Still, more studies are needed to fully understand the strategies and limitations for feminizing executive power.

The final section of each of the regional chapters sought to determine whether, once they reached the executive, women represented women and if so, how they did this and what difficulties they might have encountered.

Do women executives represent women?

It is important to note that this type of question presents researchers with a number of methodological difficulties. Given that women's access to executives is fairly recent and that there are still very few female cabinet ministers and heads of state or government, focusing on these women tends to privilege their individual experiences rather than yielding generalizable findings. Moreover, in the case of cabinets, decisions are often made collectively and behind closed doors making it difficult to determine which contributions are made by which cabinet ministers. Notwithstanding these methodological difficulties, whether female ministers represent women remains a valuable question. Cabinet plays an important role in most political regimes with regard to governance: cabinet minister introduce bills in the national legislature and possess important means by which to have them adopted. It is, therefore, interesting to know whether female ministers do in fact represent women.

To add to the aforementioned methodological difficulties, and perhaps even as a result of these difficulties, apart from studies by Atchison and Down (2009) and, to a lesser extent, Sykes (2009), no systematic research has been undertaken to determine whether women cabinet ministers represent women (in other words, whether the presence of women ministers translates into women-friendly public policy). Atchison and Down's study makes two interesting points. First, they find that women's increased presence in cabinet translated into women-friendly public policy (state-awarded parental leave) in 18 industrial democracies. Second, Atchison and Down assert that the proportion of female members in parliament has less impact on the adoption of female-friendly policies than does the proportion of female cabinet ministers. True and Mintrom (2001) make a similar observation: the proportion of women cabinet ministers has a statistically significant impact on the adoption of gender mainstreaming mechanisms, while the percentage of women parliamentarians does not have such an influence. While this second point is instructive, other variables must also be taken into account such as the government's ideological orientation.

Generally speaking, left-wing parties tend to nominate more women to cabinet and are more likely to adopt women-friendly policies than are right-wing cabinets, but is this because of higher levels of cabinet feminization or because of the parties' ideological leanings, or is it a combination of both? Sykes (2009) examines the experiences of female prime ministers in Anglo-American systems (notably Australia, Canada, Ireland, New Zealand and the United Kingdom with frequent comparisons to the United States). Her study underscores the masculinist nature of the ideologies, institutions and political practices within the Westminster regime, all the while noting that women do not form a monolithic block in politics. This certainly holds true for the substantive representation of women.

The case studies from this book do not provide a clear answer on whether female cabinet ministers (and women prime ministers and presidents) use their positions in government to represent women. What they do point out is that some female ministers represent women and others do not. It is even possible that some female ministers may support motions that go against "women's interests;"[5] Maxime Forest writes about Central and Eastern Europe that

> being often in charge of social affairs or health, female ministers in office, at least during the first decade of the transformation, share some responsibility for the elimination of many of the women-friendly aspects of social policies carried out under state socialism.

Fiona Buckley and Yvonne Galligan remind us that Margaret Thatcher merely paid lip service to women's issues when she was prime minister.

The chapters in this volume reveal that women cabinet ministers' representation of women's interests may take different institutional forms; some operate almost by default (i.e. being a role model) while others require a feminist consciousness. Several chapters cite the "role model impact" of women executives around the world. Tiffany D. Barnes and Mark P. Jones suggest that in Chile, "[t]he sustained political popularity of Bachelet and her commitment to gender equality is an archetype for future generations of female political leaders." Fiona Buckley and Yvonne Galligan maintain that as more women gain access to cabinets in Western Europe "women's political leadership becomes increasingly seen as normal and achievable." Vânia Carvalho Pinto develops a larger vision of what it might mean to represent women's interest by being a role model; in the Arab world, she suggests, female ministers are role models not only because their presence proves that women can hold high ranking positions in government, but also because it helps to strengthen women's place in society. In Burma, where there are no female ministers in the military-led government, Andrea Fleschenberg believes that activist "Aung San Suu Kyi is an outspoken leader for women's rights, participation and development and she certainly serves as a role model for her female followers in the pro-democracy movement."

Conversely, other institutional forms of women's substantive representation require a feminist consciousness. The chapters give examples of female presidents, prime ministers and cabinet ministers who have used their position to nominate other women to influential positions. Jennifer Curtin and Marian Sawer report that in Australia "women ministers were disproportionately likely to appoint women to the position of chief of staff – 71 percent of women ministers had female chiefs of staff, compared with 40 percent of ministers as a whole." Some female leaders, such as Michelle Bachelet, Gro Harlem Bruntland and Ellen Johnson Sirleaf, have named a great number of women to their cabinets.[6] (As noted previously, however, the idea that women heads of state and government will *automatically* lead to increased levels of women in ministerial positions must be, for the moment, considered cautiously.)

Female chief executives have also embraced symbolism, and notably political rhetoric, to promote women's interests. Gretchen Bauer mentions the example of Ellen Johnson Sirleaf who, in one of her first acts after becoming president of Liberia, decided "to change the inscription on the front of the Supreme Court from 'Let justice be done to all men' to 'Let justice be done to all'." Fiona Buckley and Yvonne Galligan cite a study undertaken by Mushaben which found that cabinet titles in Germany from 1998 to 2002 were changed, by adding "*innen* (the feminine noun form ending) to all job ads, political speeches, etc." During her first annual address to Congress, Michelle Bachelet of Chile reportedly pronounced the word "woman" more than 30 times. In the United States, Madeleine Albright, Condoleezza Rice and Hillary Rodham Clinton have all used their position as secretary of state to promote women's rights, often at high-profile international venues, although not all with the same conviction.

Finally, the most significant form of women cabinet ministers' substantive representation of women is to introduce measures to promote gender equality. The chapters on Norway and Sweden and Australia and New Zealand provide an abundance of examples in which women ministers have done just that. Andrea Fleschenberg finds that in Pakistan, Sherry Rehman initiated some legislative projects designed to fight discrimination against women and to better protect them against sexual harassment and domestic violence. As we all know, however, it is one thing to adopt legislative measures, and another to implement them. Vânia Carvalho Pinto notes that despite the adoption of a new Family Code in Morocco in 2004 that was designed to emancipate women from male dominance, its implementation has been met with hostility and ignorance.

In reality, several barriers may prevent female cabinet ministers and presidents and prime ministers from substantively representing women and these are described throughout the chapters in this book. For cabinet ministers, some obstacles are directly linked to the rules governing cabinets themselves. Cabinet is a collective group, with an agenda, made up of actors with varying degrees of power that operates in a broader socio-political environment, as Farida Jalalzai and Manon Tremblay explain:

> many factors may prevent women ministers from substantively representing women. Some are intrinsic to the parliamentary regime: the secrecy of cabinet discussions in conjunction with the rules of ministerial solidarity and party discipline, and the policy priorities of the first minister and her/his government team. Other factors are external to the parliamentary rules of the game.

However, the workings of cabinets and their larger operating environments are not always hostile to women's substantive representation. As Maxime Forest notes with regard to the Central and Eastern European countries, the process of European Union accession has encouraged legislative innovations in favor of gender equality. While Farida Jalalzai and Manon Tremblay note that women are often relegated to less important ministerial roles which limit their ability to represent women, Jennifer Curtin and Marian Sawer give recent examples of female cabinet ministers who "have used their positions as outer ministers or government representatives to leverage policy outcomes favorable to women."

Another obstacle that can limit female ministers' capacity to substantively represent women may be their own ideological orientations: generally, right-wing parties are more hostile to women's rights than are left-wing ones. Many chapters highlight the challenges that female executives' ideological faiths pose to women's representation. Moreover, the chapter on North America demonstrates that women on the right side of the political spectrum may have an image problem as they are often associated with personality traits that do not coincide with representing women's interests.

Finally, a number of chapters note the potential contradiction posed by women from the most elite segments of society – from which women executives often hail – representing the interests of ordinary women. Furthermore, in Asia, the Arab world and to a lesser extent Latin America, these elite executive women often belong to well-established political families thus begging the question whether they will be more influenced by familial ties (and elite status) or gender and a commitment to representing women's interests. This, of course, is an age-old debate within the literature and among and between women activists and women politicians – about who may claim to represent whose interests, what those interests are and so on and so forth.[7]

The *final* lesson of the book, then, acts as a cautionary tale with regard to the substantive representation of women (and women's participation in executives in general). Considering that there are still very few women political executives and that most have not been in office for a very long time, and considering that much of the work of political executives remains largely opaque (taking place behind closed doors – in contrast to the work of legislatures), it may be too early to determine whether the presence of women in executives is an efficient strategy for reaching gender equality – that is to say, to conclude that women executives substantively represent women. Yet the examples of Norway and Sweden and the other Nordic countries described at the end of this book suggest considerable promise. Women's presence in political executives is but one (albeit significant) piece in the larger puzzle of women's political representation and the pieces are still being assembled.

Notes

1 By mid 2010 Luísa Días Diogo was no longer prime minister of Mozambique and Michelle Bachelet was no longer president of Chile; Julia Gillard had just been elected prime minister of Australia and Mari Kiviniemi just elected prime minister of Finland. By mid 2010 Laura Chinchilla Miranda was elected president of Costa Rica and Kamla Persad-Bissessar prime minister of Trinidad and Tobago. In late 2010 Dilma Rousseff was elected president of Brazil.

2 This comparison excludes Burma. The following are the countries in which power should theoretically be shared: Australia, Canada, Croatia, Czech Republic, Germany, Lithuania, New Zealand, Norway, Spain, Sweden and the United Kingdom.

3 We did not calculate the percentage according to the open-list versus closed-list PR distinction simply because our total number of cases is too few.

4 Again, Burma has been taken out of the equation as the members of cabinet are selected from the high ranking military officers.

5 This notion is not without controversy and yields deep intellectual conflicts, mainly because it poses as universal the experiences of certain women only (particularly those living in the western world, heteronormalized and mothers), and as such pushes out any women who do not fit into these categories. However, an in-depth discussion of the notion of "women's interests" goes beyond the scope of this conclusion.

6 In their mid 1990s study of the descriptive representation of women in political executives in 72 countries, Whitford *et al.* (2007: 570) explain a ' "leader" or a "promotion" effect' to be the balance between a greater presence of women in ministerial and sub-ministerial positions.

7 In a paper published in 2002, Dovi reminds us "that some descriptive representatives are preferable to others ... and that preferable descriptive representatives possess strong mutual relationships with dispossessed subgroups of historically disadvantaged groups" (2002: 729). One might well ask whether elite women are "preferable descriptive representatives" of other women.

Bibliography

Abdullah, M.C. (2004) "Malaysia," in Friedrich Ebert Stiftung (ed.) *Southeast Asian Women in Politics and Decision-Making, Ten Years After Beijing. Gaining Ground?*, Manila: FES Philippine Office.

Aberbach, J.D., Putnam, R.D. and Rockman, B.A. (1981) *Bureaucrats and Politicians in Western Democracies*, Cambridge, MA: Harvard University Press.

Abou-Zeid, G. (2006) "The Arab Region: Women's Access to the Decision-Making Process Across the Arab Nation," in D. Dahlerup (ed.) *Women, Quotas and Politics*, London and New York: Routledge.

Abu-Lughod, L. (ed.) (1998) *Remaking Women: Feminism and Modernity in the Middle East*, Princeton: Princeton University Press.

Ackerman, R. (2009) "Rebuilding Liberia, One Brick at a Time," *World Policy Journal*, 26 (2): 83–92.

Adams, M. (2006) "Regional Women's Activism: African Women's Networks and the African Union," in M.M. Ferree and A.M. Tripp (eds) *Global Feminism: Transnational Women's Activism, Organizing, and Human Rights*, New York: New York University Press.

Adams, M. (2008) "The Election of Ellen Johnson Sirleaf and Women's Executive Leadership in Africa," *Politics & Gender*, 4 (3): 475–84.

Ahmed, K.U. (2008) "Women and Politics in Bangladesh," in K. Iwanaga (ed.) *Women's Political Participation and Representation in Asia. Obstacles and Challenges*, Copenhagen: NIAS Press.

al-Ali, N. (2003) "Gender and Civil Society in the Middle East," *International Feminist Journal of Politics*, 5 (2): 216–32.

al-Dabbagh, M. and Nusseibeh, L. (2009) *Women in Parliament and Politics in the UAE: a Study of the First Federal National Council Elections*, Dubai and Adu Dhabi: Dubai School of Government and Ministry of State for Federal National Council Affairs.

al-Kitbi, E.S. (2004) *Women's Political Role in the GCC States*, Dubai: Gulf Research Center.

Ameinfo (2006) "6689 Electoral College Members will Vote in FNC Election, Including 1189 Women," October 2. Online. Available at: www.ameinfo.com/97900.html (accessed October 2009).

Antić, M. (1999) "Slovene Political Parties and their Influence on the Electoral Prospects of Women," in C. Corrin (ed.) *Gender and Identity in Central and Eastern Europe*, London: Frank Cass.

Antić, M. (2003) "Factors Influencing Women's Presence in Slovene Parliament," in

R.E. Matland and K.A. Montgomery (eds) *Women's Access to Political Power in Post-Communist Europe*, New York: Oxford University Press.

Atchison, A. and Down, I. (2009) "Women Cabinet Ministers and Female-Friendly Social Policy," *Poverty & Public Policy*, 1 (2): 1–23.

Attanayake, A. (2008) "Elitism in Women's Political Participation in Sri Lanka within a South Asian Context," in K. Iwanaga (ed.) *Women's Political Participation and Representation in Asia. Obstacles and Challenges*, Copenhagen: NIAS Press.

Attwood, L. (1999) *Creating the New Soviet Woman: Women's Magazines as Engineers of Female Identity, 1922–53*, New York: St. Martin's Press.

Bashevkin, S. (1993) *Women and Party Politics in English-Canada*, 2nd edn, Toronto: Oxford University Press.

Bashevkin, S. (2009) *Women, Power, Politics: The Hidden Story of Canada's Unfinished Democracy*, Don Mills: Oxford University Press.

Bauer, G. (2008) "'50/50 by 2020': Electoral Gender Quotas for Parliament in East and Southern Africa," *International Feminist Journal of Politics*, 10 (3): 347–67.

Bauer, G. and Britton, H. (eds) (2006) *Women in African Parliaments*, Boulder: Lynne Rienner.

Bauer, J. (2009) "Women and the 2005 Election in Liberia," *Journal of Modern African Studies*, 47 (2): 193–211.

Becker, H. (2006) "'New Things After Independence': Gender and Traditional Authorities in Postcolonial Namibia," *Journal of Southern African Studies*, 32 (1): 29–48.

Bekoe, D. and Parajon, C. (2007) "Women's Role in Liberia's Reconstruction," *USIPeace Briefing*, May. Online. Available at: www.ciaonet.org/pbei/usip/usip10142/index.html (accessed August 2009).

Bendix, J. (2007) "Germany," in C. Hay and A. Menon (eds) *European Politics*, Oxford: Oxford University Press.

Berger, I. and White, F. (eds) (1999) *Women in Sub-Saharan Africa: Restoring Women to History*, Bloomington: Indiana University Press.

Bergman, S. (2004) "Collective Organizing and Claim Making on Child Care in Norden: Blurring the Boundaries between the Inside and the Outside," *Social Politics*, 11 (2): 217–46.

Bergqvist, C. (1998) "Frauen, Männer und die politische Repräsentation in Schweden," in B. Hoecker and G. Fuchs (eds) *Handbuch Politische Partizipation von Frauen in Europa*, Leverkusen: Verlag Leske+Budrich.

Bergqvist, C. (1999) "Childcare and Parental Leave Models," in Christina Bergqvist, Anette Borchorst, Ann-Dorte Christensen, Viveca Ramstedt-Silén, Nina C. Raaum and Auður Styrkársdóttir (eds) *Equal Democracies? Gender and Politics in the Nordic Countries*, Oslo: Scandinavian University Press.

Bergqvist, C., Blandy, T.O. and Sainsbury, D. (2007) "Swedish State Feminism: Continuity and Change," in J. Outshoorn and J. Kantola (eds) *Changing State Feminism*, Basingstoke: Palgrave Macmillan.

Bismi Infos (2007) "Le nouveau gouvernement marocain: 33 ministres dont 7 femmes." Online. Available at: www.bismi.net/articlelecture.php?id=1204 (accessed October 2009).

Black, D. (1996) *Women Parliamentarians in Australia 1921–1996*, Perth: Legislative Assembly.

Black, J.H. (2000) "Entering the Political Elite in Canada: the Case of Minority Women as Parliamentary Candidates and MPs," *Canadian Review of Sociology and Anthropology*, 37 (2): 143–66.

Black, J.H. and Erickson, L. (2000) "Similarity, Compensation or Difference? A Comparison of Female and Male Office-seekers," *Women & Politics*, 21 (4): 1–38.

Blondel, J. (1988) "Introduction: Western European Cabinets in Comparative Perspective," in J. Blondel and F. Müller-Rommel (eds) *Cabinets in Western Europe*, London: Macmillan.

Bochel, C. and Bochel, H. (2008) "Women 'Leaders' in Local Government in the UK," *Parliamentary Affairs*, 61 (3): 426–41.

Borchorst, A. (1999) "Equal Status Institutions," in Christina Bergqvist, Anette Borchorst, Ann-Dorte Christensen, Viveca Ramstedt-Silén, Nina C. Raaum and Auður Styrkársdóttir (eds) *Equal Democracies? Gender and Politics in the Nordic Countries*, Oslo: Scandinavian University Press.

Borchorst, A. (2003) *Kön, magt og beslutninger. Politiske forhandlinger om barselsorlov 1901–2002*, Aarhus: Magtudredningen.

Borchorst, A., Christensen, A.D. and Raaum, N.C. (1999) "Equal Democracies? Conclusions and Perspectives," in Christina Bergqvist, Anette Borchorst, Ann-Dorte Christensen, Viveca Ramstedt-Silén, Nina C. Raaum and Auður Styrkársdóttir (eds) *Equal Democracies? Gender and Politics in the Nordic Countries*, Oslo: Scandinavian University Press.

Borrelli, M. (1997) "Gender, Credibility, and Politics: the Senate Nomination Hearings of Cabinet Secretaries-Designate, 1975 to 1993," *Political Research Quarterly*, 50 (1): 171–97.

Borrelli, M. (2002) *The President's Cabinet: Gender, Power and Representation*, Boulder: Lynne Rienner.

Borrelli, M. (2005) "Cabinet Nominations in the William J. Clinton and George W. Bush Administrations," in S. Tolleson-Rinehard and J.J. Josephson (eds) *Gender and American Politics: Women, Men and the Political Process*, Armonk: M.E. Sharpe.

Borrelli, M. and Martin, J.M. (eds) (1997) *The Other Elites. Women, Politics and Power in the Executive Branch*, Boulder: Lynne Rienner.

Börzel, T. and Risse, T. (2003) "Conceptualizing the Domestic Impact of Europe," in K. Featherstone and C. Radaelli (eds) *The Politics of Europeanization*, New York: Oxford University Press.

Bruszt, L. and Stark, D. (1998) *Post-Socialist Pathways. Transforming Politics and Property in East Central Europe*, Cambridge: Cambridge University Press.

Buckley, F. and Galligan, Y. (2010) "Women's Political Leadership – Europe," in K. O'Connor (ed.) *Gender and Women's Leadership*, Thousand Oaks: Sage.

Burnet, J. (2008) "Gender Balance and the Meanings of Women in Governance in Post-Genocide Rwanda," *African Affairs*, 107 (428): 361–86.

Burns, N., Schlozman, K.L. and Verba, S. (2001) *The Private Roots of Public Action: Gender, Equality and Political Participation*, Cambridge, MA: Harvard University Press.

Buvinic, M. and Roza, V. (2004) *La Mujer, La Política, y el Futuro Democrático de América Latina*, Inter-American Development Bank, Social Development Division, Sustainable Development Department, Technical Papers Series, WID-108. Online. Available at: www.iadb.org/SDS/PROLEAD/index_s.htm (accessed May 2010).

Byrne, L. (2009) "Making a Difference When the Doors Are Open: Women in the Ontario NDP Cabinet, 1990–95," in S. Bashevkin (ed.) *Opening Doors Wider. Women's Political Engagement in Canada*, Vancouver: UBC Press.

Caldwell, J., Missingham, B. and Marck, J. (2001) *The Population of Oceania in the Second Millennium*, Australian National University, Health Transition Centre. Online.

Available at: http://htc.anu.edu.au/pdfs/Oceania%20manuscript.pdf (accessed April 2010).

Camp, R.A. (1979) "Women and Political Leadership in Mexico: a Comparative Study of Female and Male Political Elites," *Journal of Politics*, 41 (2): 417–41.

Carroll, S.J. (1987) "Women in State Cabinets: Status and Prospects," *Journal of State Government*, 60 (5): 204–8.

Carvalho Pinto, V. (2010) *Nation-Building, State and the Genderframing of Women's Rights in the United Arab Emirates (1971–2009)*, Reading: Ithaca Press.

Catalano, A. (2009) "Women Acting for Women? An Analysis of Gender and Debate Participation in the British House of Commons 2005–2007," *Politics & Gender*, 5 (1): 45–68.

Center for American Women and Politics (2009a) "Statewide Elective Executive Women 2009." Online. Available at: www.cawp.rutgers.edu/fast_facts/levels_of_office/documents/stwide.pdf (accessed January 2010).

Center for American Women and Politics (2009b) "Women Appointed to Presidential Cabinets," April. Online. Available at: www.cawp.rutgers.edu/fast_facts/levels_of_office/documents/prescabinet.pdf (accessed June 2010).

Center for American Women and Politics (2010) "History of Women Governors," January. Online. Available at: www.cawp.rutgers.edu/fast_facts/levels_of_office/documents/govhistory.pdf (accessed June 2010).

Center for Asia-Pacific Women in Politics (2009) "Women Heads of State," March. Online. Available at: www.capwip.org/participation/womenheadofstate.html (accessed June 2010).

Centre for Advancement of Women in Politics (2010) "Women Members of the House of Commons," 25 October. Online. Available at: http://www.qub.ac.uk/cawp/UKhtmls/MPs2005.htm (accessed January 2011).

Chowdhury, N. (2005) "Identités marginales et voix effacées des femmes au Jatiya Sangsad," in M. Tremblay (ed.) *Femmes et parlements. Un regard international*, Montreal: Remue-ménage.

Christensen, A.D. (1999) "Women in the Political Parties," in Christina Bergqvist, Anette Borchorst, Ann-Dorte Christensen, Viveca Ramstedt-Silén, Nina C. Raaum and Auður Styrkársdóttir (eds) *Equal Democracies? Gender and Politics in the Nordic Countries*, Oslo: Scandinavian University Press.

CIA (Central Intelligence Agency) (2008) *World Leaders*. Online. Available at: www.cia.gov/library/publications/world-leaders-1/index.html (accessed June 2010).

CIA (2009a) "Chiefs of State and Cabinet Members of Foreign Governments. Burma," *World Leaders*. Online. Available at: www.cia.gov/library/publications/world-leaders-1/world-leaders-b/burma.html (accessed June 2010).

CIA (2009b) "Chiefs of State and Cabinet Members of Foreign Governments. Mexico," *World Leaders*. Online. Available at: www.cia.gov/library/publications/world-leaders-1/world-leaders-m/mexico.html (accessed December 2009).

CIA (2009c) "Morocco," *The World Factbook*. Online. Available at: www.cia.gov/library/publications/the-world-factbook/geos/mo.html (accessed November 2009).

CIA (2009d) "United Arab Emirates," *The World Factbook*. Online. Available at: www.cia.gov/library/publications/the-world-factbook/geos/ae.html (accessed November 2009).

CIA (2010a) *The World Factbook*. Online. Available at: www.cia.gov/library/publications/the-world-factbook/index.html (accessed April 2010).

CIA (2010b) "Burma," *The World Factbook*. Online. Available at: www.cia.gov/library/publications/the-world-factbook/geos/bm.html (accessed June 2010).

CIA (2010c) "Pakistan," *The World Factbook*. Online. Available at: www.cia.gov/library/publications/the-world-factbook/geos/pk.html (accessed March 2010).

Cîrstocea, I. (2002) "Inventer un acteur politique: le régime communiste roumain et la 'question femme' (1945–1965)," *Revue des études sud-est européennes*, 40 (1–2): 233–56.

Corrin, C. (ed.) (1999) *Gender and Identity in Central and Eastern Europe*, London: Frank Cass.

Crowther, W. and Olson, D. (2002) "Committee Systems in New Democratic Parliaments: Comparative Institutionalizations," in W. Crowther and D. Olson (eds) *Committee in Post-Communist Democratic Parliaments: Comparative Institutionalization*, Columbus: Ohio State University Press.

Curtin, J. (1997) *Gender and Political Leadership in New Zealand*, Wellington: House of Representatives, Parliamentary Library, research note 14 1997–1998.

Curtin, J. (2008a) "Gendering Parliamentary Representation in New Zealand: a Mixed System Producing Mixed Results," in M. Tremblay (ed.) *Women and Legislative Representation. Electoral Systems, Political Parties, and Sex Quotas*, New York: Palgrave Macmillan.

Curtin, J. (2008b) "Women, Political Leadership and Substantive Representation: the Case of New Zealand," *Parliamentary Affairs*, 61 (3): 490–504.

Curtin, J. and Devere, H. (2006) "Global Rankings and Domestic Realities: Women, Work and Policy in Australia and New Zealand," *Australian Journal of Political Science*, 41 (2): 193–207.

Curtin, J. and Teghtsoonian, K. (2010) "Analyzing Institutional Persistence: the Case of the Ministry of Women's Affairs in Aotearoa/New Zealand," *Politics & Gender*, 6 (4): 545–72.

Dahlerup, D. (ed.) (2006a) *Women, Quotas and Politics*, London and New York: Routledge.

Dahlerup, D. (2006b) "Conclusion," in D. Dahlerup (ed.) *Women, Quotas and Politics*, London and New York: Routledge.

Dahlerup, D. and Freidenvall, L. (2005) "Quotas as a 'Fast Track' to Equal Representation for Women: Why Scandinavia is No Longer the Model," *International Feminist Journal of Politics*, 7 (1): 26–48.

Darcy, R., Welch, S. and Clark, J. (1994) *Women, Elections & Representation*, 2nd edn revised, Lincoln: University of Nebraska Press.

Davis, R.H. (1997) *Women and Power in Parliament: Cabinet Appointments in Western Europe, 1968–1992*, Lincoln: University of Nebraska Press.

Denmark's Governments since 1848. Online. Available at: www.statsministeriet.dk/_a_2828.html (accessed January 2010).

Devere, H. and Curtin, J. (2009) "Rethinking Political Connections: Women, Friendship, and Politics in New Zealand," in K. McMillan, J. Leslie and E. McLeay (eds) *Rethinking Women and Politics. New Zealand and Comparative Perspectives*, Wellington: Victoria University Press.

Devlin, C. and Elgie, R. (2008) "The Effect of Increased Women's Representation in Parliament: the Case of Rwanda," *Parliamentary Affairs*, 61 (2): 237–54.

Dolan, J. (2001) "Political Appointees in the United States: Does Gender Make a Difference?" *Political Science & Politics*, 34 (2): 213–16.

Dovi, S. (2002) "Preferable Descriptive Representatives: Will Just Any Woman, Black, or Latino Do?" *American Political Science Review*, 96 (4): 729–43.

Dowse, S. (2009) "A Different Kind of Politics," *Inside Story*, December 17: 1–6.

Duerst-Lahti, G. (1997) "Reconceiving Theories of Power: Consequences of Masculinism in the Executive Branch," in M. Borrelli and J.M. Martin (eds) *The Other Elites. Women, Politics and Power in the Executive Branch*, Boulder: Lynne Rienner.

Dunn, E., Beyan, A. and Burrowes, C.P. (2001) *Historical Dictionary of Liberia*, Lanham: Scarecrow Press.

Dyhouse, C. (2006) *Students: A Gendered History*, London: Routledge.

Egypt State Information Service (2009) *Women in the Executive Authority*. Online. Available at: www.sis.gov.eg/En/Story.aspx?sid=2259 (accessed October 2009).

Elgie, R. and Moestrup, S. (2008) *Semi-Presidentialism in Central and Eastern Europe*, Manchester: Manchester University Press.

Elster, J. (1995) "Transition, Constitution-Making and Separation in Czechoslovakia," *European Journal of Sociology*, 36 (1): 105–34.

Escobar-Lemmon, M. and Taylor-Robinson, M.M. (2005) "Women Ministers in Latin American Government: When, Where and Why?" *American Journal of Political Science*, 49 (4): 829–44.

Escobar-Lemmon, M. and Taylor-Robinson, M.M. (2009) "Getting to the Top. Career Paths of Women in Latin American Cabinets," *Political Research Quarterly*, 62 (4): 685–99.

Europa World Book (The) (1998) New York: Routledge.

Europa World Book (The) (2003) New York: Routledge.

Europa World Book (The) (2008) New York: Routledge.

European Commission (2008) "Discrimination in the European Union: Perspectives, Experiences and Attitudes Report," *Special Eurobarometer 296*, Brussels: European Commission.

European Commission Directorate-General for Employment, Social Affairs and Equal Opportunities (DG EMPL) (2009) *Women in European Politics: Time for Action*. Online. Available at: http://ec.europa.eu/social/main.jsp?catId=762&langId=en&furtherPubs=yes (accessed September 2009).

European Commission Directorate-General for Employment, Social Affairs and Equal Opportunities (DG EMPL) (2010) *Politics*. Online. Available at: http://ec.europa.eu/social/main.jsp?catId=774&langId=en (accessed April 2010).

Everitt, J. and Gidengil, E. (2003) "Tough Talk: How Television News Covers Male and Female Leaders of Canadian Political Parties," in M. Tremblay and L. Trimble (eds) *Women and Electoral Politics in Canada*, Don Mills: Oxford University Press.

Falkner, G. and Treib, O. (2008) "Three Worlds of Compliance or Four? The EU-15 Compared to New Member States," *Journal of Common Market Studies*, 46 (2): 293–314.

Fallon, K. (2008) *Democracy and the Rise of Women's Movements in Sub-Saharan Africa*, Baltimore: Johns Hopkins University Press.

Fauss, L. (2003) "Democracy Ideologies: Arab States," in S. Joseph and A. Najmabadi (eds) *Encyclopedia of Women & Islamic Culture: Family, Law, and Politics*, Leiden: Brill.

Feinberg, M. (2006) *Elusive Equality: Gender, Citizenship and the Limits of Democracy in Czechoslovakia, 1918–1950*, Pittsburgh: Pittsburgh University Press.

Finnish Cabinets and Ministers since 1917. Online. Available at: www.statsradet.fi/tietoa-valtioneuvostosta/hallitukset/vuodesta-1917//en.jsp (accessed January 2010).

Fleschenberg, A. and Derichs, C. (2008) *Handbuch Spitzenpolitikerinnen*, Wiesbaden: Verlag für Sozialwissenschften.

Fodor, E. (2002) "Smiling Women and Fighting Men: the Gender of the Communist Subject in State Socialist Hungary," *Gender & Society*, 16 (2): 236–59.

Folgueras, M.D. and Martin, T.C. (2008) "Women's Changing Socio-Economic Position and Union Formation in Spain and Portugal," *Demographic Research*, 19 (41). Online. Available at: www.demographic-research.org (accessed January 2010).

Forest, M. (2006a) "Emerging Gender Interest Groups in the New Member States: the Case of the Czech Republic," *Perspectives on European Politics and Society*, 7 (2): 170–85.

Forest, M. (2006b) "Les transferts institutionnels à l'usage des politiques du genre en Europe centrale," *Revue internationale de politique comparée*, 13 (2): 259–78.

Fox, R.L. and Oxley, Z.M. (2003) "Gender Stereotyping in State Executive Elections: Candidate Selection and Success," *Journal of Politics*, 65 (3): 833–50.

Franceschet, S. (2008) "La Representación Politica de las Mujeres en un País sin Ley de Cuotas: El Caso de Chile," in N. Archenti and M. Inés Tula (eds) *Mujeres Y Politica en América Latina: Sistemas Electorales Y Cuotas de Género*, Buenos Aires: Heliasta.

Fraser, N. and Navarro, M. (1996) *Evita: the Real Life of Eva Perón*, New York: W.W. Norton and Company.

Fuest, V. (2008) " 'This is the Time to Get in Front': Changing Roles and Opportunities for Women in Liberia," *African Affairs*, 107 (427): 210–24.

Funk, N. and Mueller, M. (eds) (1993) *Gender, Politics and Post-Communism: Reflections from Eastern Europe and the Former Soviet Union*, New York: Routledge.

Genovese, M. (ed.) (1993) *Women as National Leaders*, Newbury Park: Sage.

Germany (2010) *Federal Foreign Office*. Online. Available at: www.auswaertiges-amt. de/diplo/en/Startseite.html (accessed June 2010).

Gidengil, E. and Everitt, J. (1999) "Metaphors and Misrepresentation: Gendered Mediation in News Coverage of the 1993 Canadian Leaders' Debates," *Press/Politics*, 4 (1): 48–65.

Gidengil, E. and Everitt, J. (2000) "Filtering the Female: Television News Coverage of the 1993 Canadian Leaders' Debates," *Women & Politics*, 21 (4): 105–31.

Gidengil, E. and Everitt, J. (2003) "Conventional Coverage/Unconventional Politicians: Gender and Media Coverage of Canadian Leaders' Debates, 1993, 1997, 2000," *Canadian Journal of Political Science*, 36 (3): 559–77.

Gidengil, E., Everitt, J. and Banducci, S. (2009) "Do Voters Stereotype Female Party Leaders? Evidence from Canada and New Zealand," in S. Bashevkin (ed.) *Opening Doors Wider. Women's Political Engagement in Canada*, Vancouver: UBC Press.

Gidengil, E., Blais, A., Nadeau, R. and Nevitte, N. (2003) "Women to the Left? Gender Differences in Political Beliefs and Policy Preferences," in M. Tremblay and L. Trimble (eds) *Women and Electoral Politics in Canada*, Don Mills: Oxford University Press.

Gingras, F.-P. (1995) "Daily Male Delivery. Women and Politics in the Daily Newspapers," in F.-P. Gingras (ed.) *Gender and Politics in Contemporary Canada*, Toronto: Oxford University Press.

Glatzer, W., Hondrich, K.O., Noll, H.H., Stiehr, K. and Wörndel, B. (1992) *Recent Social Trends in West Germany, 1960–1990*, Montreal: McGill-Queen's University Press.

Glaurdic, J. (2003) "Croatia's Leap towards Political Equality: Rules and Players," in R.E. Matland and K.A. Montgomery (eds) *Women's Access to Political Power in Post-Communist Europe*, New York: Oxford University Press.

Goetz, K.H. (2003) "Government at the Centre," in S. Padgett, W.E. Paterson and G. Smith (eds) *Developments in German Politics 3*, Basingstoke: Palgrave.

Gouvernement du Royaume du Maroc (2006) *La liste du gouvernement*. Online. Available at: www.maroc.ma/PortailInst/Fr/MenuGauche/Institutions/Gouvernement/ La+liste+du+gouvernement.htm (accessed November 2009).

Goven, J. (1993) "Gender Politics in Hungary. Autonomy and Anti-feminism," in N. Funk and M. Mueller (eds) *Gender, Politics and Post-Communism: Reflections from Eastern Europe and the Former Soviet Union*, New York: Routledge.

Government of the Republic of Liberia Executive Mansion – President's Cabinet (n.d.) Online. Available at: www.emansion.gov.lr/content.php?sub=President's Cabinet&related=The President (accessed August 2009).

Grey, S. and Sawer, M. (2005) "Australia and New Zealand," in Y. Galligan and M. Tremblay (eds) *Sharing Power: Women, Parliament, Democracy*, Aldershot: Ashgate.

Harris, D. (2006) "Liberia 2005: an Unusual African Post-Conflict Election," *Journal of Modern African Studies*, 44 (3): 375–95.

Havens, K. and Healy, L. (1991) "Cabinet Level Appointments in Connecticut: Women Making a Difference," in D.L. Dodson (ed.) *Gender and Policy Making Studies of Women in Office*, New Brunswick: The State University of New Jersey, Center for American Women and Politics.

Heinen, J. and Matuchniak-Krasuska, A. (2002) *L'Avortement en Pologne: la croix et la bannière*, Paris: L'Harmattan, Coll. "Logiques sociales".

Heitlinger, A. (1985) "Passage to Motherhood: Personal and Social 'Management' of Reproduction in Czechoslovakia in the 1980's," in S.L. Wolchik and A.G. Meyer (eds) *Women, State and Party in Eastern Europe*, Durham, NC: Duke University Press.

Hobson, B. (2003) "Recognition Struggles in Universalistic and Gender Distinctive Frames: Sweden and Ireland," in B. Hobson (ed.) *Recognition Struggles and Social Movements. Contested Identities, Agency and Power*, Cambridge: Cambridge University Press.

Holli, A.M. (2008a) "Electoral Reform Opens Roads to Presidency for Finnish Women," *Politics & Gender*, 4 (3): 496–508.

Holli, A.M. (2008b) "Feminist Triangles: a Conceptual Analysis," *Representation*, 44 (2): 169–85.

Hoogensen, G. and Solheim, B. (2006) *Women in Power: World Leaders since 1960*, Westport: Praeger.

Howe, M. (2005) *Morocco: the Islamist Awakening and Other Challenges*, Oxford and New York: Oxford University Press.

Htun, M.N. (1997) *Moving into Power: Expanding Women's Opportunities for Leadership in Latin America and the Caribbean*, Washington, DC: Inter-American Development Bank, Social Programs and Sustainable Development Department, Women in Development Program Unit, WID97–103.

Huddy, L. and Terkildsen, N. (1993) "Gender Stereotypes and the Perception of Male and Female Candidates," *American Journal of Political Science*, 37 (1): 119–47.

Human Rights Commission (HRC) (2008) *New Zealand Census of Women's Participation*, Wellington: Human Rights Commission.

Ilonszki, G. and Montgomery, K. (2003) "Weak Mobilization, Hidden Majoritarianism, and Resurgence of the Right: a Recipe for Female Under-Representation in Hungary," in R.E. Matland and K.A. Montgomery (eds) *Women's Access to Political Power in Post-Communist Europe*, New York: Oxford University Press.

Inglehart, R. and Norris, P. (2003) *Rising Tide: Gender Equality and Cultural Change around the World*, Cambridge: Cambridge University Press.

International IDEA (2010) *Table of Electoral Systems Worldwide*. Online. Available at: www.idea.int/esd/world.cfm (accessed June 2010).

Inter-Parliamentary Union (2008) *Women in Politics. Situation on 1 January 2008*. Online. Available at: www.ipu.org/pdf/publications/wmnmap10_en.pdf (accessed October 2009).

Inter-Parliamentary Union (2009a) *Geopolitical Groups*. Online. Available at: www.ipu.org/strct-e/geopol.htm (accessed November 2009).

Inter-Parliamentary Union (2009b) *Women in National Parliaments*. Online. Available at: www.ipu.org (accessed December 2009).

Inter-Parliamentary Union (2010a) *PARLINE Database on National Parliaments*. Online. Available at: www.ipu.org/parline/parlinesearch.asp (accessed June 2010).

Inter-Parliamentary Union (2010b) *Women in National Parliaments. World Average.* Online. Available at: www.ipu.org/wmn-e/world.htm (accessed May 2010).

Inter-Parliamentary Union (2010c) *Women in National Parliaments. World Classification*. Online. Available at: www.ipu.org/wmn-e/classif.htm (accessed May 2010).

Inter-Parliamentary Union (2010d) *Women in Politics: 2010*. Online. Available at: www.ipu.org/pdf/publications/wmnmap10_en.pdf (accessed April 2010).

Inter-Parliamentary Union (n.d.) *Women in National Parliaments. Statistical Archives*. Online. Available at: www.ipu.org/wmn-e/classif-arc.htm (accessed June 2010).

Iturbe de Blanco, E. (2003) *Las Mujeres Latinoamericanas en la Alta Gestión Pública: Logros y Desafíos*, Banco Interamericano de Desarrollo, Departamento de Desarrollo Sostenible, Serie de Buenas Prácticas, SGC-103. Online. Available at: www.iadb.org/gabinete.doc (accessed June 2010).

Iwanaga, K. (2008) "Women in Thai Politics," in K. Iwanaga (ed.) *Women's Political Participation and Representation in Asia. Obstacles and Challenges*, Copenhagen: NIAS Press.

Jackson-Laufer, G. (1998) *Women Who Ruled: a Biographical Encyclopedia*, New York: Barnes and Noble Books.

Jacobsen, T. (2008) "Beyond Apsara: Women, Tradition and Trajectories in Cambodian Politics," in K. Iwanaga (ed.) *Women's Political Participation and Representation in Asia. Obstacles and Challenges*, Copenhagen: NIAS Press.

Jalalzai, F. (2004) "Women Political Leaders: Past and Present," *Women and Politics*, 26 (3/4): 85–108.

Jalalzai, F. (2008) "Women Rule: Shattering the Executive Glass Ceiling," *Politics & Gender*, 4 (2): 205–31.

Jalalzai, F. and Krook, M.L. (2010) "Beyond Hillary and Benazir: Women's Political Leadership Worldwide," *International Political Science Review*, 31 (1): 5–21.

Jalusić, V. (2004) "Gender and the Victimization of the Nation as a Preand Post-War Identity Discourse," in M. Hadžić (ed.) *The Violent Dissolution of Yugoslavia. Causes, Dynamics and Effects*, Belgrade: Centre for Civil-Military Relations.

Jancar, B.W. (1978) *Women Under Communism*, Baltimore: Johns Hopkins University Press.

Jancar, B.W. (1985) "The New Feminism in Yugoslavia," in P. Ramet (ed.) *Yugoslavia in the 1980's*, Boulder: Westview Press.

Jancar, B.W. (1990) *Women and Revolution in Yugoslavia, 1941–1945*, Denver: Arden Press.

Jensen, J. (2008) *Women Political Leaders. Breaking the Highest Glass Ceiling*, New York and Houndmills: Palgrave Macmillan.

Jibrin, I. (2004) "The First Lady Syndrome and the Marginalisation of Women from Power: Opportunities or Compromises for Gender Equality?" *Feminist Africa*, 3. Online. Available at: www.feministafrica.org/index.php/first-lady-syndrome (accessed August 2009).

Johnson Sirleaf, E. (2009) *This Child Will be Great. Memoir of a Remarkable Life by Africa's First Woman President*, New York: HarperCollins.

Jones, M.P. (1996) "Increasing Women's Representation Via Gender Quotas: the Argentine Ley de Cupos," *Women & Politics*, 16 (4): 75–98.

Jones, M.P. (2008) "The Recruitment and Selection of Legislative Candidates in Argentina," in P.M. Siavelis and S. Morgenstern (eds) *Pathways to Power: Political Recruitment and Candidate Selection in Latin America*, University Park: Pennsylvania State University Press.

Jones, M.P. (2009) "Gender Quotas, Electoral Laws, and the Election of Women: Evidence from the Latin American Vanguard," *Comparative Political Studies*, 42 (1): 56–81.

Jordan Times, The (2009) "New Ministers Sworn in," February 24. Online. Available at: www.jordantimes.com/?news=14555 (accessed November 2009).

Kandiyoti, D. (1991) "Introduction," in D. Kandiyoti (ed.) *Women, Islam and the State*, Basingstoke: Macmillan.

Karlsson, G. (1996) *Från broderskap till systerskap. Det socialdemokratiska kvinnoförbundets kamp för inflytande och makt i SAP*, Lund: Arkiv Förlag.

Karvonen, L. (1994) "Christian Parties in Scandinavia: Victory over the Windmills?" in D. Hanley (ed.) *Christian Democracy in Europe: a Comparative Perspective*, London: Printer Publishers.

Kasapović, M. (2008) "Semi-Presidentialism in Croatia," in R. Elgie and S. Moestrup (eds) *Semi-Presidentialism in Central and Eastern Europe*, Manchester: Manchester University Press.

Keiser, L.R., Wilkins, V.M., Meier, K.J. and Holland, C.A. (2002) "Lipstick and Logarithms: Gender, Institutional Context, and Representative Bureaucracy," *American Political Science Review*, 96 (3): 553–64.

Kerby, M. (2009) "Worth the Wait: Determinants of Ministerial Appointment in Canada, 1935–2008," *Canadian Journal of Political Science*, 42 (3): 593–611.

Khus, T.C. (2004) "Cambodia," in Freidrich Ebert Stiftung (ed.) *Southeast Asian Women in Politics and Decision-Making, Ten Years After Beijing. Gaining Ground?*, Manila: FES Philippine Office.

Kligman, G. (1998) *The Politics of Duplicity. Controlling Reproduction in Ceausescu's Romania*, Los Angeles: UCLA Press.

Kohn, W.S.G. (1984) "Women in the Canadian House of Commons," *American Review of Canadian Studies*, 14 (3): 298–311.

Krizsan, A. (2009) "From Formal Adoption to Enforcement. Post-Accession Shifts in EU Impact on Hungary in the Equality Policy Field," in F. Schimmel Fennig and F. Trauner (eds) "Post-Accession Compliance in the EU's New Member States," *European Integration online Papers (EIoP)*, 2 (13). Online. Available at: http://eiop.or.at/eiop/texte/2009–002a.htm (accessed March 2010).

Krook, M.L. (2006) "Reforming Representation: the Diffusion of Candidate Gender Quotas Worldwide," *Politics & Gender*, 2 (3): 303–27.

Krook, M.L. (2009) *Quotas for Women in Politics: Gender and Candidate Selection Reform Worldwide*, New York: Oxford University Press.

Krupavičius, A. (2008) "Semi-Presidentialism in Lithuania: Origins, Development and Challenges," in R. Elgie and S. Moestrup (eds) *Semi-Presidentialism in Central and Eastern Europe*, Manchester: Manchester University Press.

Krupavičius, A. and Matonyté, I. (2003) "Women in Lithuanian Politics: From Nomenklatura Selection to Representation," in R.E. Matland and K.A. Montgomery (eds) *Women's Access to Political Power in Post-Communist Europe*, New York: Oxford University Press.

Kuhar, R. (2008) "Policy Approach: Self-Discrimination. Same-Sex Partnership Legislation in Slovenia and Croatia," unpublished paper, Mannheim: Connex Network of Excellence.

Landler, M. (2009) "A New Gender Agenda," *New York Times*, August 18. Online. Available at: www.nytimes.com/2009/08/23/magazine/23clinton-t.html (accessed October 2009).

Laskier, M.M. (2003) "A Difficult Inheritance: Moroccan Society under King Muhammad VI," *Middle East Review of International Affairs*, 7 (3): 1–26.

Leira, A. (1992) *Welfare States and Working Mothers*, New York: Cambridge University Press.

Liberian Constitution and Election Laws Forum (n.d.) Online. Available at: www.liberianlegal.com/constitution1986.htm (accessed March 2010).

Lippman, T. (2004) *Madeleine Albright and the New American Diplomacy*, New York: Westview.

Liswood, L. (2007) *Women World Leaders: Great Politicians Tell Their Stories*, 2nd edn, Washington, DC: Council of Women World Leaders.

Longman, T. (1998) "Rwanda: Chaos from Above," in L. Villalon and P. Huxtable (eds) *The African State at a Critical Juncture: Between Disintegration and Reconfiguration*, Boulder: Lynne Rienner.

Longman, T. (2006) "Rwanda: Achieving Equality or Serving an Authoritarian State," in G. Bauer and H. Britton (eds) *Women in African Parliaments*, Boulder: Lynne Rienner.

Lyons, E. (1972) *Among the Carrion Crows*, Adelaide: Rigby.

McBride-Stetson, D. (2004) *Women's Rights in the USA: Policy Debates and Gender Roles*, 3rd edn, New York: Routledge.

McClelland, A. and St John, S. (2006) "Social Policy Responses to Globalisation in Australia and New Zealand, 1980–2005," *Australian Journal of Political Science*, 41 (2): 177–91.

MacIvor, H. (1996) *Women and Politics in Canada*, Peterborough: Broadview Press.

McKay, J. (2003) "Women's Quotas in Germany: Part of the Problem or Part of the Solution?" paper presented at the Conference of the European Consortium for Political Science Research (ECPR), Marburg, September.

McLeay, E. (1995) *The Cabinet and Political Power in New Zealand*, Melbourne: Oxford University Press.

McLeay, E. (2009) "Spare the Rod? The Story of How Sue Bradford, Green Party MP 1999–2009, Fought for the Rights of New Zealand Children and Changed the Law," paper presented to the Public Leadership Workshop, Australian National University, Canberra, November.

Maddy-Weitzman, B. (2005) "Women, Islam, and the Moroccan State: the Struggle Over the Personal Status Law," *Middle East Journal*, 59 (3): 393–410.

Mahbub ul Haq Development Centre (2000) *Human Development in South Asia 2000. The Gender Question*, Karachi and Oxford: Oxford University Press.

Martin, J.M. (1989) "The Recruitment of Women to Cabinet and Subcabinet Posts," *Western Political Quarterly*, 42 (1): 161–72.

Martin, J.M. (2003) *The Presidency and Women. Promise, Performance, and Illusion*, College Station: Texas A&M University Press.

Matemba, Y. (2005) "A Chief Called 'Woman': Historical Perspectives on the Changing Face of Bogosi (Chieftainship) in Botswana, 1834–2004," *JENDA: Journal of Culture and African Women Studies*, 7. Online. Available at: www.jendajournal.com/issue7/matemba.html (accessed January 2010).

Mathiason, J. with Dookhony, L. (2006) *Women in Governmental Decision-Making in the Early 21st Century. What Has – and Has Not – Been Achieved in the Post-Beijing Period*. Online. Available at: www.salzburgseminar.org/mediafiles/MEDIA28775.pdf (accessed July 2009).

Matland, R.E. (1998) "Women's Representation in National Legislatures: Developed and Developing Countries," *Legislative Studies Quarterly*, 23 (1): 109–25.

Matland, R.E. (2003) "Women's Representation in Post-Communist Europe," in R.E. Matland and K.A. Montgomery (eds) *Women's Access to Political Power in Post-Communist Europe*, New York: Oxford University Press.

Matland, R.E. (2006) "Electoral Quotas: Frequency and Effectiveness," in D. Dahlerup (ed.) *Women, Quotas and Politics*, London and New York: Routledge.

Matland, R.E. and Montgomery, K.A. (eds) (2003) *Women's Access to Political Power in Post-Communist Europe*, New York: Oxford University Press.

Matland, R.E. and Studlar, D.T. (1996) "The Contagion of Women Candidates in Single-Member District and Proportional Representation Electoral Systems: Canada and Norway," *Journal of Politics*, 58 (3): 707–33.

Mernissi, F. (2006) "Digital Scheherazades in the Arab World," *Current History*, 105 (689): 121–26.

Mills, J. (2000) "Militarism, Civil War and Women's Status: a Burma Case Study," in L. Edwards and M. Roces (eds) *Women in Asia. Tradition, Modernity and Globalisation*, Ann Arbor: University of Michigan Press.

Mi Mi, K. (1984) *The World of Burmese Women*, London: Zed Books.

Ministry of Women's Affairs (MWA) (2002) *Briefing to the Incoming Government July 2002*, Wellington: Ministry of Women's Affairs.

Misiunas, R. and Taagepera, R. (1993) *The Baltic States: Years of Dependence 1940–1990*, expanded edn, Berkeley: University of California Press.

Moghadam, V. (2008) "Modernizing Women in the Middle East," in Y.M. Choueiri (ed.) *A Companion to the History of the Middle East*, Malden: Blackwell.

Molyneux, M. (1985) "Mobilization without Emancipation? Women's Interests, the State, and Revolution in Nicaragua," *Feminist Studies*, 11 (2): 227–54.

Moncrief, G.F. and Studlar, D.T. (1996) "Women Cabinet Ministers in Canadian Provinces 1976–1994," *Canadian Parliamentary Review*, 19 (3): 10–13.

Moon, J. and Fountain, I. (1997) "Keeping the Gates? Women as Ministers in Australia, 1970–1996," *Australian Journal of Political Science*, 32 (3): 455–66.

Moore, G. and Shackman, G. (1996) "Gender and Authority: A Cross-National Study," *Social Science Quarterly*, 77 (2): 275–88.

Moran, M. and Pitcher, A. (2004) "The 'Basket Case' and the 'Poster Child': Explaining the End of Civil Conflicts in Liberia and Mozambique," *Third World Quarterly*, 25 (3): 501–19.

Muñez, M.P. (2004) "Philippines," in Friedrich Ebert Stiftung (ed.) *Southeast Asian Women in Politics and Decision-Making, Ten Years After Beijing. Gaining Ground?*, Manila: FES Philippine Office.

Murray, R. (2009) "Was 2007 a Landmark or a Let-Down for Women's Political Representation in France?" *Representation*, 45 (1): 29–38.

Mushaben, J. (2005) "Girl Power, Mainstreaming and Critical Mass: Women's Leadership and Policy Paradigm Shift in Germany's Red-Green Coalition, 1988–2002," *Journal of Women, Politics and Policy*, 27 (1): 135–61.

Naciri, R. (1998) "The Women's Movement and Political Discourse in Morocco," *United Nations Development Programme, Occasional Paper 8*, Geneva: United Nations Research Institute for Social Development. Online. Available at: www.unrisd.org/unrisd/website/document.nsf/ab82a6805797760f80256b4f005a1ab/88f77673c5a57372 80256b67005b6b98/$FILE/opb8.pdf (accessed November 2009).

Naciri, R. (2005) "Morocco," *Freedom House*. Online. Available at: www.freedomhouse.org/template.cfm?page=178 (accessed November 2009).

Nanivadekar, M. (2005) "Les quotas et la représentation politique des femmes: un tour d'horizon," in M. Tremblay (ed.) *Femmes et parlements. Un regard international*, Montreal: Remue-ménage.

Navia, P. (2008) "Legislative Candidate Selection in Chile," in P.M. Siavelis and S. Morgenstern (eds) *Pathways to Power: Political Recruitment and Candidate Selection in Latin America*, University Park: Pennsylvania State University Press.

Newbury, C. (1992) "Rwanda: Recent Debates over Governance and Rural Development," in G. Hyden and M. Bratton (eds) *Governance and Politics in Africa*, Boulder: Lynne Rienner.

Niskanen, K. (2007) *Karriär i männens värld. Nationalekonomen och feministen Karin Kock*, Stockholm: SNS.

Norris, P. (1985) "Women's Legislative Participation in Western Europe," *West European Politics*, 8 (4): 90–101.

Norris, P. (ed.) (1997a) *Passages to Power. Legislative Recruitment in Advanced Democracies*, Cambridge: Cambridge University Press.

Norris, P. (1997b) "Choosing Electoral Systems: Proportional, Majoritarian and Mixed Systems," *International Political Science Review*, 18 (3): 297–312.

Norris, P. (2004) *Electoral Engineering. Voting Rules and Political Behaviour*, Cambridge: Cambridge University Press.

Norris, P. and Lovenduski, J. (1995) *Political Representation and Recruitment: Gender, Race and Class in the British Parliament*, Cambridge: Cambridge University Press.

Norwegian Government Ministries and Offices Since 1945 (2010) Online. Available at: www.regjeringen.no/en/the-government/previous-governments/the=structure-of-the-registry/governments/modern-times/governments-since-1945 (accessed January 2010).

Norwegian Government Ministries and Offices Since 1814. Online. Available at: www.regjeringen.no/en/the-government/previous-governments.html?id=85847 (accessed January 2010).

Oakes, J.M. (1994) "The Honourable Members: Parliamentary Careers in Canada, 1958–1993," unpublished thesis, University of Toronto.

Official Website of the Government of Rwanda – Cabinet (n.d.) Online. Available at: www.gov.rw/page.php?id_article=67 (accessed August 2009).

Olson, D. (1980) *The Legislative Process: a Comparative Approach*, New York: Harper & Row.

O'Malley, E. (2006) "Ministerial Selection in Ireland: Limited Choice in a Political Village," *Irish Political Studies*, 21 (3): 319–26.

Opfell, O. (1993) *Women Prime Ministers and Presidents*, Jefferson: McFarland and Company.

Otieno, A. (2008) "Gender Mainstreaming through Women's Leadership: the Liberian Example," *Critical Half* [Women for Women International], 6 (1): 29–35.

Pankhurst, D. (2002) "Women and Politics in Africa: the Case of Uganda," in K. Ross (ed.) *Women, Politics and Change*, Oxford: Oxford University Press.

Parpart, J. (1988) "Women and the State in Africa," in D. Rothchild and N. Chazan (eds) *The Precarious Balance: State and Society in Africa*, Boulder: Westview Press.

Paxton, P. and Hughes, M.M. (2007) *Women, Politics and Power. A Global Perspective*, Los Angeles: Pine Forge Press.

Paxton, P. and Kunovich, S. (2003) "Women's Political Representation: the Importance of Ideology," *Social Forces*, 82 (1): 87–114.

Payne, J.M., Zovatto, G.D. and Diaz, M.M. (2007) *Democracies in Development: Politics and Reform in Latin America, Expanded and Updated Edition*, Washington, DC: Inter-American Development Bank.

Pearson, E. and Powley, E. (2008) "Demonstrating Legislative Leadership: the Introduction of Rwanda's Gender Based Violence Bill," *The Initiative for Inclusive Security*. Online. Available at: www.huntalternatives.org/download/1078_rwanda_demostrating_legislative_leadership_updated_6_20_08.pdf (accessed August 2009).

Pennell, C.R. (2000) *Morocco since 1830: a History*, London: Hurst.

Perrotino, M. (2000) "La persistance du parti communiste de Bohême et de Moravie," *Transitions*, 41 (1): 85–100.

Phillips, A. (1998) "Democracy and Representation: Or, Why Should it Matter Who Our Representatives Are?" in A. Phillips (ed.) *Feminism and Politics*, Oxford: Oxford University Press.

Posner, D. and Young, D. (2007) "The Institutionalization of Political Power in Africa," *Journal of Democracy*, 18 (3): 126–40.

Powley, E. (2004) "Strengthening Governance: the Role of Women in Rwanda's Transition. A Summary," *United Nations OSAGI*. Online. Available at: www.un.org/womenwatch/osagi/meetings/2004/EGMelectoral/EP5-Powley.PDF (accessed August 2009).

PROLID (2007) *Base de Datos de Ministras de Estado en América Latina*, Washington, DC: Banco Interamericano de Desarrollo. Online. Available at: http://iadb.org/SDS/PROLEAD/index_s.htm (accessed June 2010).

Putnam, R.D. (1976) *The Comparative Study of Political Elites*, Englewood Cliffs: Prentice-Hall.

Raaum, N. (1999) "Women in Parliamentary Politics: Historical Lines of Development," in Christina Bergqvist, Anette Borchorst, Ann-Dorte Christensen, Viveca Ramstedt-Silén, Nina C. Raaum and Auður Styrkársdóttir (eds) *Equal Democracies? Gender and Politics in the Nordic Countries*, Oslo: Scandinavian University Press.

Raaum, N. (2005) "Gender Equality and Political Representation: a Nordic Comparison," *West European Politics*, 28 (4): 872–97.

Real-Dato, J. (2009) "Intra-Party Conflict and Cabinet Dynamics in Democratic Spain 1977–2008," paper presented at the Conference of the European Consortium for Political Science Research (ECPR), Berlin, September.

Republic of South Africa Government Communications (2009) Photo Gallery – Faces of Government. Online. Available at: www.gcis.gov.za/resource_centre/multimedia/audio_visual/photo_galley/faces/index.html#sec1 (accessed August 2009).

Reynolds, A. (1999) "Women in the Legislatures and Executives of the World: Knocking at the Highest Glass Ceiling," *World Politics*, 51 (4): 547–72.

Richter, L. (1991) "Explaining Theories of Female Leadership in South and South East Asia," *Pacific Affairs*, 63 (4): 524–40.

Rincker, M.E. (2009) "Masculinized or Marginalized: Decentralization and Women's Status in Regional Polish Institutions," *Journal of Women, Politics and Policy*, 30 (1): 46–69.

Ríos Tobar, M. (2007) "Chilean Feminism and Social Democracy for the Democratic Transition to Bachelet," *NACLA Report on the Americas*, 40 (2): 25–9.

Ríos Tobar, M. (2008) "Seizing a Window of Opportunity: the Election of President Bachelet in Chile," *Politics & Gender*, 4 (4): 509–19.

Robinson, G.J. and Saint-Jean, A. (1996) "From Flora to Kim: Thirty Years of Representation of Canadian Women Politicians," in H. Holmes and D. Taras (eds) *Seeing Ourselves: Media Power and Policy in Canada*, 2nd edn, Toronto: Harcourt Brace.

Robinson, G.J. and Saint-Jean, A. with Rioux, C. (1991) "Women Politicians and Their Media Coverage: a Generational Analysis," in K. Megyery (ed.) *Women in Canadian Politics: Towards Equity in Representation*, Toronto: Dundurn Press.

Roces, M. (2000) "Negotiating Modernities: Filipino Women 1970–2000," in L. Edwards and M. Roces (eds) *Women in Asia. Tradition, Modernity and Globalisation*, Ann Arbor: University of Michigan Press.

Rock, D. (1987) *Argentina 1516–1987: From Spanish Colonization to Alfonsin*, Berkeley: University of California Press.

Rose, R. (1976) "On the Priorities of Government: a Developmental Analysis of Public Policies," *European Journal of Political Research*, 4 (3): 247–89.

Rouse, S. (2004) *Shifting Body Politics. Gender, Nation, State in Pakistan*, New Delhi: Women Unlimited Feminist Fine Print.

Rueschemeyer, M. and Wolchik, S. (eds) (2009) *Women in Power in Post-Communist Parliaments*, Bloomington: Indiana University Press.

Rule, W. (1987) "Electoral Systems, Contextual Factors and Women's Opportunities for Election to Parliament in Twenty-Three Democracies," *Western Political Quarterly*, 40 (3): 477–98.

Russell, C. and DeLancey, M. (2002) "African Women in Cabinet Positions – Too Few, Too Weak: a Research Report," *Asian Women*, 15: 147–63.

Sabbagh, A. (2005) "The Arab States: Enhancing Women's Political Participation," in J. Ballington and A. Karam (eds) *Women in Parliament: Beyond Numbers*, Stockholm: International Institute for Democracy and Electoral Assistance. Online. Available at: www.idea.int/publications/wip2/upload/WiP_inlay.pdf (accessed November 2009).

Sainsbury, D. (1999) "Gender and Social-Democratic Welfare States," in D. Sainsbury (ed.) *Gender and Welfare State Regimes*, Oxford: Oxford University Press.

Sainsbury, D. (2004) "Women's Political Representation in Sweden: Discursive Politics and Institutional Presence," *Scandinavian Political Studies*, 27 (1): 65–87.

Sainsbury, D. (2005) "Party Feminism, State Feminism and Women's Representation in Sweden," in Joni Lovenduski, Claudie Baudino, Marila Guadagnini, Petra Meier and Diane Sainsbury (eds) *State Feminism and Political Representation*, Cambridge: Cambridge University Press.

Sampert, S. and Trimble, L. (2003) "'Wham, Bam, No Thank You Ma'am': Gender and the Game Frame in National Newspaper Coverage of Election 2000," in M. Tremblay and L. Trimble (eds) *Women and Electoral Politics in Canada*, Don Mills: Oxford University Press.

Sapiro, V. (1984) *The Political Integration of Women. Roles, Socialization and Politics*, Urbana: University of Illinois Press.

Savoie, D.J. (1999) *Governing from the Centre. The Concentration of Powers in Canadian Politics*, Toronto: University of Toronto Press.

Sawer, M. (2009) "Women and the 2007 Federal Election," *Australian Cultural History*, 27 (2): 167–74.

Sawer, M. (2010) "Women and Elections," in L. LeDuc, R.G. Niemi and P. Norris (eds) *Comparing Democracies*, 3rd edn, London: Sage.

Sawer, M. and Simms, M. (1993) *A Woman's Place: Women and Politics in Australia*, 2nd edn, Sydney: Allen & Unwin.

Sawyer, A. (2008) "Emerging Patterns in Liberia's Post-Conflict Politics: Observations from the 2005 Elections," *African Affairs*, 107 (427): 177–99.

Saxonberg, S. (2000) "Women in East European Parliaments," *Journal of Democracy*, 11 (2): 145–57.

Schmidt, J. (2008) "Naher und Mittlerer Osten – Sheherazade im Parlament?" in A. Fleschenberg and C. Derichs (eds) *Handbuch Spitzenpolitikerinnen*, Wiesbaden: VS.

Schüler, D. (2006) "The Uses and Misuses of the Gender-related Development Index and Gender Empowerment Measure. A Review of the Literature," *Journal of Human Development*, 7 (2): 161–81.

Schwindt-Bayer, L.A. (2007) "Women in Power: How Presence Affects Politics," paper presented at the Inter-American Dialogue, Inter-American Development Bank, League of Women Voters of the United States, and Organization of American States sponsored conference "Women in the Americas: Paths to Political Power," Washington, DC, March.

Schwindt-Bayer, L.A. (2008) "Women and Power in the Americas: a Report Card," in *Women in the Americas: Paths to Political Power. A Report Card on Women in Political Leadership*, Washington, DC: Inter-American Development Bank: 5–18. Online. Available at: www.thedialogue.org/page.cfm?pageID=5 (accessed December 2009).

Sczesny, S., Bosak, J., Neff, D. and Schuns, B. (2004) "Gender Stereotypes and the Attribution of Leadership Traits: a Cross-Cultural Comparison," *Sex Roles*, 41 (11): 631–45.

Segovia, C. (2005) "Hacia la Presidencial del 2005. Cambios en las Preferencias de la Opinión Pública 2001–2004," in *Centro de Estudios Públicos Puntos de Referencia 277*. Online. Available at: www.cepchile.cl (accessed October 2009).

Shaheed, F., Zia, A. and Worraich, S. (1998) "Women in Politics: Participation and Representation in Pakistan with Update 1993–1997," *Special Bulletin*, Lahore, April.

Shaheen, A.R. (2009) *Saudi Arabia Appoints First Woman Minister*. Online. Available at: http://gulfnews.com/news/gulf/saudi-arabia/saudi-arabia-appoints-first-woman-minister-1.51705 (accessed October 2009).

Sharabi, H. (1988) *Neopatriarchy: a Theory of Distorted Change in Arab Society*, New York: Oxford University Press.

Siaroff, A. (2000) "Women's Representation in Legislatures and Cabinets in Industrial Democracies," *International Political Science Review*, 21 (2): 197–215.

Šiklová, J. (1993) "Are Women from Central Europe Conservatives?" in N. Funk and M. Mueller (eds) *Gender and Post-Communism: Reflections from Eastern Europe and the Former Soviet Union*, New York: Routledge.

Silverstein, J. (1990) "Aung San Suu Kyi. Is She Burma's Woman of Destiny?" *Asian Survey*, 30 (10): 1007–19.

Skjeie, H. (2001) "Quotas, Parity, and the Discursive Dangers of Difference," in J. Klausen and C.S. Maier (eds) *Has Liberalism Failed Women? Assuring Equal Representation in Europe and the United States*, New York: Palgrave.

Smith, M. (2009) "Historical Institutionalism in Contemporary Political Science: Diversity and Canadian Political Development: Presidential Address to the Canadian Political Science Association, Ottawa, May 27, 2009," *Canadian Journal of Political Science*, 42 (2): 831–54.

Soetjipto, A. (2004) "Indonesia," in Friedrich Ebert Stiftung (ed.) *Southeast Asian Women in Politics and Decision-Making, Ten Years After Beijing. Gaining Ground?*, Manila: FES Philippine Office.

Sörensen, K. and Bergqvist, C. (2002) *Gender and the Social Democratic Welfare Regime*, Stockholm: Institute for Workinglife.

SOU (2007) 42. *Från statsminister till president? – Sveriges regeringschef i ett jäm-förande perspektiv*. Online. Available at: www.sweden.gov.se/sb/d/8586/a/84336 (accessed June 2010).

Statistics Canada (2005) *Women in Canada: a Gender-Based Statistical Report*, Ottawa: Statistics Canada.

Staudt, K. (1987) "Women's Politics, the State, and Capitalist Transformation in Africa," in I.L. Markovitz (ed.) *Studies in Power and Class in Africa*, Oxford: Oxford University Press.

Stauffer, B. (2006) "Women's Rights in Morocco: New Family Code Faces Many Hurdles," *Qantara*. Online. Available at: www.qantara.de/webcom/show_article.php/_c-478/_nr-545/i.htm (accessed November 2009).

Steegstra, M. (2009) "Krobo Queen Mothers: Gender, Power and Contemporary Female Traditional Authority in Ghana," *Africa Today*, 55 (3): 105–23.

Stein, E. and Tommasi, M. (eds) with Spiller, P.T. and Scartascini, C. (2008) *Policymaking in Latin America: How Politics Shapes Policies*, Washington, DC: Inter-American Development Bank.

Stevens, A. (2005) "In Rice's Speech, Listeners Hear Rights, Rhetoric," *Womensenews.org*, June 24. Online. Available at: www.womensenews.org/story/the-world/050624/rices-speech-listeners-hear-rights-rhetoric (accessed October 2009).

Stjórnarráð Íslands. Online. Available at: www.stjornarrad.is/Rikisstjornartal (accessed January 2010).

Stoeltje, B. (2003) "Asante Queen Mothers: Precolonial Authority in a Postcolonial Society," *Research Review*, 19 (2): 1–19.

Stokes, W. (2005) *Women in Contemporary Politics*, Cambridge and Malden: Polity Press.

Storm, L. (2007) *Democratization in Morocco: the Political Elite and Struggles for Power in the Post-independence State*, London: Routledge.

Studlar, D.T. and Moncrief, G.F. (1997) "The Recruitment of Women Cabinet Ministers in the Canadian Provinces," *Governance: an International Journal of Policy and Administration*, 10 (1): 67–81.

Studlar, D.T. and Moncrief, G.F. (1999) "Women's Work? The Distribution and Prestige of Portfolios in the Canadian Provinces," *Governance: an International Journal of Policy and Administration*, 12 (4): 379–95.

Suffrage Universel: Citoyenneté, démocratie, ethnicité et nationalité en France (2009) *Nafissa Sid Cara*. Online. Available at: www.suffrage-universel.be/fr/sidecara.htm (accessed October 2009).

Svanström, Y. (2004) "Criminalising the John – a Swedish Gender Model?" in J. Outshoorn (ed.) *The Politics of Prostitution. Women's Movements, Democratic States and the Globalisation of Sex Commerce*, Cambridge: Cambridge University Press.

SVD (2009) Online. Available at: www.svd.se/naringsliv/nyheter/artikel_3452389.svd (accessed January 2010).

Sweden (2007) *Governments and Prime Ministers since 1900*. Online. Available at: www.sweden.gov.se/sb/d/4136 (accessed June 2010).

Sweden DS (2001) 64. *Ändrad ordning. Strategisk utveckling för jämställdhet*. Online. Available at: www.riksdagen.se/Webbnav/index.aspx?nid=3271&dok_id=GPB464 (accessed January 2010).

Sykes, P.L. (2008) "Women Leaders and Executive Politics: Engendering Change in Anglo-American Nations," paper presented at the Australian Senate Lecture Series, Canberra, Australia, March 7. Online. Available at: www.aph.gov.au/SEnate/pubs/occa_lect/transcripts/070308/index.htm (accessed December 2009).

Sykes, P.L. (2009) "Incomplete Empowerment: Female Cabinet Ministers in Anglo-American Systems," in J. Kane, H. Patapan and P. t'Hart (eds) *Dispersed Democratic Leadership: Origins, Dynamics and Implications*, New York: Oxford University Press.

Tahri, R. (2003) "Women's Political Participation: the Case of Morocco," paper presented at the Parliamentary Forum Conference on the Implementation of Quotas: African Experiences, Pretoria, November. Online. Available at: www.quotaproject.org/CSCS_Morocco_tahri_27_7_2004.pdf (accessed November 2009).

Tambiah, Y. (2002) "Introduction," in Y. Tambiah (ed.) *Women & Governance in South Asia. Reimagining the State*, Colombo: ICES.

Theakston, K. (1987) *Junior Ministers in British Government*, New York: Basil Blackwell.

Tonguthai, P. and Putanusorn, S. (2004) "Thailand," in Friedrich Ebert Stiftung (ed.) *Southeast Asian Women in Politics and Decision-Making, Ten Years After Beijing. Gaining Ground?*, Manila: FES Philippine Office.

Touahri, S. (2007) "Sept femmes nommées à des postes ministériels stratégiques au Maroc," *Magharebia*, October 17. Online. Available at: www.magharebia.com/cocoon/awi/xhtml1/fr/features/2007/10/17/feature-01 (accessed October 2009).

Tremblay, M. (1998) "Do Female MP's Substantively Represent Women? A Study of Legislative Behaviour in Canada's 35th Parliament," *Canadian Journal of Political Science*, 31 (3): 435–65.

Tremblay, M. (2003) "Women's Representational Role in Australia and Canada: the Impact of Political Context," *Australian Journal of Political Science*, 38 (2): 215–38.

Tremblay, M. (2008a) *Women and Legislative Representation. Electoral Systems, Political Parties, and Sex Quotas*, New York: Palgrave Macmillan.

Tremblay, M. (2008b) "Introduction," in M. Tremblay (ed.) *Women and Legislative Representation. Electoral Systems, Political Parties, and Sex Quotas*, New York: Palgrave Macmillan.

Tremblay, M. (2008c) *100 questions sur les femmes et la politique*, Montreal: Remueménage.

Tremblay, M. (2008d) "Conclusion," in M. Tremblay (ed.) *Women and Legislative Representation. Electoral Systems, Political Parties, and Sex Quotas*, New York: Palgrave Macmillan.

Tremblay, M. (2010) *Quebec Women and Legislative Representation*, Vancouver: UBC Press.

Tremblay, M. and Mullen, S. (2007) "Le Comité permanent de la condition féminine de la Chambre des communes du Canada: un outil au service de la représentation politique des femmes?" *Canadian Journal of Political Science*, 40 (3): 615–37.

Tremblay, M. and Pelletier, R. (2000) "More Feminists or More Women? Descriptive and Substantive Representations of Women in the 1997 Canadian Federal Elections," *International Journal of Political Science*, 21 (4): 381–405.

Tremblay, M. and Trimble, L. (2004) "Still Different After All These Years? A Comparison of Female and Male Canadian MPs in the Twentieth Century," *Journal of Legislative Studies*, 10 (1): 97–122.

Trimble, L. (1993) "A Few Good Women: Female Legislators in Alberta, 1972–1991," in C.A. Cavanaugh and R.R. Warne (eds) *Standing on New Ground: Women in Alberta*, Calgary: University of Alberta Press.

Trimble, L. (1997) "Feminist Politics in the Alberta Legislature, 1972–1994," in J. Arscott and L. Trimble (eds) *In the Presence of Women. Representation in Canadian Governments*, Toronto: Harcourt Brace & Company.

Trimble, L. (1998) "Who's Represented? Gender and Diversity in the Alberta Legislature," in M. Tremblay and C. Andrew (eds) *Women and Political Representation in Canada*, Ottawa: University of Ottawa Press.

Trimble, L. and Tremblay, M. (2005) "Representation of Canadian Women at the Cabinet Table," *Atlantis: A Women's Studies Journal*, 30 (1): 31–45.

Trimble, L., Treiberg, N. and Girard, S. (2010) " 'Kim-Speak:' Gendered Mediation of Kim Campbell during the 1993 Canadian National Election," *Recherches féministes*, 23 (1): 29–52.

Tripp, A.M. (2001) "The New Political Activism in Africa," *Journal of Democracy*, 12 (3): 141–55.

Tripp, A.M. and Kang, A. (2008) "The Global Impact of Quotas: On the Fast Track to Increased Female Legislative Representation," *Comparative Political Studies*, 41 (3): 338–61.

Tripp, A.M., Konate, D. and Lowe-Morna, C. (2006) "Sub-Saharan Africa: On the Fast Track to Women's Political Representation," in D. Dahlerup (ed.) *Women, Quotas and Politics*, London and New York: Routledge.

Tripp, A.M., Casimiro, I., Kwesiga, J. and Mungwa, A. (2009) *African Women's Movements: Changing Political Landscapes*, Cambridge: Cambridge University Press.

True, J. and Mintrom, M. (2001) "Transnational Networks and Policy Diffusion: the Case of Gender Mainstreaming," *International Studies Quarterly*, 45 (1): 27–57.

UAE Cabinet Official Website (2008a) *Cabinet Members*. Online. Available at: www. moca.gov.ae/english/cabinet_member.asp (accessed November 2009).

UAE Cabinet Official Website (2008b) *Constitution of the United Arab Emirates*. Online. Available at: www.moca.gov.ae/english/constitution_1_4.asp (accessed November 2009).

Uhrová, E. (2005) "Narodní fronta žen a Rada československých žen: dva proudy ženského hnutí v českých zemích a jejích zájem o sociální a pravní postavení žen, květen 1945 – únor 1948" ["The National Front of Women and the National Council of Czechoslovak Women: Two Streams of the Czech Women's Movements and their Interest for the Social and Juridical Position of Women, May 1945–February 1948"], in Z. Karnik and M. Kopeček (eds) *Bolševismus, komunismus a radikální socialismus v Československu* [*Bolshevism, Communism and Radical Socialism in Czechoslovakia*], Prague: Ústav soudobé dějiny [Institute of Contemporary History].

UNESCO (Institute for Statistics) (2010) *Global and Internationally Comparable Statistics on Education, Science, Culture and Communication*. Online. Available at: www. uis.unesco.org/ev.php?ID=2867_201&ID2=DO_TOPIC (accessed June 2010).

UNICEF (n.d.) Online. Available at: www.unicef.org (accessed June 2010).

UNICEF (2010) "At a Glance: Spain." Online. Available at: www.unicef.org/infobycountry/spain_statistics.html#70 (accessed June 2010).

United Nations (1991) *The World's Women 1970–1990. Trends and Statistics, Social Statistics and Indicators*, New York: United Nations, Series K no. 8.

United Nations Development Fund for Women (UNIFEM) (2009a) *Progress of the World's Women 2008/2009*. Online. Available at: www.unifem.org/progress/2008/media/POWW08_chap02_politics.pdf (accessed November 2009).

United Nations Development Fund for Women (UNIFEM) (2009b) *Women in Ministerial Positions: 1 in 3 at Best*. Online. Available at: www.unifem.org/progress/2008/vs_politics7.html#vstats (accessed November 2009).

United Nations Development Programme (UNDP) (1995) *Human Development Report: Gender and Human Development*. Online. Available at: http://hdr.undp.org.en (accessed June 2010).

United Nations Development Programme (UNDP) (2005) *Arab Human Development Report: Towards the Rise of Women in the Arab World*, New York: United Nations Publications. Online. Available at: www.arab-hdr.org/publications/other/ahdr/ahdr2005e.pdf (accessed November 2009).

United Nations Development Programme (UNDP) (2009a) *Human Development Reports*. Online. Available at: http://hdr.undp.org.en (accessed June 2010).

United Nations Development Programme (UNDP) (2009b) *Human Development Reports. Myanmar*. Online. Available at: http://hdrstats.undp.org/en/countries/data_sheets/cty_ds_MMR.html (accessed June 2010).

United Nations Development Programme (UNDP) (2009c) *Human Development Reports. Pakistan*. Online. Available at: http://hdrstats.undp.org/en/countries/data_sheets/cty_ds_PAK.html (accessed June 2010).

United Nations Development Programme (UNDP) (2009d) *Human Development Reports. Statistics. Getting and Using the Data*. Online. Available at: http://hdr.undp.org/en/statistics/data/ (accessed June 2010).

United Nations Development Programme (UNDP) (2009e) *Human Development Reports. United States*. Online. Available at: http://hdrstats.undp.org/en/countries/country_fact_sheets/cty_fs_USA.html (accessed June 2010).

United Nations Development Programme (UNDP) (2009f) *Indicators – Human Development Report*. Online. Available at: http://hdrstats.undp.org/en/indicators/ (accessed November 2009).

Veneracion-Rallonza, L. (2008) "Women and the Democracy Project: a Feminist Take on Women's Political Participation in the Philippines," in K. Iwanaga (ed.) *Women's Political Participation and Representation in Asia. Obstacles and Challenges*, Copenhagen: NIAS Press.

Vickers, J.M. and Brodie, M.J. (1981) "Canada," in J. Lovenduski and J. Hills (eds) *The Politics of the Second Electorate. Women and Public Participation*, London: Routledge & Kegan Paul.

Wängnerud, L. (2000) "Testing the Politics of Presence: Women's Representation in the Swedish Riksdag," *Scandinavian Political Studies*, 23 (1): 67–91.

Watson, P. (1997) "Civil Society and the Politics of Difference in Eastern Europe," in C. Kaplan, D. Keates and J. Scott (eds) *Transitions, Environments, Translations: Feminisms in International Politics*, New York: Routledge.

Watson, R., Jencik, A. and Selzer, J. (2005) "Women World Leaders: Comparative Analysis and Gender Experiences," *Journal of International Women's Studies*, 7 (2): 53–76.

White, G. (2005) *Cabinets and First Ministers*, Vancouver: UBC Press.

Whitford, A., Wilkins, V. and Ball, M. (2007) "Descriptive Representation and Policymaking Authority: Evidence from Women in Cabinets and Bureaucracies," *Governance: an International Journal of Policy, Administration, and Institutions*, 20 (4): 559–80.

Wiesinger, B.N. (2008) *Partisaninnen: Widerstand in Jugoslawien 1941–1945*, Wien, Köln and Weimar: Böhlau.

Wilson, J. and Black, D. (2009) *Women Parliamentarians in Australia 1921–2009*, Canberra: Parliament of Australia, Parliamentary Library. Online. Available at: http://parlinfo.aph.gov.au/parlInfo/download/library/prspub/7N3T6/upload_binary/7n3t64.pdf (accessed June 2010).

Wolchik, S. and Meyer, A.G. (eds) (1985) *Women, State and Party in Eastern Europe*, Durham, NC: Duke University Press.

Women Environment and Development Organization (WEDO) (2007) "Getting the Balance Right in National Cabinets." Online. Available at: www.wedo.org/wp-content/uploads/5050_cabinetsfactsheet021.pdf (accessed June 2010).

Women for Women International (2004) "Women Taking a Lead: Progress Toward Empowerment and Gender Equity in Rwanda," *Women for Women International Briefing Paper*. Online. Available at: www.womenforwomen.org/news-women-for-women/files/RWpaper.pdf (accessed August 2009).

World Development Indicators (n.d.) Online. Available at: http://siteresources.worldbank.org (accessed January 2010).

Worldwide Guide to Women in Leadership (2007) *The Kingdom of Morocco*. Online. Available at: www.guide2womenleaders.com/Morocco.htm (accessed November 2009).

Worldwide Guide to Women in Leadership (2008a) *Republic of Sudan*. Online. Available at: www.guide2womenleaders.com/sudan.htm (accessed November 2009).

Worldwide Guide to Women in Leadership (2008b) *United Arab Emirates*. Online. Available at: www.guide2womenleaders.com/United_Arab_Emirates.htm (accessed June 2010).

Worldwide Guide to Women in Leadership (2009a) *First Female Ministers*. Online. Available at: www.guide2womenleaders.com/First-female-ministers.htm (accessed October 2009).

Worldwide Guide to Women in Leadership (2009b) *The Islamic Republic of Mauritania*. Online. Available at: www.guide2womenleaders.com/Mauritania.htm (accessed November 2009).

Worldwide Guide to Women in Leadership (2009c) *The Republic of Lebanon*. Online. Available at: www.guide2womenleaders.com/lebanon.htm (accessed October 2009).

Worldwide Guide to Women in Leadership (2009d) *Republic of Liberia*. Online. Available at: www.guide2womenleaders.com/Liberia.htm (accessed August 2009).

Worldwide Guide to Women in Leadership (2009e) *Rwanda*. Online. Available at: www.guide2womenleaders.com/Rwanda.htm (accessed August 2009).

Worldwide Guide to Women in Leadership (2009f) *United States of Mexico*. Online. Available at: www.guide2womenleaders.com/Mexico.htm (accessed December 2009).

Worldwide Guide to Women in Leadership (2009g) *Women in Power. Africa*. Online. Available at: www.guide2womenleaders.com/africa.htm (accessed May 2010).

Worldwide Guide to Women in Leadership (2010) *Worldwide Guide to Women in Leadership*. Online. Available at: www.guide2womenleaders.com/ (accessed June 2010).

Worldwide Guide to Women in Leadership (n.d.) *Woman Ministers and Woman Heads of Government*. Online. Available at: www.guide2womenleaders.com/women_heads_of_governments.htm (accessed 2010).

Yi Yi, M. (2000) *Myanmar Gender Profiles*, unpublished report, January.

Young, L. and Cross, W. (2003) "Women's Involvement in Canadian Political Parties," in M. Tremblay and L. Trimble (eds) *Women and Electoral Politics in Canada*, Don Mills: Oxford University Press.

Zahab, M.A. (2005) "D'une rhétorique gouvernementale de façade à la mobilisation du mouvement des femmes en faveur des quotas," in M. Tremblay (ed.) *Femmes et parlements. Un regard international*, Montreal: Remue-menage.

Zetterberg, P. (2008) "The Downside of Gender Quotas? Institutional Constraints on Women in Mexican State Legislatures," *Parliamentary Affairs*, 61 (3): 442–60.

Zia, S. and Bari, F. (1999) *Baseline Report on Women's Participation in Political and Public Life in Pakistan*, Islamabad: Aurat Foundation.

Akční program Česko-slovenského Svazu Žen [*Action Plan of the Czecho-slovak Women's Union*] (1968) Adopted June 26, 1968, Prague: Mona.

Zpravodaj Česko-slovenský Svaz Žen [Gazette of the Czechoslovak Women's Union] (1968) 3.

Index

Note: Page numbers in *italic* denote tables.

Printed by Publishers' Graphics Kentucky